P9-CRT-877

Rediscovering Our Roots,
Recharting Our Routes

Gerard
Kelly

InterVarsity Press
Downers Grove, Illinois

InterVarsity Press
P.O. Box 1400, Downers Grove, IL 60515
World Wide Web: www.ivpress.com
E-mail: mail@ivpress.com

This edition published by arrangement with Monarch Books, Angus Hudson Ltd., Concorde House, Greenville Place, Mill Hill, London NW 7 3SA. Originally published under the title Get a Grip on the Future Without Losing Your Hold on the Past.

InterVarsity Press® is the book-publishing division of InterVarsity Christian Fellowship/USA®, a student movement active on campus at hundreds of universities, colleges and schools of nursing in the United States of America, and a member movement of the International Fellowship of Evangelical Students. For information about local and regional activities, write Public Relations Dept., InterVarsity Christian Fellowship/USA, 6400 Schroeder Rd., P.O. Box 7895, Madison, WI 53707-7895.

Cover photograph: Chigmaroff/Davison/SuperStock

ISBN 0-8308-2264-X

Printed in the United States of America ∞

Library of Congress Cataloging-in-Publication Data

Kelly, Gerard, 1959-
  Retrofuture : rediscovering our roots, recharting our routes / Gerard Kelly.
    p. cm.
  Includes bibliographical references.
  ISBN 0-8308-2264-X (paper : alk. paper)
    1. Social history—20th century. 2. Social change. 3. Technology and civilization. 4. Religion and culture. I. Title.

  HN17.5 .K439 2000
  306'.09'04—dc21
                                                                                    00-040947

| 15 | 14 | 13 | 12 | 11 | 10 | 9 | 8 | 7 | 6 | 5 | 4 | 3 | 2 | 1 |

| 12 | 11 | 10 | 09 | 08 | 07 | 06 | 05 | 04 | 03 | 02 | 01 | 00 |

To Joseph, Aaron, Anna and Jacob

Contents

Acknowledgments

If it takes a village to raise a child, it takes a city to write a book. There are literally hundreds of people whose friendships, conversations, ideas and inspiration have played a part in shaping this project. Special thanks are due to those who helped to bring the book to birth: Chrissie Kelly, Tony Collins at Monarch (U.K.), Dan Reid at IVP (U.S.A.), Ben Wickham for research, and Tom and Christine Sine for friendship and many encouragements. Thanks to the members of the Cyberpub for world-class conversation; the members of café.net for support, encouragement and prayer; our church family at Chawn Hill Christian Centre; the Leadership and Head Office Teams of Spring Harvest; and all involved in the Youth and Rage Programmes. This being the digital age, there's no one to thank for the typing.

Introduction

The future is too important to be left to chance.
CHARLES HANDY, *The Future of Work*

A few miles north of my home in the West Midlands stands one of the most enduring monuments to the great age of British road building. Comprising 24,000 tons of steel, 230,000 tons of concrete and 270,000 tons of earth, and $13 million in the making, it operates on six levels and brings together eighteen route options. It bears the official title of Junction 6 of the M6 freeway, but within days of its opening it had earned the name by which it is now universally known: Spaghetti Junction. The most complex traffic interchange in the U.K., Spaghetti Junction is a Medusa of the freeway, throwing a shadow of grayness over the small community of Gravely Hill. By reputation, it is one of the easiest places in England to get lost.

Spaghetti's American cousin is the 5/22/57 Interchange in Orange County, California, known to all as Orange Crush Junction. This asphalt panic attack rises to a mere two levels but all the same manages to knot together thirty-four route options, with a total of sixtysix lanes of traffic. Each day Orange Crush Junction contributes to the success or failure of some 690,000 separate journeys.

Similar junctions could be identified in every nation of the developed world. Wherever high-volume, high-speed traffic management is needed, there will be the twisting form of the interchange—a writhing snake pit of cars and concrete that increases in equal measure both traffic capacity and driver stress. The freeway interchange is an abiding symbol of our age.

This book is a response to the existence of another sort of interchange. Complex, threatening, unprecedented in its scale, it is just as real as Spaghetti and Orange Crush, but it exists in our cultural rather than our physical geography. As a new century is born, movements of significant change are surfacing in unconnected areas of our lives, like multilane highways converging around us. Gathering pace and complexity, disparate changes compound one another to add up to a corporate "change of life," an interchange in the traffic of society. Changes are not happening one after the other on a single level but simultaneously on many levels. Diverse fields of inquiry are finding unexpected connections and spinning off in radical new directions. Like drivers in the approach to Spaghetti Junction, we see the signs of change flash by with increasing frequency—we are aware of options offered, of choices demanded, of life-changing decisions ahead. Choose your route, or the road will choose it for you. We are caught up in the knots of a culture junction.

RetroFuture is an exploration of this historic interchange, which will demand of us both rerouting and rerooting. Rerouting because every area of our lives will be touched in the coming two decades by intense social change, forcing upon us a choice of road. Rerooting because beyond the interchange we will need to find access in a new cultural landscape to resources deep enough and rich enough to fund our future journey. To embrace the future with no regard for the past is to throw away centuries of learning and development—and to risk making again the mistakes by which history has tried so hard to teach us. Our best course, rather, is to carry with us into the future the very best of past experience, to be rooted in something deeper than the surface currents of change. The challenge before us is to embrace all that the future offers without losing our hold on the riches of the past. If the culture junction demands that we reroute, at the same time survival demands that we reroot.

Previewing *RetroFuture*

Our exploration of the culture junction will fall into three distinct parts.

Part one, "Root Change," introduces the theme of social transformation and argues that the changes we face, growing faster, wider and deeper by the day, add up to a broad cultural shift—a societal "change of life." We will set out the unique situation of two generations. Generation X was the last generation to become adult in the twentieth century, just as the Millennial generation will be the first young adults of the twenty-first. Together these are the junction generations, those who are leading us into our culture's interchange and those who will lead us out of it. The question of the future shape of culture is essentially a question of these two generations.

Part two, "Root Causes," will examine five of the currents of change set to shape the first two decades of the new century: the five "posts" of Generation X and beyond. Each taking a different perspective or emphasis, the five "posts" together offer a framework through which to explore the horizons of the future. The five-posts framework describes the emerging culture in which the junction generations will live out their adult years. These "posts" are the following:

☐ postindustrial technology: remolding society and transforming our lives through the shift from machine technology to digital processing

☐ postliterate communication: shifting the Western knowledge base, learning styles and methods of interaction from those founded on the authority of printed text to those of image and hypertext

☐ postmodern philosophy: undergirding social change with a shift in popular worldview from the certainties of the Enlightenment to a new adventure of ambiguity, uncertainty and diversity

☐ postimperial politics: shifting from the old order of political empires, colonies and monocultural rule to the new paradox of globalization and fragmentation—the fast-growing commercial empires of McWorld in the competitive multiplicity of the planetary marketplace

☐ post-Christian spirituality: moving popular piety on from the orthodoxy of Christian and other established faiths to the plurality of individualized, experiential faith expressions[1]

In each of these five areas, we will explore the implications of rerouting (the choices and changes offered to us) and of rerooting (the prospects for Generation X and the Millennials).

Part three, "Root Growth," will draw together these many threads to offer resources for the management of change. How can individuals, families and communities embrace, manage and survive the process of change? We will look in particular at the following questions:

☐ Rebirth or retrenchment? How well do we deal with change, individually and corporately? Can we get from where we are to where we will be without drowning?

☐ Remote controllers or resourceful friends? What kind of leaders will the new environment call for?

To facilitate the journey through the text, three types of links will occasionally appear. The first type is called "definition.link." These will appear where it is valuable to focus on the core definition of terms used in a given chapter. The next type is called "word.link." These represent occasional forays into the Bible, taking a meditative approach to key passages that relate to the areas under discussion. And last, there is the type called "creative.link." These are passages where the material is approached through a different type of prose.

The notes offered in this book contain both publication details and, where available, Internet addresses. It will be clear even at a glance that certain books and web sites crop up frequently. If you want to explore further the themes of this book, these titles and references offer proven entry points. I encourage you to use them to the full. If you have comments or questions on the content of *RetroFuture,* I am happy to receive them. You can e-mail me directly at <retro@cafe-net.org.uk> or visit the book's Web page at <www.cafe-net.org.uk>. This is the Web site for the European edition of the book, published as *Get a Grip on the Future.* From this site there will be links to response and discussion zones for *RetroFuture.*

Laying Out My Assumptions

Before we set out on the journey we will share, there are four assumptions I have made that are better spelled out now than stumbled over later.

1. Faith matters. As a practicing Christian, I write from a perspective informed by the traditions and discoveries of that faith. As an evangelical, I have lived for twenty-five years in the section of the Christian community that, while not the largest group, probably makes the most noise. It is inevitable that my own exploration of cultural change will tend toward seeking out the implications for the Christian church. I am naturally concerned for the future of my own faith community. However, this is not a journey on which only those of that community are invited. I hope that this book will be of use to many people whose interests are not exhausted by concern for the church—the parents of children who show all the signs of having been born on another planet, businesspeople and employers steering small and large organizations through the whitewater rapids of corporate change, ordinary people battling the daily dilemmas and choices of a culture dizzy with transition. I do not apologize for mentioning the church so often, but I do hope that those for whom this is unfamiliar ground will be able all the same to benefit—to distinguish principle from application and apply it elsewhere. If this book doesn't produce some pointers for the future of the church, I will have failed, but equally it ought to throw up a few other ideas along the way.

2. Perspective colors perception. As well as being informed by my twenty-five-year Christian journey, I am also inevitably shaped by my location. Having lived for five years of my childhood in Canada, I spent my adult years in Britain and France. This book is, in that sense, a European book. I have spent enough time in North America, and working with North Americans, to know that there are both differences and similarities between these two continents. My conclusion is that the similarities can be of value because we can learn from one another's successes and failures, and that the differences can also be of value because a voice that comes to us from "the outside" may often help us see our own situation more clearly. It is my hope, therefore, if you are reading this book in a setting different from that in which it was written, that you will forgive the misunderstandings, enjoy the comparisons and benefit from the contrasts. Many of the challenges we face are global in scale and scope, and we have much to learn from intercultural exchange.

3. Change demands a response. One school of thought holds that the church, rooted as it is in centuries-old tradition, needn't concern itself with minor external diversions such as social transformation. Even if a case can be made for the existence of a cultural interchange somewhere between now and the near future, there is no implication that anything need be done about it. Businesses need to change; schools must follow suit; but the church exists on a higher plane where such imperatives don't apply. Individuals who crave the same immunity need only huddle under the benevolent umbrella of the unchanging church—to cling like Quasimodo to the altar and cry, "Sanctuary!" I do not hold this view. I believe that the church *must* change. The church is not trend-driven; it is God's family and lives by other rules. But it is also a cultural and social institution, rooted in a given place and time. If we have any concern for the rising generations—and for those who will follow them—we must look with urgency to the future shape of our church. To resist change is to remain relevant to a world that no longer exists. Tom Sine's much-quoted warning in *Wild Hope* is worth repeating here. "Every denomination and religious organisation I have worked with does long-range planning. Ironically, they do long-range planning as though the future will simply be an extension of the present. . . . As a result, we are chronically surprised by change. In the future, we can no longer afford this luxury."[2]

4. Fear is natural. The fourth assumption necessary for this journey is that it's OK to be afraid. Freeway driving is never more stressful than in the negotiating of a major interchange. Likewise the culture junction offers us a speeding blur of choices, demanding that we make them fast. Around us others are tackling change in their own way—some bursting ahead with confidence, swapping lanes and making turns like they were born to it; others crawling in the slow lane in a blind panic; still others pulling over or reversing down an on-ramp to be finished with the whole thing. Away in the distance we catch sight of those who have made their choices and sped on. Are they halfway home or hopelessly lost? Should we follow them or take a different course? As I have discussed cultural change with individuals and groups in recent years, I have met many who are caught in this fear and are genuinely unsure of where to turn. Change brings with it uncertainty, apprehension and sometimes panic. But it can be the stimulus we need to reach new heights of creativity, opening up new avenues to explore. Change can be approached in two ways—primarily as threat or primarily as opportunity. I hope that this book will be of help to some in shifting the balance. The fear is real, but it need not be terminal.

These assumptions made, my prayer is that this will be a stimulating, enjoyable and ultimately useful journey.

PART 1

Root Change

*An Age
of Social Transformation*

No Small Change

In One Era
& Out the Other

The greatest of all illusions is the illusion of familiarity.
G. K. CHESTERTON, *Everlasting Man*

This is a kairos time, a time to influence and inspire our land for a generation to come. . . . May the Holy Spirit show us what may change, what must change, and what must not change.
SAM HUTCHINSON

This morning you woke up on a new planet.

Imagine for one moment that you are a Russian cosmonaut, trained to endure months if not years in the weightlessness of space. The year is 1988. You are sent to live on the space station Mir, ostensibly for a period of six months. But something goes wrong in the administration. You are asked to work at first a double shift and then a triple, until in the end it is over three years before you set foot again on solid ground. You are well rewarded for your hard work and welcomed back to earth a national hero, but nothing has prepared you for the world to which you return.

The Iron Curtain, which was the defining reality of your youth, has fallen. The Berlin Wall has been broken into a million pieces, carted off as souvenirs to every corner of the world. In a secret meeting in a forest dacha outside the city of Brest, Boris Yeltsin has met with the leaders of Ukraine and Belarus to frame a declaration that will tell the world, "The Union of Soviet Socialist Republics, as a subject of international law and a geopolitical reality, is ceasing its existence."[1] What began as a few hesitant steps of *glasnost* and *perestroika* has grown into the full-scale democratization of Mother Russia. At least in your part of the world, communism of the one-party-rule variety is a fast-fading memory. Your universe has changed—more than you thought it could and in ways you could never have imagined. You have experienced, at first hand, the faster, wider, deeper change that is the overarching icon of our age.

Preaching just after World War II, at the midpoint of the twentieth century, theologian Paul Tillich saw the first indications of this flood of change and called it "the shaking of the foundations."[2] Fifty years later it seems that more than ever we are shaken, destabilized, by the turbulence that social change brings. Introducing its 1997 White Paper on Education, "Excellence in Schools," the British government warned, "At all levels society is undergoing massive economic, technological, social and political changes that challenge traditional values, beliefs and institutional arrangements."[3]

Management guru Peter Drucker concurs. "Every few hundred years in Western history," he says, "there occurs a sharp transformation. . . . Within a few short decades, society rearranges itself—its worldview; its basic values; its social and political structure; its arts; its key institutions. Fifty years later, there is a new world. And the people born then cannot even imagine the world in which their grandparents lived and into which their own parents were born. We are currently living through just such a transformation."[4] The discovery of fire, the first-ever transition from hunter-gatherers to settled community, the Industrial Revolution, the coming of the railways to the Western United States—previous watersheds such as these give an indication of the scope and depth of change we can expect to see.

Dee Hock, the outspoken founder of the Visa Corporation, the world's most successful virtual business, uses more dramatic imagery to make much the same observation. "We are in the midst of a global epidemic of institutional failure," he says. "This next decade and maybe the one after that will be the decades that people will look back to over a thousand years and say—that was the melting pot."[5]

Whether analyzed through a theological, sociological, technological or philosophical lens, it is clear that our turn-of-the-century world is turbulent with social change.

A Personal Journey

My own awareness of the scale and complexity of the changes we face began in a front-line encounter with new technology in the mid-1980s. For eighteen months I served as personnel and training manager for Syco Systems, Ltd., in London. Syco was a high-tech retailer of musical instruments, founded in 1980 by rock star Peter Gabriel and built initially on the Fairlight CMI—the world's first computerized musical instrument. For several years the company led the field in the emerging technologies of computers and music. Every product carried was, in its own right, a technological breakthrough.

As Syco's training manager, part of my job was to research the wider context in which the company was developing. Over a relatively short period, from 1979 to around 1986, we had seen the music industry revolutionized before our eyes. Until this point the recording of music had been based entirely on the manipulation of analogue signals—electronic signals captured on tape as magnetic impulses. The recording process set strict limits on what was possible in composition, reproduction and performance; much of the paraphernalia of the studio had less to do with creativity and music than with overcoming these technical limitations. In the 1970s musicians who were computer-literate and programmers who were musically aware both began to experiment, composing and recording by an entirely new process. Sounds could be sampled by a computer and converted into digital information—the millions of binary digits on which all computing is based. This information could be manipulated almost without limit. The key was to work not with an electronic signal but with strings of binary code. Once reconverted to the analogue domain, new sounds would then emerge for performance and recording.

Working with digital code allowed for degrees of flexibility and precision never before achieved, and the change in technology brought with it an explosion of possibilities. A simple sequence of notes could be looped to create an instant rhythm track. Drum patterns well beyond the capacity of a two-armed human drummer could be built up, layer on layer. Any sound—whether musical in origin or not—could be captured, assigned to a keyboard and converted into melody. The whole process could be delivered to disk without ever leaving the digital domain. A new language, MIDI (Musical Instrument Digital Interface), was created so that keyboards, drum machines and other instruments could talk to each other and in turn relate to PCs carrying the relevant software. A new creative landscape was opening up before the writers, performers and producers of popular music.

Fifteen years later, MIDI is a standard feature of even home-based computers, and these changes are a part of music history. At the time they seemed almost miraculous. Their impact was felt immediately in all aspects of music making, transforming known styles, creating new ones and putting number crunching at the heart of the creative process. Before long, as memory became cheaper and applications more sophisticated, it was possible to create state-of-the-art, full-scale compositions just by sitting at a workstation. The music industry would never be the same again.

The importance of this experience for me was that I saw firsthand the speed at which change could sweep through a whole domain of culture. Reading around the subject, it became clear that this new level of change was affecting not only music and musicians; it was one application or footprint of a much larger process. All around us, change on a similar scale was taking hold. And it was not just in technology. Somehow—in ways that were on occasion too bizarre to even think about—these technological changes were part of, or related to, wider social changes. Attitudes and beliefs were changing. Philosophy was involved, and religion too. A new phenomenon called the New Age movement had grown up from nowhere and was gaining ground fast. There were political implications. Before long the Iron Curtain—that great and terrible symbol of old certainties— would fall, changing the face of the planet in an impossibly short period of time. What began for me as an object lesson in musical technology grew into an awareness of global change on a remarkable scale. My personal journey resonates with that of many others I have known or read of in recent years. I came away from the Syco experience convinced that a form of cultural meltdown had begun. Nothing that has happened since has lessened that conviction.

It is not the fact of change that demands special attention in our age—this has been implicit throughout history. It is in its order of magnitude that change is reaching new heights. Like the McDonald's empire or Michael Dell's bank balance, change has been big for a while, but today it is bigger than ever. It is this mind-numbing *volume* of change that has come to mark the past two decades and seems set to mark the next two. Put simply, change is growing faster, wider and deeper by the day.

Faster Change: The Shock of the New

The most helpful model for understanding the increasing speed of change remains the one introduced in the late 1960s by Alvin and Heidi Toffler. The Tofflers sensed a paradox in the way technological change was affecting Western society. Technology was supposed to be delivering an upbeat future of laborsaving devices and consumer comforts—but that was not what most people were *feeling*. Instead, there was a strange but widespread dread in the face of life's accelerating pace. In 1969 the Tofflers linked this dread to "the premature arrival of the future" and called it "future shock." This became the title of a book in the following year, giving the Tofflers the first of many global bestsellers and introducing a new way of understanding the effects of social change.[6]

Future shock is a form of culture shock that you experience without ever leaving home. It is defined as "the shattering stress and disorientation that we induce in individuals by subjecting them to too much change in too short a time."[7] It is what happens when your own culture changes so fast that you become, in effect, a foreigner within it. "It arises from the super-imposition of a new culture on an old one. It is culture shock in one's own society."[8] Not only will this new condition be as keenly felt as culture shock might be, but its prognosis might be much worse. With culture shock I have the reassurance of knowing that the old, familiar world I have left behind still exists somewhere and that one day I may get back to it. Future shock affords me no such hope. The past is gone, vaporized. The future I was hurtling toward has come to meet me head-on, and I must learn to live with it now. Even ET could phone home, but the victims of future shock cannot.

The Tofflers' analysis remains relevant today for two reasons. The first is that many people, perhaps especially in the church, have never really caught up with this important idea. The second is that its effects are greater than ever. If future shock was already visible in 1969, when Bill Gates was chewing pencils and dreaming of becoming a railroad conductor, how much more will it be seen and felt in the twenty-first century and beyond? Not only is the pace of change accelerating but the rate of acceleration is itself increasing. Change is getting faster, and it is getting faster *faster*.

Wider Change: It Takes a Village

Not only must we come to terms with change that is *faster* than ever before; we also need to see that it is *wider*. This operates in three distinct dimensions. Geographically, socially and culturally, the changes we presently face have a breadth to them that goes way beyond our experience to date.

Geographically wider. We are dealing, perhaps for the first time, with truly global patterns of change. There have always been changes that over a period of time spread their influence over large segments of the planet's population, but history shows this to be a slow and laborious process, taking generations to filter through. Today's changes, by contrast, are being faced simultaneously by a much higher proportion of the world's people. Marshall McLuhan's famous term "the global village," which first captured this strange notion of cultural proximity overcoming geographical separation, has been updated by users of the Internet, who are now beginning to talk of a "global mind," as individuals participate in new forms of discourse that know neither cultural nor national boundaries.

Socially wider. There is a social breadth to change that is breaking new ground. Every level of society is being touched, and every one of us is involved. No recent event could more perfectly express this than the incredible scenes in Great Britain in 1997 following the death of Diana, Princess of Wales. In the full glare of international publicity, the royal family were stopped in their tracks by a tidal wave of public emotion. Such was the strength of conviction displayed that the reigning sovereign was forced to abandon aspects of protocol that had been observed for centuries and looked set to stay forever. No amount of wealth, nor of power, nor of prestige could preserve one of the world's most privileged dynasties from the impact of social change. The rich and the poor, the employed and the unemployed, the owners of the means of production and the workers who own nothing, the influential and the unknown—all will be touched by the turbulence of history at this critical time. Those who walk regularly in the corridors of power, whether in politics, business or community life, or for that matter in the church, would do well to learn by heart the mantra of change in our day: "None of us is immune."

Culturally wider. In cultural terms, change is leaving a wide and growing footprint in our lives. Technological change is an obvious starting point, but it is by no means the only field of change. The need to reimagine human culture, implied by the sheer scope of the changes taking place, will hold true for businesses, for families, for churches and for social institutions. It will affect children in the classroom and their grandparents negotiating the erratic aisles of Wal-Mart; it will affect workers in the workplace and homemakers in the home. Town planning will change. Transport will change. The arts will change. Religion will change. Perhaps most important, *people* will change. Indeed, people are already changing in assumptions and attitudes, in lifestyles and timestyles, in the relationships they build or break and the choices they avoid or make. Culturally, socially and geographically, change is getting *wider* by the day.

Deeper Change: Following the Fault Line

If change is *faster* than we had imagined and *wider* than we had assumed, it is also proving to be *deeper* than we at first suspected. Sociologists and cultural pundits have been used to measuring social change against a fairly short time scale—the decade of this, the generation of that, the year of the other. But it now seems that we are seeing change that will be measured against cycles of centuries. Beliefs, traditions and practices that have held good for hundreds of years—that have been the shaping ideologies of our lives—are being questioned and revisited. Terms such as *postindustrial* and *postmodern*, which we will explore in some depth later, are an indication of this much larger time scale.

Imagine for a moment that you live on the fifteenth floor of a high-rise apartment building. You begin to become concerned because cracks have appeared in your walls, and they are widening. Your windows rattle. Your floorboards creak more than usual. In time your concern spills over into action, and you begin to search for the cause. You examine the walls, only to find that none of the cracks have their origin in your apartment—they all begin somewhere deeper. You visit the apartment on the fourteenth floor. Hearing your request, its occupant lets you know that she too is worried. Widening cracks, rattling windows, creaking floors—the same mysterious story as your own. But she too has established that the problem is deeper than her floor. Together you descend to floor thirteen, then floor twelve and so on down through the building. Each floor checked confirms that the cracking has a deeper source or cause than you imagined. You end up, with fourteen of your anxious coresidents, in the basement—armed with shovel and pickax, hacking away at the very foundations of the building. What you initially perceived as an annoyance on a domestic scale has grown, as you have worked your way down, into something much greater. It has drawn in more and more families; its implications have magnified; you begin to sense danger. In the end it is a matter not of comfort but of life and death, affecting not your apartment alone but the whole block.

This is the kind of journey that those investigating social change have found themselves taking in recent years. Every small change proves to be a symptom of some larger transformation, and the stakes just get higher and higher. The further back in history you go to find the source of the cracks, the greater you can assume the impact will be. It is simply not possible for a culture to abandon beliefs held for centuries and not be deeply affected. This is change comparable to the discovery that the world is not flat—change whose depth is all but unfathomable.

Faster change, wider change, deeper change: these are the parameters that mark out social transformation in our age. Together they add up to a kind of cultural millennopause, a "change of life" producing a wide range of signs and symptoms and varying degrees of trauma. Beyond the transformation: new ways of living. Between here and there: changes, more changes and changes still to come.

The X Files
A social transformation of this magnitude will take several decades to run its course, and for the generations at its heart these will be

decades of turbulence and uncertainty. In our own case it is those coming into adulthood in the years immediately before and immediately after the turn of the century, Generation X and the Millennials, for whom these changes will have the greatest significance. There is no clear consensus on whether the current levels of change will slow down in the foreseeable future or whether the transitional generations will simply adapt to change and accept it as the norm. Either way, it is in the coming two decades that the river of history will cross the rapids of change—and nowhere will this have a greater impact than in the lives of these two generations. Nowhere will the cutting edge of the future, for good or ill, be sharper. All of us are affected by change, but Gen Xers and the Millennials are at its fulcrum. We begin our exploration of a culture in transition by knocking on the door of Generation X.

creative.link
john one
by Lynda Marshall

hey, in the beginning which was before or yesterday there was the reason why. the reason why washing powder, the reason why cornflakes, the reason why trees, grass, flowers break into purple, VW Beetles, feet on babies, faces—hey, faces—there was a reason why when in a moment before now, that which was not, big black all over became . . . us.

by us I mean the one to one squillion ape-likes, wondering why they like a bad cigarette lighter were snapped into a blue second, and a moment later which was always too soon, not sometimes even able to inhale they more or less were caught and blown away.

the reason why became flesh and made his dwelling among the TV sets and buildings with no windows and we did not recognise, kept eyes on green screens, quiz shows, news, news blow over our heads, movies—good feelings, happy endings, never thinking of this end, this matchstick flame of a life we were decreasing.

hey, stood next to my shoulder this reason why, but I weren't looking over.

saw him in our sid carrying a board strapped on shoulder said on it "Jesus, Jesus". old sid who offered me a satsuma on a hot afternoon when I sat on a step with my heart twisted over.

"he loves you", he said.

saw it in a girl in the classroom who we pitied because she never once rolled over with no boy in an old cortina with a broken back seat. never once sucked on the stub of a cigarette until her eyes spotted, but one time, one time danced and I wasn't sure whether her feet actually touched the ground. she had a colour on her I had never seen, it was red green purple yellow blue.

i found it in he who sat next to me unexpected on a beach and breathed into me . . .

yeah the reason why became flesh and we have seen him, the glory of the one and only, woke up life and the colours in my eyes were red green purple yellow blue purple yellow orange as the world cracked open . . .

made his dwelling within me.[9]

Homo Xapiens
The New Prototype

---

*Even the much-heralded, sex-drenched 1960s look like a real dump in
retrospect: cars stank, people didn't take care of their bodies,
photocopiers resembled Trabants and just try finding a push-button
phone to enter your answering machine's access code. Ugghh.*
DOUGLAS COUPLAND, "The Past Sucks"

*Our kids may be younger than us, but they are also newer. They are the latest
model of human being and are equipped with a whole lot of new features.*
DOUGLAS RUSHKOFF, "Playing the Future"

The reworking of the opening chapter of John's Gospel on pages
30-31 is the work of Lynda Marshall, a twenty-four-year-old student
from York in England. The exceptional tone of these words—rooted in
contemporary culture, carrying messages of both familiarity and of
strangeness, at once both prophetic and nostalgic—says two things
about their author. First, she is a writer of great promise and talent, but
second, she writes from the heart of Generation X.

It has proved notoriously difficult to define, in any systematic way, what it is that makes Gen Xers different, though millions of words and countless ad agency research budgets have been expended in the attempt. What pundits across the cultures of the developed world agree on is that there is something extraordinary about this age group, the children of the postwar Baby Boomers. Born somewhere between 1960 and 1979, they are the last generation to come of age in the twentieth century. As with the writing of Lynda Marshall, you can spot Generation X when you see it, even if you don't know why. Bemused, pithy, streetwise, rootless, adventurous, exploratory, by turns delirious and despairing, caught between ecstasy and existential angst, Gen Xers wander the urban jungles of the Boomer generation as if they'd just landed from a far-distant planet. Like the "family" of the TV show *Third Rock from the Sun*, they engage with the host culture without ever being fully at home—domestic life is a role to be played; planet earth is just one rock among a million; the old and familiar is new and strange and reevaluated from a wry outsider's perspective. Fake father, fake son—is there anything you can actually call *real* anymore?

Sales for an Accelerated Coupland

Generation X was the name of a short-lived punk band in the late 1970s. Over the ensuing decade the term surfaced from time to time among media experts and advertisers struggling to win over the youth market and encountering not so much rejection as indifference. It remained in the shadowlands of such professional specialization until 1991, when Canadian author Douglas Coupland found it, dusted it off and used it as the title for a book.

Coupland was born in 1961 and raised, for the most part, in Vancouver. He traveled and studied in Hawaii, Italy and Japan and fell by chance into journalism. When his interest in the traits and trends of his own generation surfaced in an article for the periodical *Vancouver,* his concept of Generation X was born, growing up through a cartoon strip in the short-lived *Vista* magazine. Before long Coupland was asked by a New York publishing house to write a "guide to Generation X," modeled on the 1989 *Yuppie Handbook*. He declined the commission but accepted the hint and moved to California to write his first novel.

Generation X: Tales for an Accelerated Culture has little by way of plot but offers a string of snapshots of the lives of twentysome-things Andy, Dag and Claire as they swap stories, compare disillu-sionment and gleefully deconstruct the strange planet, 1990, on which they find themselves. The book was an overnight success in North America, and soon a bestseller around the world. It was closely followed by *Shampoo Planet* (1992), *Life After God* (1994), *Polaroids from the Dead* (1996) and *Girlfriend in a Coma* (1998), all of which continue Coupland's explorations of the post-Boomer culture of the 1990s.

While all six novels chart the journeys of the generation Coup-land belongs to and has named, he has always resisted being cited as its spokesman, claiming, "I speak for myself; not for a generation. I never have."[1] But there is no doubt, whether by accident or design, that Coupland's work has captured the spirit and ethos of his age. He has been translated into twenty-four languages; he is quoted almost endlessly as an indispensable and insightful chronicler of the 1990s; TV Journalist John Fraser has described him as "the Dalai Lama of the twenty-something generation";[2] Generation X has become a term as widely used as *teenager* and *rock 'n' roll* ever were; and many of the author's ironic definitions have effortlessly entered the linguistic gene pool. Witness, for instance, "McJob—a low-pay, low-prestige, low-dignity, low-benefit, no-future job in the service sector. Frequently considered a satisfying career choice by people who have never held one." Or try "Air Family: describes the false sense of community experienced among co-workers in an office environment."[3]

Coupland's Generation X are adrift in a world that has plenty of color but little coherence, in which the bold dreams of its Baby Boom architects have produced a hollow shell. This is a world long on options, short on substance, offering an unprecedented array of goods and experiences but little that is rooted in the permanent or meaningful. Culture past and present is a supermarket shelf of choice and opportunity—nothing is "yours" until you choose to buy it, and then it's yours only until another purchase takes its place. Immanence is on overdrive; transcendence has taken a long holiday. Coupland quotes Al Gore as saying, "The accumulation of material goods is at an all-time high, but so is the number of people who feel emptiness in their lives."[4] In the newly liberated Berlin, he asks, "What is it we can now desire, now that things, objects—stuff— have failed us?"[5] He has become one of that rare breed of writers who, by being at the right place at the right time, pen or PowerBook in hand, touch such a nerve in contemporary culture as to give a name to history. Pundits will argue endlessly on just what is so "X" about this generation, but since Coupland, no one will say it doesn't matter.

Generation Games

Broadly speaking, Gen Xers are those born in the 1960s and 1970s—the teenagers of the 1980s and 1990s and, by implication, the last generation to become adults before the turning of the century. They are approximately equivalent to the generation labeled "Busters" by American sociologists—those born between 1965 and 1983, the children and younger siblings of Boomers (1946–1964) and the grandchildren of Builders (1927–1945).[6] Cyber journalist Douglas Rushkoff succinctly describes Xers as "people who are too young to remember the assassination of President Kennedy and too old to have totally missed disco."[7]

Boom or Bust?

Much of the sound and fury surrounding Generation X relates to the inability of Boomers to come to terms with their own progeny. Gen Xers are not for the most part in open conflict with the institutions of their parents' generation, but they have a sophisticated and worldly wise way of dismantling the values around which those institutions have been formed. As Kevin Ford says, "They disregard rather than distrust authority—distrust is too active a word."[8] Ford characterizes Generation X as being shaped by three overwhelmingly negative assumptions: "The world is not user friendly; the world is not simple; the world has no rules."[9]

Gen Xers cohabit the environment of their Boomer parents but interpret it very differently. They accept the surface forms of the culture they have inherited but divorce these from any assumed inner meaning. They will work the jobs and buy the products of the Boomer age; what they won't do is believe in it. Market analyst Karen Ritchie sums up Boomers as "idealistic, manipulative, flashy and headstrong" and Xers as "streetwise, pragmatic and suspicious."[10]

For Douglas Rushkoff, this standoff is central to the emergence of Generation X. "Gen X as a term came up," he says,

> because a bunch of very wealthy, well-paid public relations experts kept failing to reach a certain demographic, so they went back to their bosses and said, "Oh, no, it's not us, it's not our techniques, it's this generation. They're just X; they don't care. They don't care about anything." Meanwhile these same kids have higher rates of volunteerism than during the peace corps era. It's not that they don't care, it's that they don't listen to this packaged programming anymore.[11]

The Boomer project was working; the consumer engine was purring like a Cadillac—nobody expected the new generation to see things so differently. The very existence of the term Generation X points to a gulf—in lifestyle, values and understanding—between two generations that many had assumed would be continuous. Meaningful or invented, the term marks a schism in cultural history. Somewhere between the Boomer generation of Woodstock, Vietnam and Watergate and the Busters of Madonna, MTV and McWorld, a change has surfaced in Western culture significant enough to leave two generations barely able to understand one another. This is expressed clearly in the Japanese term equivalent to Generation X, *shinjinrui,* meaning literally "a new kind of human being."[12]

Hinge Generation

The sheer scale of this schism—the depth and breadth of the Generation X divide—points to changes that run deeper by far than the so-called "generation gap." Something bigger is happening here than a simple evolution in fashions and values. InterVarsity worker Jimmy Long, who recently completed a D.Min. program on Gen Xers, describes his own discovery of this deeper level of change:

> When I started this study project (in 1992), I was content to focus on Generation X. My goal was to study the characteristics of this generation, compare it with my baby-boomer generation, and make some suggestions for ministering to this generation. The more I studied, the more I began to feel . . . that I did not have the whole picture. Something was missing. I became more and more convinced that something more than the generational transition from boomers to Xers was affecting this present student generation.[13]

For Long, the nature of this larger change became clear through reading David Bosch's *Transforming Mission.*[14] Bosch applies scientist Thomas Kuhn's theories of paradigm shifts to human culture, describing the societal paradigm shifts to which history bears witness. In such shifts it is not just a generation or subculture but a whole culture that changes its ways of thinking and of being. It is a shift of this magnitude, Long claims, that lies beneath the Generation X fault line. The concept is captured perfectly by Graham Cray when he describes the X generation as a "hinge generation." "Western culture is undergoing a fundamental shift," he says. "It is both a shift in the shape and organisation of society and the way people find their identity within it, and in the paradigm or worldview by which people make sense of society and make their decisions."[15] It is this deep shift, more than fashion, trend or generational whim, that has put the X into Generation X.

Straddling a cultural shift, Xers have been raised in a context that is still engaging with the "old" even as the "new" is born and finds its feet. They are tied to both, just as a hinge is held to both door and doorpost. If it is true, as Walter Truett Anderson says, that "we have passed, like Alice slipping through the looking glass, into a new world,"[16] then it is Gen Xers who must make sense of the wonderland. Behind the mirror, in a world at once both familiar and strange, both recognized and unknown, Gen Xers must survive in a new and strange environment. Whatever the roots and routes of our social transformation—whatever the culture junction is all about—Generation X is at the heart of it.

Emigration X

It is important to take seriously this linking of Generation X to a wider societal paradigm shift. For those observing the changes evident in this generation, the link is significant because of the following:

1. Gen Xers aren't coming home. The temptation with short-term generational labeling is that we simply wait for the latest generation of rebels to grow up, come to their senses and rejoin the society and culture of their parents. If Gen Xers are, as we are claiming, a hinge generation—the last of the old and the first of the new—then such an expectation will in their case be illusory. If Generation X says nothing else to us, it says, "Life will never be the same again."

2. Gen Xers are a wake-up call to Western culture. If the turbulence of the Generation X transition is symptomatic of a wider societal paradigm shift, then we need to move urgently from observing generational distinctives to understanding the deeper changes. Gen Xers are significant not only for their *characteristics* but also for their *context*—at the apex of change. Their very existence speaks to us of the transforming journey on which Western culture has embarked.

3. Gen Xers are the place to start in understanding this cultural transformation. If Xers are the last of the old and the first of the new—the hinge generation—then their attitudes and activities will be indicative, to some extent, of future directions. In the way Gen Xers are thinking and behaving, and in the choices they are making now, there will be clues as to where our culture will move in the early years of the twenty-first century.

4. Gen Xers are the key to understanding, and perhaps healing, the pain of the Western church. For those carrying a faith commitment, this is an added dimension of significance to the Generation X phenomenon. One of the contexts in which Graham Cray has applied the "hinge generation" analogy is in the discussion of the postevangelical movement in the United Kingdom. "Is it possible," he asks, "that post-evangelicals are the Generation X or 'baby-busters' of the evangelical world?"[17] Church leaders are wringing their hands and wondering why so many in their twenties and thirties are asking unanswerable questions, rejecting or deconstructing key aspects of their faith and choosing to live out their pilgrimage in a wilderness outside of any communal church commitment. Were they to better understand the magnitude of the cultural transition that underpins these changes of attitude, they might well be less discouraged and less threatened—and better able to help.

Gen Xers are the icebreakers of the new, the generation at the bow of societal change who will be the first to forge into the emerging world. Whatever has been until now ends with them. Whatever is to come has begun in them already. Those of us who are concerned to anticipate the emerging culture must start by better understanding and serving Generation X. If we cannot understand Generation X, we will in all likelihood fail to understand their successors. The key to winning a significant presence for the church in the emerging culture is to win a significant presence for Generation X in the church.

A Word to the Ys

In this global transition Generation X will stand alongside those immediately beyond, their younger siblings born between 1980 and

1999: We have already called this group the Millennials; other suggested labels include Generation Y, Generation Next and the Mosaics (in honor of their capacity to think in mosaic rather than linear forms). This is broadly the generation currently in childhood, the oldest of them slogging through school while their Gen X elders are out making sense—or nonsense—of higher education and the world of work. They will be the first teenagers of the twenty-first century, the first generation to come of age in the third millennium.

Most attempts to date to ride in the wake of Coupland's "Generation X" with an incisive profile of the Millennials are speculative and premature—it will take a Douglas (or perhaps Daphne) Coupland of 2011 to catch the zeitgeist of Generation Y. All the same, there are ways in which we can begin, intuitively, to reach toward the lives these post-X young people will live. Some of the key factors in this are the following:

1. The Ys are different already. Much of what Millennials will be is present already in what they are—the potential hidden in the actual. Even in childhood, contextual and behavioral changes can point toward the shape of teenage and adult lives to come.

2. The Ys are more X than the X. What has begun in Generation X will go much further among Millennials—the influence of the previous culture all but wiped out by the time they reach maturity. Boomer culture will be as far removed from Millennials as World War II, Frank Sinatra and corned beef have been from Xers.

3. The Ys have a new normative environment. The social influences that have been new phenomena during the lives of Gen Xers— the Internet being the supreme example—will be taken for granted by Millennials. In an accelerated culture, the novel becomes the normal in the space of just a few years.

4. The Ys have a special task. Like Generation X, the *context* of the Millennials will greatly influence their *character.* Just as Gen Xers are taking us into the "change of life," it is the creativity and skill of this younger group, who will live all of their adult lives in the new millennium, that will lead us *out* of it.

5. The Ys live at the dawn of a new day. There is an important difference between living at the end of a century and living at its beginning. Where Gen Xers have lived in the apocalyptic shadow of the end of the world, Millennials will become adults in the wide-open spaces of a dawning century. This may prove to be the defining factor of their age. An evening generation will give way to a morning generation.[18]

These two generations are central to our thinking about social change, just as social change is central to their lives. That which Xers have experienced in early adulthood the Millennials have watched as children. What they, in turn, will live through in their crucial teenage and early adult years will be the first two decades of a new century. The contours of social change by which these decades are shaped will be the contours of these new young adults' lives.

word.link: Re:generation
We will tell the next generation the praiseworthy deeds of the LORD, his power, and the wonders he has done. . . . They would not be like their forefathers—a stubborn and rebellious generation, whose hearts were not loyal to God, whose spirits were not faithful to him.—**Psalm 78:4, 8**

When I was engaged full time in youth ministry, this psalm was one of my greatest sources of encouragement. It records the rollercoaster reality of the history of Israel: a people who waxed and waned, generation by generation, in their devotion to their God. Two truths leap out from these verses for me.

First, generational distinctives were not invented in the twentieth century. The idea that a new generation can be different from the last, that it must travel its own journey and face its own challenges, is inherent in this psalm. There was no Hebrew concept of Generation X, but there was an abiding, deeply held notion of transition. The gospel is not given to be held on to but to be passed on, transmitted, recontextualized for a new generation.

Second, and most important, God is in the business of renewing his work in each new generation. Where there is disobedience, where hearts have become cold toward Yahweh, where we have not walked in his ways, one of his strategies is to make a fresh approach to a new generation. The renewal of the work of God continues, generation by generation. The pivotal words of this psalm are found in verse 8: "they would not be like their forefathers." They will be different. This is not only a sociological or descriptive statement; it is a cry of hope and longing. They *will be* different. This is the hope—the only hope—of the Western church.

Seven Seas of Why

Charting Currents of Change

It is the social transformations, like ocean currents deep below the hurricane-tormented surface of the sea, that have had the lasting, indeed the permanent, effect.
PETER F. DRUCKER, "The Age of Social Transformation"

There is no lighthouse keeper. There is no lighthouse. There is no dry land. There are only people living on rafts made from their own imaginations. And there is the sea.
JOHN DOMINIC CROSSAN, *The Dark Interval*

W *aterworld* is not a great movie by most objective standards. At its release it was the most expensive film project in history (later surpassed by the equally watery *Titanic*). Within the industry the on-set gossip is generally believed to be more entertaining than the script: the delays in filming due to Kevin Costner's seasickness; the day a freak storm sank the whole multimillion dollar set; the legendary conflicts between the two Kevins—Costner the star and Reynolds the director. But for all the mixed reviews, there is a level at which *Waterworld* holds extraordinary power, and that is in its visual and intuitive portrayal of our contemporary situation.

Whether by default or by design, *Waterworld* offers a rich fund of imagery and nuance to better understand the junction generations. Seven images in particular set the film apart as a parable of change in our day. I offer them here, not in any attempt at systematic social analysis, but more as an emotional journey—not so that we *know* more but so that we might *feel* more of the challenges these generations face. Let's allow a creative product of the 1990s to deepen our intuitive grasp of a culture in transition.

Image 1: A Past Flooded Out by the Future

Waterworld takes place on planet Earth in an imagined future in which the icecaps have melted. The world's surface has been covered by water, and those who once lived with their feet on terra firma must adapt to living at sea. This marks a subtle departure from Hollywood's habitual postapocalyptic scenario, in which the earth is all but destroyed by nuclear holocaust, planetary collision or alien invasion. The difference in *Waterworld* is that the old civilization has not been destroyed so much as made redundant. It remains—for the most part intact—beneath the waves. A new world has washed over the old, rendering it uninhabitable.

This echoes the Tofflers' definition of future shock arising from "the superimposition of a new culture on an old one."[1] The survivors are those who have been lifted by the floodwaters high above what were once their rooftops. So it is with culture shift—it is something that grows around us, begins to lift us from familiar moorings, changes us before we know we're changing. These generations are not different because of some huge, momentary crisis; they are different because a different world carries them. They are seaborne, and the assumptions of the landlocked no longer hold the power to inspire.

Image 2: Losing the Dry Ground of Certainty

Waterworld's survivors must adapt to a new place in which to be human and to new ways of being human. Their points of reference, their laws, their notions of civilized behavior are all called into question by their seaborne lifestyle. They float on the undulating sea, at the mercy of its winds and currents—there is no fixed point to cling to.

As these generations journey through culture shift, they too are on uncertain ground. There is a rocking motion. Nausea is possible. There are storms. Structures may fall. Older generations, who have prided themselves on their capacity to survive and thrive on land, may be surprised by their own vulnerability. The sea exposes the weaknesses of those who appeared strong when they had something strong to stand on. New skills are needed for a life, for the time being, without moorings. "Postmodern surfaces are not landscapes but wavescapes," writes Leonard Sweet, "with the waters always changing and the surface never the same. The sea knows no boundaries."[2]

Image 3: The Emergence of Transitional Communities

Human beings are, by nature, culture formers. A pioneer wagon train, even if made up of total strangers, would form a defensive circle at night. Men and women are driven to band together for mutual protection and prosperity. Waterworld is no exception as new cultures and communities are formed. Some choose to bolt and buckle together their assorted floating structures to form an outer shell and, within it, to create some semblance of civic life. Others occupy huge abandoned ships, moving together across the oceans as mass pilgrims in search of a better future. Still others choose the lone call of the high seas but live all the same by agreed-upon codes and norms. What these responses have in common is that they are transitional social structures. They are temporary adaptations, responding to immediate need without laying down foundations for permanence. No one knows quite what the long-term future will hold. For some, the search for the legendary Dryland is enough to render any other lifestyle temporary.

Equally, among the junction generations, the new cultural forms that emerge in new structures and patterns of behavior may well be temporary and experimental. When old clothes wear out, many new outfits might be tried on before the best is found. Meanwhile, we will continue to be dazed and confused by the often bizarre choices of generations in transition.

Image 4: Be Safe—Be Surface

In a flooded world, deep is dangerous. Stay too long and deep is dead. Preserving life means staying surface.

Channel hopping, Net surfing, multitasking, mosaic thinking, sampling, pick-and-mix—these generations are famous already for their capacity to engage with the surface level of culture but move on before getting deep.[3] This is an offense to land dwellers, who live by laying foundations, putting down roots, digging deep. But these generations have learned to hop like water bugs across the surface because that is the only safe way to negotiate a flood. This is not some deficiency in their attention span; it is an appropriate adaptation to an entirely new environment. If they learn to seek internal depth, they must do it even as they remain, externally, at surface level. "Just like ocean surfing," writes Douglas Rushkoff, "the habitual channel surfing of our TV-fixated youth is as lamented by parents as it is valuable to us all as an example of thriving on chaos. Just like the ocean or the man-made cityscape, the modern mediaspace, too, is a chaotic system, and subject to the same laws of dynamics."[4] Digging is not a valuable skill in Waterworld.

Image 5: Plundering the Past to Fund the Future

In one of the genuinely moving scenes of *Waterworld*, Mariner (Costner) allows his newfound companion to join him, via a makeshift diving bell, as he heads far below the surface to explore the skyscrapers and cathedrals of what once was Dryland. No words are spoken, and the enormity of the change that has swept the planet is brought home to us in the murky but recognizable shapes. Mariner has made it his habit to dive deep into these flooded ruins, always surfacing with some gadget or memento—a fragment of the old world to bring color to the new.

This image of diving deep into the past to seek some sign, some clue to the present and future, is a powerful metaphor for the strange life of the junction generations. Many in Boomer culture are surprised that young people, with such a new and different future opening up before them, are drawn to explore the past. In particular, the deep history and traditions of premodern and aboriginal peoples are newly and unexpectedly popular. These generations sense two things above all others: that the current culture is coming to an end, and that its replacement has not yet fully emerged. The principal has announced his retirement at the end of the school year, and a successor has not yet been appointed. In the meantime, with the future unknown and the present unreliable, the past is a storehouse of ideas to explore. In the turmoil of today, the young rummage through yesterday in search of keys to tomorrow.

Image 6: Adapted to Two Worlds, at Home in None

A sixth compelling image from *Waterworld* is that of Mariner himself. For all that the character is defined by Costner's action-figure antics, Mariner has something else that sets him apart from the crowd: he has gills. A byproduct of an evolutionary aberration the script never quite explains, Mariner is a mutant: half man, half fish. He lives among the surface community but is just as at home under water. Thus adapted to the new watery conditions of the world, Mariner is unable or unwilling, when Dryland is finally located, to resettle with his human friends. As the credits roll, he leaves them to their newfound paradise and sets sail, alone, for the high seas once more.

No less mutant, the junction generations understand intuitively that they must live in two worlds. Generation X, especially, born when the continental plates of history were already on the move, have been forced to adapt to this dual reality. Many have become bilingual, speaking the language of the past among their elders and of the future among their peers. They know just enough of both worlds to know that they are at home in neither. Rootless and restless, they wander both worlds as strangers, inexplicably driven by a longing for home.

Image 7: And a Little Child Shall Lead Them

One final image from *Waterworld* that carries remarkable power at this transitional stage in history is that of the map of the future. The film's plot finds its focus in the quest for the legendary Dryland. Real or mythical, the very idea of Dryland is enough to fuel a lifetime's searching. The search, in turn, becomes centered on an old map—the only remaining clue to where Dryland might lie. But the map does not exist on paper; it is tattooed on the back of a child. Only by keeping the child with them, as they seek to understand the map, can the straggling survivors hope to reach their goal. The child, without knowing it, holds the key to the future.

This is a powerful parable for the junction generations. Though they may not know it, our children already hold the keys to reading the future. Without them, the older generations cannot hope to decode the blinding array of signals with which the new century bombards them. The young are uniquely equipped for the environment they will meet. But they need help to read the maps they hold. The wisdom of the past without a vision of the future is irrelevant, or worse still, deadening. But a vision of the future ignorant of the lessons of the past is irresponsible. What is needed is that the two should unite, the generations overcoming the culture gap and working together to construct the new. This proves the key to success for the straggling survivors of Waterworld, and it stands as the best hope in our own, more real dilemmas. Many in the older generations need to face the truth that those younger than themselves hold the keys; many in the younger generations need to admit their need of help. Only as the two stand together will the map of the future be intelligible. As the film's promotional slogan says, "Beyond the horizon lies the key to a new beginning."

PART 2

Root Causes

The Five "Posts"
of Generation X & Beyond

4

New Tools,
New Rules
Postindustrial Technology

---

*The things that got you to where you are today are not the things that
will get you to where you need to be tomorrow.*
GEORGE BARNA, *The Second Coming of the Church*

*In acquiring new productive forces men change their mode of
production; and in changing their mode of production, in changing the
way of earning their living, they change all their social relations. The
hand-mill gives you society with the feudal lord; the steam-mill, society
with the industrial capitalist.*
KARL MARX, *The Poverty of Philosophy*

Online trading is like the Old West. The slow die first.
FIDELITY.COM, advertising copy

History has long acknowledged James Watt as the father of steam power. I remember being told at school that he watched his mother's kettle boil and was inspired on the spot to invent the railroad train. The truth is never that simple, but Watt was a pioneer who saw the vast potential in the everyday act of applying heat to water. His business partner, without whom he might never have left the kitchen, was Matthew Boulton—a pioneer of economics rather than of science. The inventor put up the ideas, the businessman put up the money, and in 1775 the Boulton and Watt factory opened in Birmingham, England. Pushing available technology to the limits of innovation, the factory was the first in the world to manufacture steam-powered "prime movers" on an industrial scale. History records Matthew Boulton's profound faith in the new venture—a faith proved when King George II of England paid a visit to the site. "Your Majesty," Boulton said, "I have at my disposal what the whole world demands; something which will uplift civilisation more than ever by relieving man of all undignified drudgery. I have steam power."[1]

Fastforward 220 years. For Matthew Boulton read Bill Gates, founder of the giant Microsoft Corporation. For steam power read digital processing. For the rest, the parallels are clear: the same buoyant optimism; the same zealous faith in the upside of technology; the same potent cocktail of investment and innovation, with rich rewards for the pioneers. "A whole generation of us computer guys, all over the world, dragged that favorite toy with us into adulthood," Gates has said. "We caused a kind of revolution—peaceful, mainly—and now the computer has taken up residence in our offices and in our homes."[2]

What unites this pair, Boulton and Gates, across two centuries is that they are both actors in the early years of a technological earthquake. The first Industrial Revolution brought *mechanization* to a culture dependent on agriculture. Within decades the face of human society was substantially remodeled, until it bore little resemblance to the rural idyll of its past. Most of what we take for granted in our culture has come to us because of this revolution—we are the children of the Industrial Age. The second revolution is happening now. The era of Boulton and Watt has always been referred to as *the* Industrial Revolution, as if we weren't expecting another, but the evidence that innovation is moving us on once again is now overwhelming. "The law of acceleration now hurtles us into a new age," Harvard historian Arthur Schlesinger Jr. has written. "The shift from a factory-based to a computer-based economy is more traumatic even than our great-grandparents' shift from a farm-based to a factory-based economy. The Industrial Revolution extended over generations and allowed time for human and institutional adjustment. The Computer Revolution is far swifter, more concentrated, and more dramatic in its impact."[3]

At first some of us mistakenly thought of the computer as a machine because it lived in a metal box and was plugged into the wall. But it has shown itself to be something quite different: a whole new revolution. Machines and mechanism are being replaced by information and digital code as the genetic imprint of our economy and culture. Our world is once more in for a face-lift; change is once more at work. The early generations of millennium three will be children of a second Industrial Revolution, and the coming two decades, at the very least, will be marked by ongoing and exponential technological change.

definition.link: *Postindustrial*

The world of Generation X and beyond will be postindustrial in the following senses:

1. A primary driver of change is technology, in its influence on economics and the world of work and its subsequent impact on lifestyle.

2. The role of machinery and mechanization as a central icon in the shaping of society has been superseded.

3. In its place, new economic, cultural and social structures are growing around the central influence of digital processing, enabled by fast-developing information technology.

4. The influence of this new technological icon will be as widely and keenly felt as that of machine technology has been and as that of agriculture once was, shaping not just economic activities but a whole range of social and cultural structures.

Three questions confront us if we are to better understand this particular current of change:

1. What's happening? What is the evidence that this transition is already under way? Is this a major shift or just another flurry of inventions?

2. What's next? What further changes will the technologies currently in development bring? How will tomorrow's postindustrial technology be *more* postindustrial than the postindustrial technology of today?

3. What does it matter? What social forms will these changes bring? How will they impact Gen Xers and the Millennials? What specific challenges will the spread of postindustrial technology present to our culture?

The first two of these questions will be tackled in the rest of this chapter; the third will form the basis of chapter five.

What's Happening: The Digital Wormhole

It is impossible to discuss postindustrial society without coming across the name of Peter Drucker.[4] Widely credited as the father of contemporary management studies, Drucker was raised and educated in Austria and Germany but has lived in the United States for most of his adult life. He has been observing, analyzing, informing and shaping the world of work in Western culture for over four decades, and much of this time he has been dedicated to understanding the changes sweeping through industrialized cultures. Drucker's take on the theme of technological transition is that we are moving into the "knowledge society."

A change in the human condition. Drucker has traced the growth and decline of the Industrial Revolution of Boulton and Watt by examining the types of employment dominant in society. "By 1900," he says, " 'industrial worker' had become synonymous with 'machine operator' and implied employment in a factory along with hundreds if not thousands of people."[5] By 1950, such workers had become the largest single group in every developed country and mass-production industry was the dominant economic factor. But this peak was to be the last great hour of industrialism. In the forty years that followed, the growth of knowledge-based and service-oriented industries transformed employment and economics. "Whereas industrial workers who make or move things had accounted for two fifths of the American workforce in the 1950's," Drucker says, "they accounted for less than one fifth in the early 1990's—that is, for no more than they had accounted for in 1900, when their meteoric rise began. . . . By the year 2000 or 2010, in every developed free market country, industrial workers will account for no more than an eighth of the work force."[6]

In their place, our economies are now dominated by "knowledge workers"—those whose role is not to make or move things but to process information and offer services. "Knowledge workers . . . will give the emerging society its character, its leadership, its social profile. They may not be the ruling class of the knowledge society, but they are already its leading class."[7]

Drucker's analysis offers compelling evidence of a major shift in the way we live and work. He is describing social and economic patterns on the grandest scale—changes that affect whole nations in their development. "This is far more than a social change," he summarizes. "It is a change in the human condition. What it means—what are the values, the commitments, the problems of the new society, we do not know. But we do know that much will be different."[8] For management consultant Terence Ryan, this difference can be measured in one simple assertion. "The symbol of this new era is at hand," he says. "Today, for the first time in history, the world's wealthiest man, Bill Gates, is a knowledge worker and not a petroleum magnate, as had been the case for the past hundred years."[9]

Birth of a revolution. The transition from an industrial to a knowledge-based economy began while the old technologies were still dominant, just as industrialization had begun when agriculture was still the majority occupation. The increasing levels of information being handled by the new knowledge workers called for new tools and a new concept: information processing. In exploring this new field, researchers began to unlock the secrets of digital code and "computation," and before long a new technology was born. Tools invented to solve the problems of the old order served to accelerate its evolution to a new order. What began in the 1950s and 1960s as a tentative shift from manufacture to information revealed itself, with the launch of the IBM personal computer in 1981, to be the revolution we now know it to be. Digital technology was not in itself the origin of this "change in the human condition," but it has become the driving force behind it. A society shifting from mechanism to information in the 1950s and 1960s set its sails toward the knowledge culture, and the digital technology of the 1980s and 1990s became the wind that filled them—a gentle breeze at first, but before long, a gale-force wind.

Just as mechanical technology was applied at first to making agriculture more efficient, but in time spawned whole new industries of its own, so digital technology, the child of industry, is growing up to transform the very society that gave it birth. "The forces of digitalization act like the gravity of a 'wormhole' in *Star Trek,*" one recent report said, "pulling recognizable industries through it and transforming them into something unrecognizable on the other side."[10] Another prominent management theorist, Charles Handy, describes this transformation in terms of "discontinuous change."[11] We live, Handy argues, in the "Age of Unreason," when each small technological breakthrough can have dramatic effects, changing us in ways from which we will never return. This is, as the French magazine *Capital* proclaimed in August 1998, "one of the fastest revolutions in human history."[12]

Brute force to brain force. The recognition that the Industrial Age was coming to an end formed the basis of the second bestseller from *Future Shock* authors Alvin and Heidi Toffler. *The Third Wave,* published in 1980, presents "a model of historical and social change,"[13] built on the simple and compelling argument that human history has been dominated by three great waves of technology. "The first wave corresponds to the agricultural revolution which dominated human history for thousands of years. The second wave—industrial civilization—is now playing itself out after 300 years of dominance. The Third Wave is crashing over us right now, having started with the birth of a post-industrial, high-technology, information economy in the 1950s."[14]

The Tofflers go well beyond simply telling us that this revolution is happening; they have gathered a whole range of evidence to help us see what it will *mean.* Their claim is that we are moving "from a brute-force economy to a brain-force economy"[15] and that this will have enormous implications not just for the way we work and do business but for the way we live. Central to the Tofflers' approach is an appreciation of the extent to which our lives are shaped by the dominant technology of the day. Technology gives birth to economic activity, which in turn configures social structures and arrangements. Consider, for example, the vast array of geographical, social and legal conditions that have arisen from our mastery of the internal combustion engine, of powered flight and of satellite communications. In significant areas of our lives, the tools create the rules.

The hugely successful British film *The Full Monty* offers a remarkable view of this process at work. The group of men around whom the film revolves are seen to change not only their occupation but also their attitudes on such matters as gender roles and childcare, sexuality, and their own self-image and social role. But all these changes are rooted in a technological shift: the closing of the Sheffield steelworks.

Riding the wave. When I first read *The Third Wave* in the late 1980s,

I found myself reflecting on the extent to which machine technology had influenced the culture in which I was raised. I had to agree with the authors that mechanization was a central icon, a kind of invisible genetic code, to industrial society. Somehow its imprint had gone beyond the immediate shaping of the industrial process—the design of assembly lines, factories and machine parts—to influence much wider social structures: schools, town planning, housing, unions and organizations of every type, families and, yes, churches. Terence Ryan cites the work of early industrial engineer Frederick Winslow Taylor—founder of "scientific management," later called time and motion study—to illustrate this power of the machine as social icon. Scientific management, Ryan suggests, increased productivity "by making each worker conform to a scientifically prescribed form of work, as mechanical as that of a machine." The influence of this went well beyond the factory walls. "So persuasive was the idea of scientific management," Ryan writes, "that it spread without question from the industrial sector right across all aspects of social organisations. Writing in 1910 Taylor suggested that the lessons of scientific management 'can be applied to all social activities: to the management of our homes, the management of our farms, the management of the business of our tradesmen, large and small; of our churches, our philanthropic institutions, our universities and our government departments.' "[16] The limitations of such a mechanistic view of society are captured in the words of Taylor himself, who said in 1900, "The antithesis of our scheme is asking the initiative [of our workers] . . . their workmanship, their best brains and their best work. . . . Our scheme does not ask any initiative in a man."[17]

If the Tofflers, Ryan and others are to be believed, we are now experiencing the demise of these principles—the corporate, social equivalent of a heart transplant—as digital code displaces machinery as the imprint at the very core of our social arrangements. The nature of this imprint, and how the digital revolution will change it, is what makes the shift to a postindustrial society so important. If the adoption of machine technology has lead to a machinelike understanding of work, of education and of culture—even of the human condition—then what changes in understanding will the adoption of digital technology bring? "If we look back on this period in a hundred years from now," the Tofflers argue, "the historians will say . . . the most important thing that happened in that period was the emergence of a new civilization. You can call it post-industrial, Third Wave or technotronic."[18] If we are to take seriously the impact of technological change, we will need to look well beyond the realm of industry and work. Digital technology is not only changing the way we earn our keep; it is changing the way we live. In chapter five we will explore the implications of this change, not least for Gen Xers and the Millennials. But first we must take a brief look at the revolutions that are still to come, as the postindustrial "third wave" goes beyond the boundaries of our present experience.

What's Next 1: Cyberoptic Fiberspace

If the names of Toffler and Drucker have been associated with analyzing the early decades of postindustrialism, one name that is inseparable from its future is that of Bill Gates. Head of the mammoth Microsoft Corporation and reportedly the richest man in the world, Gates has written extensively of the unfolding history of digital technology. In *The Road Ahead* he tells the inside story on some of the milestones in the personal computer revolution, but he stresses that the biggest leap forward is in the future. This will be associated not primarily with computation but with communication, when the present-day Internet evolves into the "information superhighway." "We stand on the brink of another revolution," Gates writes. "This one will involve unprecedentedly inexpensive communication. All the computers will join together to communicate with us and for us. . . . When communication gets inexpensive enough, and is combined with other advances in technology, the influence of interactive information will be as real and as far-reaching as the effects of electricity."[19]

Using fiber-optic cables, the information superhighway offers

high-capacity, multilane links for potentially billions of users, carrying a vast array of information from one to the other. "Fibre optics is
going to render bandwidth and hertz virtually free," technoevange-
list George Gilder has claimed. "One thread of glass the width of a
human hair can carry one thousand times the content of today's
entire radio spectrum."[20] The new networks carry not just text and
voice but also broadcast-standard audio and video, full-length movies, whole libraries compressed into a few seconds of transfer time.
Cables currently being laid beneath the Pacific Ocean will have the
capacity to carry eight million voice or data conversations at any one
time—compared to just forty thousand on the existing, first-generation fiber cables.[21] "We can no more imagine what the broadband
information highway will carry in twenty-five years," Gates says,
"than a Stone Age man using a crude knife could have envisioned
Ghiberti's Baptistry doors in Florence."[22]

The advent of the information superhighway is creating a whole
new realm in which to live, work and make social contacts: cyberspace. A concept that first appeared in the science fiction of William
Gibson,[23] cyberspace gets more real by the day. It is the new territory in which social interaction will thrive. "Cyberspace," Michael
Malone predicts, "will be a world twenty-first century man will feel
at home in."[24]

Already, business pioneers are staking their claims to cyberspace
in what commentators have called "the Internet gold rush." A flood
of Internet business start-ups, dubbed dot.com companies, is creating hundreds of millionaires, often within a colossally short time
frame. A historic example is Netscape—chief competitor, in the
browser business, to Microsoft—for whom "the Initial Public Offering (IPO) was held only 16 months after the company had been
formed. The stock was offered at $28, already a high price, but
demand quickly pushed it to $71. Netscape, after a single day of
trading, was worth $4.4 billion."[25] "We believe that Web sites are
essentially real estate lots in an unbounded territory on a new continent,"[26] says Toby Corey, former vice president of industry giant

Novèll. To read magazines such as *Wired* and *Fast Company* is to be plunged headlong into this new world, which barely existed half a decade ago and yet which is growing at an unimaginable rate. While for some the Internet is still seen as a future technology, for increasing numbers it is very much a present experience. Michael Dell—at thirty-four, reputedly the fifth-richest man in America—is host to the world's largest and busiest Internet shopping site, generating sales estimated at $30 million a day. He puts the future of business in stark terms: "I think that every company has to be an internet company, or it won't be a company at all."[27] "Ultimately," says journalist Michael Moon, "what emerges is the global Interopolis—a new, rapidly expanding republic of information."[28]

The changes we've seen so far, dazzling as they are, are just the beginning—a dress rehearsal for what happens when cyber meets fiber to bring exponentially faster, and cheaper, communications. "A machine that transforms communication impinges far more radically on people's lives than one that transforms computation," *The Economist* tells us. "You do not have to be a nerd or a mystic to see that historians will look back upon the emergence of 'cyberspace' as a turning point no less decisive than the advent of the computer itself."[29]

And there is more to come. The year 2000 was slated to see advanced trials of a second-generation Internet, known as Internet2 (I2), or "Abilene," after the railhead that opened up the American West. Built on an advanced Internet Protocol, IPv6, Abilene currently links together 150 U.S. universities. It will be bigger, more reliable and, most important, faster than today's Internet. IPv6 is already used by radio stations for audio webcasting, and will almost certainly bring us real-time Web TV. It will be capable of transferring data at the astounding speed of 2.4 gigabits per second—forty-five thousand times faster than today's average modem, and the equivalent of sending ten full encyclopedias around the world in one second. Abilene's research team is already working on the transmission of holographs and—ultimately—a sense of touch.[30]

The first adult generations of the new millennium will witness—
and be impacted by—the most significant development in communications technology since the creation of the alphabet. "The information superhighway is more than a short-cut to every book in the
Library of Congress," writes researcher Nicholas Negroponte. "It is
creating a totally new, global social fabric."[31] In chapters six and
seven we will explore the impact of these changes on the ways in
which we communicate, as well as the place in our lives of text and
print. For the moment, it is crucial that we appreciate the sheer scale
of this revolution, as the planet is hard-wired into a single, interactive, high-capacity communications web.

What's Next 2: The Talking Fridge

Physicist Michio Kaku is one of the brightest scientists on the
planet. He has written extensively on superstrings, quantum field
theory, hyperspace, the tenth dimension and other concepts that
most mere mortals don't even pretend to understand.[32] His most
recent book, a bestseller on both sides of the Atlantic, offers a
guided tour of the future from the perspective of research science.
Rather than blindly predict what might happen Dr. Kaku wrote
Visions: How Science Will Revolutionize the Twenty-First Century
by asking 150 of the world's leading researchers what *is* happening.
The result is a book that anticipates rather than predicts, based on
research projects that are already under way and products that exist
already in prototype form. *Visions* foresees three revolutions in the
coming century.

In the realm of medicine and physiology, the *biomolecular revolution* will change society forever and "ultimately give us the power
to alter and synthesize new forms of life, and create new medicines
and therapies."[33] By 2003 the Human Genome Project will have
sequenced all one hundred thousand human genes. By 2020 a doctor
will be able to take a tiny fragment of a patient's skin, analyze it
and hand over a CD-ROM containing a complete genetic profile.
Treatment will be as likely through gene manipulation as through

drugs. Diseases for which no cure currently exists will be treated genetically. Even aging, the ancient enemy, may be rendered treatable.

In the realm of physics, the *quantum revolution* will transform our capacity to manipulate matter. "Nanotechnology is a field that promises perhaps the smallest of all possible machines: molecular machines," Dr. Kaku writes.[34] Invisible to the human eye, these tiny agents will perform complex tasks, opening up a whole new world of micromanagement.

The *computer revolution* will come about through the workings of Moore's Law, which demonstrates the accelerating capacity of computer memory.[35] "To appreciate the remarkable increase in computer power that is propelling us from one phase to the next," Dr. Kaku writes, "it is important to remember that from 1950 to the present, there has been an increase in computer power by a factor of about ten billion. At the heart of this explosive growth is Moore's law, which states that computer power doubles every eighteen months. A rapid increase in power on this scale is almost unheard of in the history of science."[36] Greater chip power means lower memory cost. As Moore's law pushes the power of computers in one direction, there is an equal and opposite force pushing their price in the other. Once microchips cost less than a penny, below the current price of a sheet of paper, Dr. Kaku predicts that the personal computer will be replaced by millions of tiny intelligent systems, embedded in our environment: in clothes, jewelry, glasses, cars, furniture and walls. These will be voice-responsive, carrying out simple commands. In time, perhaps within the first two decades of millennium three, microchips will be as common as writing and electricity.

Of these three, the cyber future will be the first to be widely experienced—and the most significant to our current exploration of social change. At Media Lab—one of the world's leading research agencies, founded by Nicholas Negroponte in 1985 and based at MIT[37]—over 330 researchers work at the pioneering edge of computing. Their most cherished goal is "ubiquitous computing"—the

official term for the "chips with everything" future that Michio Kaku
is predicting, when processing power breaks out of the computer
itself to be implanted in the ordinary objects of everyday life—creating a physical environment as intelligent and responsive as the
motherboards of today. "Ubiquitous computing was conceived in
1988; it may take until the year 2003 to begin to see these ideas
affect our lives in an appreciable way. And it may be years after that
before they reach 'critical mass' and ignite the marketplace. But by
2010, one can expect to see ubiquitous computing becoming of age.
By 2020, it will dominate our lives."[38]

Ubiquitous computing will put *digital processing* at the heart of a
vast array of objects and products. Processes that in current technology are essentially mechanistic—unable to respond to choice and
change—will be rendered intelligent. Examples of this change can
be seen in some of the products in production or foreseen even at
this very early stage of the revolution These include the following:

☐ the talking fridge—a part-PC, part-icebox appliance that keeps
everything cool but also stores recipes, offers cooking advice, and
logs onto the Web to transmit a shopping list

☐ intelligent ink—an electronic system with the capacity to print
text into a standard book format, then refresh the content by downloading from the Internet

☐ toilets that analyze whatever lands in them and alert the user to
health concerns

☐ ski jackets with built-in communications facilities, including sat-
ellite-linked e-mail, so no skiers need ever go so far off the trail that
they cannot be found

☐ contact lenses that receive e-mail and display a miniature Internet
screen

☐ head scarves that release micro quantities of perfume when
brushed against human skin

☐ robot pets—second-generation Tamagotchis, with limbs, fur and
independent movement—that respond to their keepers' personalities

☐ a coffee machine that registers the preferences of each person in the household and matches the drink to the voice[39]

Ubiquitous computing will be as far beyond the current capability of PCs as domestic electricity is beyond a first-generation steam traction engine. It will take the shift from machines to digital technology and spread it into every corner of our lives. Whatever else it achieves, the "chips with everything" revolution will increase and deepen the impact of the Third Wave technological shift.[40]

These two "revolutions yet to come," the information superhighway and ubiquitous computing, will consolidate the place of digital technology at the very heart of the twenty-first century. Computing and communications technologies, as they evolve, will be among the most powerful shaping forces in the lives of the transitional generations. As much as the twentieth century reflected the characteristics of industrial mechanism, so will the twenty-first reflect information processing—from the macro scale of multinational corporations to the micro scale of a lone teenager logging on to the Web. It's time to ask, what does it matter? What are the implications of the information revolution for the Homo xapiens experience?

High-Cyber Diet

Living with
Postindustrial Technology

It is not only our material environment that is transformed by our machinery. We take our technology into the deepest recesses of our souls. Our view of reality, our structures of meaning, our sense of identity—all are touched and transformed by the technologies which we have allowed to mediate between ourselves and our world.
DAVID LOCHHEAD, "Technology and Interpretation"

You can no longer remain unconscious where you slept before; one way or another, you are creating your future. Wake up before you find that the devils within you have done the creating.
STEPHEN L. TALBOTT, *The Future Does Not Compute*

Technological change does more than thrust upon us a new set of tools. It invites us, tools in hand, to participate in the reshaping of society. The growth of new technology is relevant to more than just commercial interests. In a complex chain of relationships that takes in economic activity, demographics, social structures, educational provision and domestic arrangements, a shift in technology sends out coded signals that trigger a cascade of other changes. These signals reflect, somehow, the nature of the technology at work. If the processing of information is different in essence from the manufacture and sale of goods, then the culture that grows up around it—the digital society—will be a very different culture. It will bring changes in behavior and values right across the postindustrial world—changes that are already surfacing in the lives and attitudes of Gen Xers and Millennials. It will be to these changes that the church of century twenty-one will be called to respond. This chapter will explore three of the key changes that this journey will bring.

Key Change 1: The Triumph of Hyperchoice

Postindustrialism will dismantle many aspects of the Industrial Age, but the consumer economy is not one of them. What the industrial society has aspired to in terms of consumer choice digital technology is at last able to deliver. The customer is king, with almost unlimited choice of where to spend his money, and what on—with the miracles of digital processing to cope with the complexities of servicing the choices made. The age of hyperchoice consumerism is upon us.

What is true in the marketplace of goods and services is spilling over into the marketplace of ideas, with philosophical and religious choices increasingly subject to the same consumer criteria. Today's creedal consumer browses the shelves of the faith hypermarket, unwilling to make a purchase until her customer needs—personal, specific and complex—have been fully met. Every attempt to force a sale is repelled with the mantra of the age, "I still haven't found what I'm looking for." Shop around; try before you buy; check out the brochure; keep your consumer options open: the philosophical shoppers of postindustrialism are as tough to please as a customer ever was. What they come to expect in the marketplace they will increasingly also expect in their relationships with social institutions, including the church.[1] Some of the implications of hyperchoice consumerism in the realm of faith are those that follow:

Acceptance of competition as normative. In many areas of life, *competition* was once a dirty word. In hyperchoice consumerism it is seen as the necessary companion of quality and value. For better or worse, the economies of the developed world are shifting more and more into a hypercompetitive free market. The spillover of this development into the realm of faith and ideas does not mean, by definition, that churches must compete with one another—all institutions have a choice as to where they operate on the competition-cooperation continuum. What it does mean is that their customers— their members and potential members—are more likely to have *checked out* the competition and will reserve the right to choose from a competitive short list. A recent investigation of the "Net-powered generation" polled eighty-five hundred Americans between the ages of sixteen and twenty-two. The survey revealed five key characteristics of these "new consumers" that will set the tone for marketing in the coming decade:

☐ The Net-powered generation expects accurate information to be constantly available, irrespective of geographical location.

☐ People now believe that choice is a human right. Customization will be taken for granted.

☐ Personal information is valuable and should be used accordingly. The Net-powered generation will expect salespeople to "know them better than just another customer." Mass marketing is out; pinpoint marketing is in.

☐ The Net-powered generation believes there *is* such a thing as a free lunch. What's more, people will expect to taste or try before they will commit. Free is in.

☐ The Net-powered generation will change our concept of relationships. E-mail correspondence is surprisingly casual; trust will be built over phone lines rather than with a handshake.

The Net-powered generation survey concerned itself with marketing, not with faith, but how many of these changing attitudes will also impact the way faith decisions are made? What kind of society emerges when almost every process is menu-driven, with options, opportunities for customization and the ever-present Back, Undo and Escape commands to protect the unwary consumer?

An increasing hunger for experience. The experience of buying has become more important than the product bought, leading to the assertion that "the experiential consumer" has arrived. What is true in commerce and industry is also increasingly true in leisure, in relationships and in religion—it is *experience* rather than *content* that provides the criteria by which a social transaction is evaluated. The generations of the postindustrial twenty-first century will increasingly evaluate every product, including public faith, in terms of their experience of it.

Loyalty earned, not given. One of the features of hyperchoice consumerism is the loyalty program. Frequent flyer miles, club card points, fidelity schemes—almost every industry sector that thrives on repeat business is working to *create* rather than *assume* loyalty. The principle is that a single purchasing decision does not commitment make. Consumers not only have the right to put their initial business wherever they want to; they reserve the right to switch horses at whatever stage in the race it seems beneficial to do so. What will this mean in the realm of faith? That we can expect to see increased "horse switching" in terms of congregational, denominational and even creedal commitments. And that we can expect faith adherents to self-audit their experience more frequently. I made the decision *then,* but is it still working for me *now?* Loyalty is not absent in Gen Xers and the Millennials, but it is a hard-won prize.

Made-to-measure expectations. At its height, the Industrial Age was marked by the mass production of standardized goods, immortalized in Henry Ford's words "You can have it in any color you want, as long as it's black." More recent developments have worked toward greater diversity and increased design options. In many industries, digital technology is now delivering a level of consumer choice that comes close to made-to-measure solutions. This raises customer expectations and creates suspicion of standard designs, off-the-shelf solutions and ready-made packages. What works for customer A may not work so well for customer B, and those who provide services are increasingly expected to adapt them to the individual.

"It ain't sold until I buy it!" The customers of hyperchoice consumerism are self-aware, well informed and in control. They want product information, they will seek sales advice, but they will not be coerced into a purchase. The self-service megastores of Virgin and Ikea are as much a symbol of this new age as door-to-door insurance salesmen were of the old. Hyperchoice consumers want to see what's available; they want to ask difficult questions about it; they want time and space to reflect without pressure. The first sign of a pressurized sale will having them saying no just for the sake of it. "Techniques of coercion and trying to coerce a culture aren't going to work anymore," Douglas Rushkoff has said. "What you have to do is just make a good product, tell us what it does and charge a good price."[2]

Key Change 2: Asynchronous Lifestyles and Timestyles

The standard definition of a machine is that formulated by German engineer Franz Reuleaux (1829–1905): "A machine is a combination of solid bodies, so arranged as to compel the mechanical forces of nature to perform work as a result of certain determinative movements."[3] "Solid," "arranged," "determinative"—a machine can achieve its allotted task only with the right components in the right place at the right time. For an assembly line to operate, it is necessary that a set number of workers present themselves for duty at the set time and work at the line's designated pace until the set time to finish. Built as it is on machine technology, the growth of industrialism throughout Western culture brought with it an increased emphasis on determined, synchronized movement. Engineers such as Frederick Wilson Taylor brought new profits to employers through their systems of "applying machine-type processes to human labour"[4]—kicking off a chain reaction that resulted in "Newton's concept of the perfect machine . . . fully realized and expanded into the human sphere."[5] Industrial society became dependent on *spatial and temporal synchronism*—a large number of people being in the same place at the same time. Commuting, the rush hour, the school timetable, bank holidays, shopping hours—all these are spinoff products of industrialism's need for fixed times and places. When an assembly line is the culture's idea of excellence, then uniformity, standardization and synchronism will rule.

Digital technology is undoing this with great speed. As Paul Saffo, director of the Foundation of the Future has said, it is "the solvent leaching the glue out of old, much-cherished social, political and business structures."[6] Social interaction no longer requires geographical proximity nor synchronous timing. An e-mail network might draw together participants from every continent; a web page will sit, available to all, day and night. The new standard for customer service is "24/7"—twenty-four hours a day, seven days a week. The global credit clearance systems operate all hours, making "banking hours" a quaint memory. Telephone service centers in Dublin or Barcelona will handle customer calls rerouted from every part of Europe. A business on one side of the Atlantic will download its day's trading figures to a data processor on the other, to be computed "overnight" and presented as summarized accounts before the opening of business the following "day." More and more workers are offered flex-time contracts; more and more professionals are telecommuting. It is less and less likely that you will live next door to someone who lives according to the same time-style as you do.

One of the slowest institutions to become aware of this change, it seems, is the church, which for the most part still assumes that the faithful will gather in a fixed place at a fixed time. A minority of churches are breaking the pattern, but it remains true that for the vast majority Sunday is the day on which God's business is done. To outside observers, a Sunday congregation is the primary visible manifestation of church. Church is a physical place that people "go to." Like an industrial plant, the church seems able to function only if its "components" are in the right place at the right time. For many churches, the pattern even predates industrialism, stemming from an era in which most of the congregation lived, worked, married, bore children and died without ever leaving the parish. Leith Anderson points out in *Dying for Change* that most American churches meet at a day and hour suited to the needs of dairy farmers—they just have time to get the milking done before the family outing "to church." As a contemporary church leader, Anderson muses that neither he nor the vast majority of his congregation have ever milked a cow in their lives.[7]

If the church continues to insist on synchronism in an asynchronous culture, it will lose contact with the growing numbers of people whose lifestyle and timestyle patterns no longer fit the old norms. With timestyles personalizing and diversifying, it will be increasingly difficult for a local church to *ever* gather all its members in one place. A church that genuinely adapts to postindustrial culture will find that it must accept the following:

☐ *The end of roll-call worship.* Being visible in a Sunday congregation will no longer be the acid test of commitment. Being "all together in one place" will be the exception rather than the norm, and it may never happen. So what will being a member mean?

☐ *The end of one-size-fits-all ministry.* Congregations as diverse as a midmorning shoppers drop-in, a lunchtime workplace study group, an early dawn rave worship experience and a cyber-linked diaspora will all seek the support and blessing of the same local church structures. Will those structures have the necessary flexibility to respond?

☐ *Discipleship through mousegroups.* If cyberspace grows to become a genuine meeting place for the community,[8] pastors will find themselves building relationships with people they have never met and perhaps never will. Do we have ministry models that will cope with this?

☐ *The end of the "local" church.* In a geographically diverse culture, "local" is increasingly defined in terms of interest groups rather than neighborhoods. Can the church accept this as a valid basis upon which to build congregations? "People don't work in their neighborhoods," says Bob Buford. "People don't shop in their neighborhoods. People don't go to the movies in their neighborhoods. So why should anyone expect them to go to church in their neighborhoods?"[9]

The end of synchronism does not simply mean that *everyone* will opt out of church in the "real world" and head off into virtual reality. It is not about the demise of the physical church. But it does mean that the physical church will have to become more flexible, diverse, adaptable and responsive than it has been for many generations. "The mainline denominations are bleeding," writes Charles Trueheart. "Their churches have more pew than flock, and unless they change, they have more history than future."[10] To adapt to changing times will not mean becoming less biblical but more so. The Jerusalem church of Acts 2:46, in which "every day they continued to meet together in the temple courts . . . [and] broke bread in their homes and ate together," almost certainly represents one of the most adaptable, open-to-change communities ever.

Key Change 3: Migration from Suburbia to Cyberia

Cyberia is the name given by author Douglas Rushkoff to the world inhabited by users of the Internet.[11] It is cyberspace once it has been colonized. While Microsoft, Dell, Amazon and their like explore the potential of the Net as a commercial arena, there are millions exploring it as community. "In America," Rushkoff says, "we've destroyed virtually every civic space. . . . America is suburb strip mall hell. There's nowhere to go and nothing to do. I see interactive media as a remedial help for a society that really doesn't have any more open conversations. I think it's working for young people as a community space."[12] More and more people are being drawn to this "new place to be"—not just to do business but to interact socially, to build relationships and make human contact.

From its inception the World Wide Web had an anarchic, uncontrolled side. While its fastest growth is in the commercial sector, there are nonetheless millions exploring its potential for community rather than commerce. And the anarchy goes on. Take Dale Ghent, just out of high school when he hit on the idea of registering a domain name: <www.billgates.com/>. Ghent's site features only a blank screen with a single button marked "mail," and to date he has collected over seventy thousand e-mails intended for the Microsoft supremo. "It's a kind of hobby," Ghent explains. "I'm just hanging out in cyberspace."[13]

Or take Jennifer Ringley, the first to come up with the idea—now much imitated—of putting her everyday, ordinary life on the Web. Her "Jennicam" site offers "a real-time look into the life of a young woman, an undramatized photographic diary for public viewing via the net." Bizarre? Perhaps. But the Jennicam site averages 5 million hits per day.[14]

Tim Berners-Lee is the researcher who first proposed the creation of a World Wide Web in 1989, when he was working at the Geneva-based European Laboratory for Particle Physics (CERN). Known as the "father of the Web," Berners-Lee envisaged a "universal space" in which "collaborative thinking" could take place, irrespective of geography and distance. Empowered by HTML, the hypertext language that makes surfing possible, the Web would create a world in which "the regular person has been re-enabled as a writer, a thinker and a linker, rather than just a clicker."[15] Now working with the MIT-based World Wide Web Consortium, Berners-Lee has commented on the extent to which the Web has moved beyond his expectations to become a new and creative communal space. "My original vision for a universal web was as an armchair aid to help people do things in the web of real life. It would be a mirror, reflecting reports or conversations or art and mapping social interactions. But more and more, the mirror model is wrong, because interaction is taking place primarily on the web. People are using the web to build things they have not built or written or drawn or communicated anywhere else."[16]

As Cyberia becomes more populated, it will present the church with a new and uncharted missionary challenge. How can the church become incarnate in the cultures of Cyberia? It will do so only by recognizing the importance and urgency of the need.

Last time around, rural church leaders and members took generations—almost centuries—to accept that industrialization and urbanization were transforming human culture and that a response was needed. Thousands upon thousands of workers and their families were left to migrate into the cities without the pastoral support of the church. Where the churches did respond, they often did so by transferring to the urban context the models, concepts and calendar of ministry that had worked so well in the countryside for generations. No wonder the years of urbanization have been years of decimation for the Christian faith. Even today, many church congregations cling to rural models of faith that are irrelevant in the communities in which they live and work. Procrastination gripped the church again when "youth culture" first emerged in the post-war years; only through the visionary determination of pioneers such as Billy Graham were the new "youth missionary" organizations born. As culture moves on once more, and thousands migrate to Cyberia,[17] we need to face the challenge sooner, faster and more effectively than our forebears. We will do this only by doing the following:

☐ *Taking the territory seriously.* Pioneer missionary William Carey, widely cited as the inventor of modern-day Protestant missions, spent years trying to persuade his fellow Baptists in England that Africa and India mattered to God. We may face a similar battle for Cyberia, but we must recognize now that it is a real place, that people live there, that it is a milieu in which matters of faith can appropriately be expressed.

☐ *Learning the language and culture.* Contemporary missionaries know that they must be skilled in cultural anthropology—that they must listen, learn and understand before ever they have the right to speak. If Cyberia grows to become a significant continent of century twenty-one, we need a generation of missionaries to begin their learning process now.

☐ *Letting go of old-world assumptions.* If Cyberia offers a new language to learn, it also challenges us to unlearn the old. Those working to carry the life of the church into Cyberia will have to abandon many habits, assumptions and distinctions. In Cyberia, for instance, there is no "abroad"—home and overseas are one seamless unity. Cultural groupings that form on the Net are defined by many forms of commonality, but geographical location—which to date has been the primary definer of church loyalty—is the least of them. Cyberia is an egalitarian society, at least in terms of access and the right to speak. The opinions of a learned professor take just as many bytes to transmit as those of a creative novice— and in many cases you won't know which you are in touch with. Some distinctives of Cyberia are trivial; others are fundamental— the new country will demand that you abandon long-cherished assumptions from the old country.

☐ *Aiming for an indigenous church.* We are only just beginning to see what church planting in Cyberia might mean, with experiments such as Charles Henderson's "First Church of Cyberspace," <www.godweb.org>. But early as these offerings are, it is essential that we gain an understanding of how church life might function in this new realm. There will be a section of the next century's population who will not join any other church. Internet mission is about more than buying Web space to advertise existing churches. Don't go to Cyberia to plant churches for suburbia.

☐ *Mobilizing Gen Xers and the Millennials.* Cyberia is a young space. It would be a mistake to claim that all those born since 1960 feel, by definition, more at home in cyberspace than in physical space. But there is an increasing number who do, and most have a more immediate, intuitive grasp of the culture than their elders. Many are bilingual, living daily in both suburbia and Cyberia, fluent in the language of the church and the language of the Web. Many churches are losing these young people because they don't value or validate their Cyberian experience. In doing so they lose not only the individual but also a potential link into this new, emerging world. The church's own Gen Xers and Millennials need permission—and with it encouragement and resources—to be pioneer missionaries to Cyberia.

The Years Ahead

The rise of Cyberia, the end of synchronism and the triumph of hyper-choice will be three "big apples" in the fruit basket of the postindustrial society. All three will deeply influence the emerging generations, presenting new and unique challenges to the church. There will be other significant changes, and somewhere in all of them the imprint of digital technology will be seen. In summary, the years ahead will be postindustrial in the sense that they will do the following:

☐ The years ahead will see the ongoing progress of the revolution that has already begun, the transition from the industrial society dominated by machine technology to the knowledge society dominated by digital processing.

☐ The years ahead will be further rocked by two yet-to-be revolutions: the advent of Cyberia, when billions of computers go to live on a super-fast, broadband, globally interactive network, and the growth of ubiquitous computing, when chips are embedded in every nook and cranny of our homes and surroundings, extending the impact of digital technology and rendering the human environment intelligent.

☐ The years ahead will see a remodeling of social and cultural institutions and norms in ways that reflect this shift from an industrial to a postindustrial paradigm.

☐ The years ahead will witness in the maturing of Gen Xers and the coming of age of the Millennials the emergence of cultural and behavioral patterns shaped by the new technological paradigm.

word.link: Get Up and Eat, Version 1

The angel of the LORD came back a second time and touched him and said, "Get up and eat, for the journey is too much for you."—1 Kings 19:7

First Kings 19 records an episode in the life of the prophet Elijah when he had reached the end of his tether. Battling for God in a hostile culture, he was worn out by persecution and opposition, isolated and underresourced, aware only of his own weakness and the enormity of the task before him. Despite all the great victories he had seen, he sat under a tree and asked to die. Falling into a deep sleep, he was twice woken by an angel, who brought food and said, "Get up and eat, for the journey is too much for you."

There are many within the Western church who sense it is at the end of its tether. Exhausted, we are worn down by battling the hostility of a culture turned against us. Bankrupt, we are aware only of our scant resources in the face of an overwhelming task. Some within the church have prayed for a quiet death; others wait patiently to be whisked away to glory on a cloud. But while we slumber on, God is sending angels to wake us. "Get up and eat," they say, "for the journey is too much for you."

Far from giving up on Western culture, God is inviting us to journey farther with him—to run into the deserts of the twenty-first century, strengthened by his presence and sustained by the food of angels. Only he knows what we will find there. Our response is not to give up but to get up. Get up and eat, Western church, there is a journey to be undertaken.

The digital revolution is not only dismantling the social structures of the Industrial Age and undermining mechanization; it is also on the verge of dethroning another age-old technology. It is a technology that has dominated Western society not for three centuries but for five (some would say since 1438), and it runs so deeply through our culture that it is hard to imagine life without it. But imagine it we must. The writing is on the video wall—the future is a whole new chapter for the book.

It is to this second "post" of the emerging world that we now turn.

6

Gutenberger & Fries

Postliterate Communications

· *Encyclopaedia Britannica has announced an end to printing books after 200 years.*
LONDON EVENING STANDARD, July 28, 1999

Our books better communicate something more than a Web page does, too. We have to understand what it is a book can do . . . or quit cutting down trees for no reason.
DOUGLAS RUSHKOFF, "Information Revolution"

When I was a little over two years old, my parents bought a cottage in County Wexford in the Republic of Ireland. It was one of around twelve dwellings stretched along a mile of potholed lane. There was an electrical supply, but we were not connected to the water main. The farmer at the top of the lane was fortunate enough to have a well in his yard; everyone else had two choices for obtaining fresh water. The first was to collect it in barrels whenever it rained; the second was to walk or cycle half a mile to the nearest municipal pump. On our property, my father arranged for a deep well to be drilled, an electric pump to be installed, and piping and drainage to be laid. Ours was the first home on the Ford of Ling to have hot and cold running water.

What strikes me in the distant memory of this time was the effect that the limited supply of water had on those forced to live with it. The barrels and buckets of collection and delivery were a valued part of daily life. Different sources of water were allocated to different tasks—pumped water for drinking, rainwater for washing, ditch water for the livestock and flowers. Children were taught early to treat water with respect and not to waste it. Such was the value of freshwater that our nearest neighbor, a merchant seaman with a good line in Polish vodka, would regularly swap my father two bottles of vodka for a bucketful of water.

All this changed overnight when water mains were installed. The old barrels were left to rot or painted as ornaments; gossip at the village pump had to find some other focus; domestic routines were transformed. Who would heat a tub of bath water in the kitchen when there's a bath with plumbing upstairs? What girl will wash her hair once a week in rainwater when she can wash it every day over the sink? The simple technological shift of making that which came in bucketfuls available on tap changed everything for this rural population. And if information is water and books are buckets, much the same is happening to us now. We have collected knowledge by the barrel load; very soon it will be there for us on tap.

The Gutenberg Galaxy

We have already seen that the marriage of computing power with fiber-optic technology and ultracheap communication links will create a whole new media realm—the new land of Cyberia. A wide range of commentators are now comparing this moment to the birth of the print age, and suggesting that we are becoming postliterate.

The era of literacy was born in 1438, when "Johannes Gutenberg wanted a cheaper way to produce hand-written Bibles. His movable type fostered a spread in literacy, an advance of scientific knowledge, and the emergence of the industrial revolution."[1]

The breakthrough into print technology had an almost immeasurable impact on Western culture. According to communications theorist Marshall McLuhan, it carried us into "the Gutenberg galaxy."[2] For McLuhan, "print as a technology is the catalyst that allowed the emerging mechanistic, linear, individualistic tendencies of the modern period to become the integrated, dominant pattern of our time."[3]

The electronic era is something else entirely—a culture dominated not by the printed word but by multimedia, interactive, free-flowing information. The revolution that began with broadcast radio picked up the pace with television and found a running mate in satellite and cable capabilities will hit breakneck speed in cyberoptic fiberspace. The final effect this will have on the ways we think, communicate and learn is as yet unknown—the digital revolution is still relatively young. But it is clear that there *will be* an effect. If we are concerned to relate to the world of the new century, if the lives of Gen Xers and the Millennials mean anything to us, then we must give time to exploring the implications of this shift beyond the literate. We are about to leave the Gutenberg galaxy, traveling at warp speed. Can we even begin to anticipate what new corner of the universe we will arrive in?

definition.link: *Postliterate*

The world of Generation X and beyond will be postliterate in the following senses:

1. A primary driver of change will be the changing communication media.

2. The role of printed text as the primary medium of communication, of learning and of information storage and transfer is superseded.

3. In its place, new cultural, educational and popular forms emerge around the availability of interactive media, made possible by digital technology.

4. The impact of this technological shift will be widely and keenly felt—in the ways people learn, in the ways they communicate and in the shape and nature of the ideas that influence them.

5. The emergence of new communication paradigms will be seen first in the transitional generations: caught in the tension of dual citizenship; speaking the old language, but increasingly attracted to the new.

Our purpose in this section will be to explore this "change of galaxies" and to ask the questions that follow:

☐ What are the key differences between print-based communication and interactive media?

☐ What effect will these differences have on the transitional generations?

☐ What challenges will this present to the Christian faith community?

Once again, we will deal with the first two of these questions in the current chapter, leaving the important themes of the third to chapter seven.

The Virtual McCoy

It is fairly straightforward to describe just what it was that Gutenberg hit on—the dissemination of ideas and information through printed text. The methods were slow at first but soon gained the speed and capacity of a bulk technology, creating human culture's first experience of mass communication. Print technology's abiding symbol is the book—a bound and defined repository of words, associated with authority, learning, scholarship and sophistication. Postliteracy, fast replacing print as the dominant communications ethos, is not the result of any one technological change but of several. These changes include the following:

☐ the shift from word to image, as transmitted by photography, television, video and the computer screen and empowered by digital technology's image-manipulation capacity and bit-stream delivery;

☐ the transition from text to hypertext brought by the computer's capacity to both write and read in nonlinear forms;

☐ the power of digital technology to combine word, image and sound as multimedia communication;

☐ the interconnectedness and interactivity of Cyberia; and

☐ the relative ease with which a PC, CD-ROM drive and modem put all this into the hands of the individual.

The dominance of image has been with us for some time—initially in cinema, more recently in television and supremely in the advertising industry both have played host to. But it is the power of digital encoding, unlocking the problems of bandwidth, speed and capacity, that signals most strongly the end of the print age. If there is any one development that history will credit as decisive in this leap, it is likely to be the marriage of cyber and fiber referred to in chapter four—the birth of cyberoptic fiberspace. But the impact of these changes on human culture and behavior—already visible in the X and Millennial generations—rests with the combined influence of these different elements. Postliteracy is not a single drink but a cocktail: the taste of instant communication blending with the potency of the moving image, laced with the spice of interaction.

Some of the characteristics of the postliterate era that will set it apart from the age of print are the following:

1. Capacity and scope. First, in terms of storage, when Bill Gates wanted to demonstrate the capacity of the CD-ROM, he had himself photographed sitting on a fifty-five-foot-high pile of paper. A total of 330,000 sheets of single-spaced text still could not match the CD's hunger for data. With more encyclopedias now being sold in digital format than as books, the huge reference potential of the medium is clear. Add to that the development of DVD technology and the increasing possibility of downloading directly from the Internet, and the measure of information instantly available to a PC user starts to run into millions rather than thousands of pages.

Second, in terms of experience, computers are more than just reference tools. Cyberpunk author William Gibson says that electronic communication provides "a sensory expansion for the species by allowing people to experience an extraordinary array of things while staying geographically in the same spot."[4] Those who have tended to use the term *virtual reality* in a dismissive sense—to describe a reality that is less real than real reality—may need to think again as increasing numbers find it very real indeed. Cyberia is a *different* reality, but for those who experience it, it is no less real.

Third, in terms of access, the electronic arena puts something approaching broadcast technology in the hands of the individual citizen. Bill Gates points out that "on a bulletin board, all you have to do is type your message in once and it's available for everybody you want to reach."[5] Never before has the scope to talk to the whole world been so accessible. David Lochhead says, "Everyone can have a web page, can tell their own story, promote their own version of the truth for all the world to hear."[6] The ongoing communications revolution will offer the rising generations access to an unprecedented store of information and to unimagined communications opportunities—as far beyond print as an ocean is beyond a glass of water. How might this change their perceptions of truth and the value of words—and of books?

2. Speed and transience. An unexpected spinoff of the communications revolution has been an increase to unprecedented levels in the global consumption of printing ink and paper. With cheap printers, easy-to-use software and a torrential outpouring of information, homes and offices are printing like never before. But what they publish may not last very long. Where the hard work of producing books afforded them protected status, the ease of printing information is now having the reverse effect. Information is disposable, transient, out-of-date within hours. You can print it, but somehow the act of printing no longer confers authority—the rarity and mystique are gone. There is a flow to electronic information; it's not static anymore. "Print was designed to convey fact—solid, stable fact," David Lochhead has written. "Print could hold a proposition, freeze it so that it could be studied, dissected, verified. The electronic media were designed to convey news, information that moved so quickly that by the time it could be confirmed or denied, it was no longer news."[7] How might the rising generations, skilled in dealing with information that is fluid and transient, deal with questions of universal or long-term meaning?

3. Multiplicity and diversity. The term *multimedia* is now much used and abused, but it does describe one of the most salient features of electronic communication: its capacity to blend and mix image, text and sound in the service of a given message. Marshall McLuhan claims that the electronic media render words "tactile"—open to being grasped as much by the senses as by the intellect.[8]

In the office of the very near future, Bill Gates has predicted that "a significant percentage of documents . . . won't be fully printable on paper. You'll still be able to print out a two-dimensional view, but that will be like reading a music score instead of listening to a recording."[9] Already, according to advertising executive Jim Carroll, "young consumers are more visually articulate . . . more adept at handling visual ideas."[10] Neville Brody, the art director behind the revolutionary lifestyle magazine *Face*, explains further, "The way we absorb information changes: with digital technology and interactive cable our behavior is totally different from the past in the way we read text and images, the way we experience visual language."[11]

A pioneer in moving artistic expression onto the Internet, designer Auriea Harvey pushes the very boundaries of multimedia in self-expression. Her Web site[12] has won numerous awards and is cited in several books on site design. "With text everyone feels they 'know' what you are saying," she says. "With images it is left more to interpretation."[13] She recognizes that this is not just an extension of existing media but a whole new way of working. "It took years for me to learn to paint. I imagine the web will take equally as long to become a real means of expression to me."[14]

Adapting to this multiplicity of information sources, young people are fast becoming "mosaic thinkers," able to "integrate disparate
information into new perspectives on reality."[15] They are quickly
losing the memory of monomedia communication and are comfortable with the multisensory. Presented with a range of simultaneous
sources—image, text, voice, sound, movement—they will take
threads from each and weave them into meanings, often in patterns
that don't exist in any one of the source "tracks." They are able "to
put information together in new patterns, often arriving at unusual,
novel, or surprising conclusions."[16]

The more accustomed young people become to multimedia, the
more necessary it will be for a given message to be reinforced
through more than one voice. Monomedia communication can
quickly appear one-dimensional and uninspiring compared to this
"total experience that is brighter, louder and larger than life itself."[17]
It is not in the script, the image or the music that contact is made, but
in the collusion of all three. There is a remarkable new area of communication opening up in random, unpredicted connections—a
computer graphic left to make its own connection with the music;
the soundtrack from one film played over the images of another;
speech, image and rhythm brought together in unrehearsed sym-
phony. In such experiences, the message is discovered rather than
dispatched and has as much to do with intuition as intellect. Rave
culture thrives on this randomness, as DJs search for new connections of beat and melody, and dancers find their own rhythmic space
within them. Multimedia communication, like a net or a web, finds
its strength not in strings but in knots—it is the intersections that
matter most. But how quickly will those of us used to text and voice
learn to handle the new language of multimedia? It's one thing to
juggle with one or two information sources; what skills will we need
to keep eight in the air?

4. Interaction and response. Alongside multimedia capabilities it
is the interactivity of the new communication that marks its departure from the linear, predetermined nature of traditional text. In print

the power to set meanings belongs not to the receiver but to the sender. Electronic and image-based communications, by contrast, invite the receiver to share in the task of creating the message. As young people grow increasingly accustomed to this invitation, they become resistant to messages in which they have no such cocreative role.

The medium of CD-ROM can combine "music, graphics, animation and video clips to create a new level of multi-media interactivity."[18] Mike Large, director of operations for Peter Gabriel's Real World studio, gives an excellent definition of interactive communication in describing Gabriel's project *Eve*. He explains that Gabriel "has always wanted his audience to experience his work from the inside, rather than being passive observers or listeners. . . . The disc will enable the users to transform and create their own versions of the images and music as they explore the world that has been created."[19]

This "option expansion" is not the only aspect of the new media that is interactive; there is also the very real sense in which the Net is drawing people into increased interaction in "cyber communities." Douglas Rushkoff insists that this, rather than machine-driven interaction, is the real thing. "Interactivity does not mean interacting with a machine," he says, "however real it might feel. . . . I suggest that interaction with machines, however temporarily novel, will reveal itself as a poor substitute for using machines to interact with one another."[20] The Internet provides for the possibility of living "not in an information age; [but] in an interactive one"[21] in which the new media are simply the devices through which we communicate with other living beings. "To me the internet is teeming with life, buzzing with thought," he says. "All of this terrific spirit, however, comes from us. We are the life coursing through our datasphere's veins."[22]

For Rushkoff and the many co-Cyberians who have made this strange new world their home, interactivity is the sum and substance of the Net. It is not simply a new means for advertisers to get products into our homes but a genuine opportunity to multiply human interchange. Communication is the essence of community, and whether interaction lies in the options offered by a CD-ROM or in the interconnectedness of the Net, it restores the possibility of response to much of our communicating. There can be no doubt that it will bring deep and lasting changes to our culture.

Implications of the Changes

Capacity and scope, speed and transience, multiplicity and diversity, interaction and response—already these characteristics of postliterate communications are making a difference in the lives of the transitional generations. Some of the more significant implications of this are the following:

The demystifying of authority. Douglas Rushkoff has written extensively on the power of Cyberian technology to demystify the "magic box" of television, taking away its almost priestly power. "If you're actually moving around the pixels yourself on the screen, you no longer see television as the mystical act," he says. "You don't see it as the gospel truth being pumped into your home."[23] David Lochhead sees the same process attacking the authority of text. "Text can carry a sense of authority because it is 'given,' " he says. "The printed text is solid, unchanging, real. . . . With the computer, the text is always tentative. . . . In this medium, I control the text. The text does not control me."[24] Media that for generations have enjoyed priestly status are being stripped of their privileges and left to stand naked.

The reinvention of writing. Jay David Bolter describes the computer as "a new writing surface that needs conventions different from those of the printed page."[25] Hypertext, increasingly replacing text as the standard means of writing on a computer, allows the reader to determine where the beginning, middle and end of a piece will lie, plotting their own path of clicks and links through the textual landscape. American author Bob Arellano's novel *@ltamont*, published on CD-ROM, offers two beginnings. Readers who click on "Innocence" read about a young couple's first kiss; those who click on "Experience" read about a murder.[26] Such novels are, in sales terms, a minority interest, but as the influence of the Internet grows that may change. Bolter says, "Sedate rows of linear text are becoming the exception rather than the rule."[27]

Charles Henderson has experimented with a hypertext reading of Psalm 23. Among other features, this offers the "reader" links to Web sites offering a complete listing of all biblical references to the word *shepherd,* a visit to the Sistine Chapel ceiling to view Michelangelo's paintings of the life of Moses, a visit to the Vatican's sculpture of *The Good Shepherd* and the home page of a modern-day working shepherd.[28]

Writing has been at the heart of our notion of civilization for centuries—and computers are changing the way we write. "What needs to be clear," David Lochhead explains, "is that digital text is not print. Our relation to text in a digital culture will be very different to the relation that was created by print technology." Not only are the new media adding a whole range of information sources alongside text, but in addition they are transforming the way we deal with text itself. Tom Hohstadt has written, "This new reality means we are also speaking a new language—not just new words, but a new way of using words. Implicit words are replacing explicit words. Metaphoric words are replacing literal words. Endless flowing images are replacing orderly ideas. Experience is replacing reason. And feeling is replacing form."[29]

The redefining of the book. Charles Handy, among others, has been quick to point out that the electronic media are transforming rather than displacing the book. "The telecommunications revolution will add to the ways we get and pass information—it won't replace them," he says. "They said that television would make books unnecessary, but instead we found the television actually bred books, sending people off to read *Pride and Prejudice* who would not previously have dreamt of reading it for pleasure."[30] Early evidence of the effects of the Internet confirms this: the easy access and searchable databases of online bookshops are already leading to a minirevival in sales from publishers' backlists. "Just when it appears that a new medium is going to replace its predecessor," Douglas Rushkoff has said, "we tend to figure out the true value of the older."[31]

A helpful analogy might be that of horseback riding. When the internal combustion engine replaced horses as the best means of getting from *a* to *b,* that didn't mean the end of human interest in horses. Far from it. Relieved of the drudgery of pulling carts, horses were seen to possess grace, strength and beauty, and the activities that emphasized these qualities grew. Blacksmiths lost jobs, but the racing, show-jumping, trekking and weekend riding industries thrived. It is quite possible that the postliterate future will usher in a golden age of literature, as the book is released from its tedious duty as conveyor of information to become an object of pleasure. "A book has totemic value," Rushkoff claims. "Like a photograph or a piece of jewelry, the impression of ink on paper creates physical connection with its author. . . . Computers and the Internet may have taught or at least reminded us of the special ability of books to provide a kind of experience you can't get anywhere else."[32]

While the notion of the book will almost certainly survive, and many readers will retain their love of ink on paper, recent technological developments make it unlikely that this will be the only way to read. "Reading on paper is so much a part of our lives," Bill Gates has written, "that it is hard to imagine anything could ever replace inky marks on shredded trees."[33] But e-books, which will complement and might even replace ink on paper, *are* being imagined—by researchers at MIT, Microsoft and a hundred other labs. "You will get instant delivery from your web bookshop to your e-book," Gates has written, "and be able to store hundreds of novels on a device the size of a paperback, . . . an entire library in your pocket. Or you can keep it on your PC. A modern laptop can hold more than 30,000 books. . . . Your children will be able to listen to unfamiliar words pronounced for them. . . . You will have unabridged audio synchronized to the text, so you can continue the story in situations where you are unable to read."[34] Add to this hyperlinks within the text and to outside sources, support for images and sounds, the capacity to add personal annotation and hyperlinks—and you have the creation of an entirely new medium that will, according to Gates, "revolutionize the way the world reads."[35]

In the meantime, just as the capacity of engines is still measured in horsepower, so electronic communications will continue to borrow the language of "pages," "publishing" and "typefaces." But don't be fooled by the continuance of terminology—the new forms of communication opening to us will be as different from the printing of books as driving a Mercedes S-class automobile is from riding a donkey. "If it's in a book, it must be true" will mean nothing to the rising generations of century twenty-one.

The reevaluation of oral traditions. The speed with which print came to dominate our culture centuries ago meant that skills associated with oral communication were quickly lost. Centuries earlier, Plato had used the character of the king of Egypt to ask whether the invention of writing itself would "produce forgetfulness in the minds of those who learn to use it, because they will not practice their memory. Their trust in writing, produced by external characters which are no part of themselves, will discourage the use of their own memory within them."[36] To the skills of memory, self-expression and storytelling kept alive by the oral tradition, Gutenberg's movable type dealt the final deathblow that the king of Egypt had feared. But the transition we are now seeing includes, according to Stephen Toulmin, a shift "from the written to the oral, from the universal to the particular, from the general to the local and from the timeless to the timely."[37] Delivered from the illusion that printed text is the all-in-all of communication, young people are rediscovering the power of the oral tradition. Perhaps the single most potent sign of this rediscovery lies in the explosive growth of noncelebrity TV chat shows. Presenters such as Oprah Winfrey, Rikki Lake and Jerry Springer have become multimillionaires through a formula that in essence invites ordinary people to "tell their story" to the world. There is a never-ending stream, it seems, of people willing to do so, and a global audience of millions clamoring ready to listen.

The reordering of social skills. In the age of print, society's glittering prizes were awarded to those adept at handling text. As Colin Morris—for many years the head of religious broadcasting for the BBC in London—has written, "For the first time in five hundred years those groups and professions in society who live by mastery of the spoken and written word no longer dominate our culture."[38] In their place, a new range of skills will create a new range of skill bearers. Some of these will be developments from existing vocations—artists become cyber artists, musicians producing CD-ROMs—but there will also be entirely new social functions. One of these will be the "information filter"—the communicator who is able to dive deep into the information ocean to bring up the treasures relevant to a given social group. Weekly and monthly magazines are increasingly fulfilling this function. This is a new kind of bucket or barrel, needed not because information is in short supply but because there is too much of it to process or control. An indication of the sheer scale of the task is given by the early developments in software "censorship" packages, designed to filter out selected material on the Internet. According to a report, "The US market for filtering software was worth more than $14m in 1997."[39] The Cyber-NOT list, used by the market-leading package Cyber Patrol, includes a staggering 4.5 million banned Web sites.[40] Censorship is just one aspect of filtering, as parents, businesses, social groups and consumers increasingly seek help on prioritizing and processing an overwhelming data flood. Functioning in terms of quantity, quality and consumer preference, information filters will be in great demand in the coming years.

The reimagining of education. The 21st Century Learning Initiative is a global network of thinkers and practitioners in education. Terence Ryan, one of the Initiative's key researchers, has written extensively of the impact of predigital technologies on schooling. "Education has been modelled on the work paradigm of mass production," he says. "Throughout this century in industrialised nations the management practices of factories have been directly applied to the management of children's learning in schools."[41] A linear, deterministic understanding of text has fostered learning in its own image. Digital technology's introduction of new paradigms both for management and for communication are set to dramatically change this picture. According to John Abbot, director of the Initiative, "The emerging, multi-layered knowledge economy . . . requires creativity, flexibility, collaboration and the practical skills of the entrepreneur. . . . Learning has to be about more than schooling."[42] In *The Knowledge Society,* Peter Drucker tells us, "Increasingly, an educated person will be somebody who has learned how to learn."[43] This same theme has been taken up by Gunther Kress, a professor of the London-based Institute of Education and one of Britain's leading commentators in the field. Kress questions the emphasis on reading skills in a world moving swiftly into postliteracy. "What preparation does the highly traditional literacy agenda that dominates the public debate provide for the demands of that new world?" he asks. "There are things that images can do which writing cannot, and these things will be central to an economy built on the management of vast amounts of information."[44] Professor Kress offers a detailed analysis of education in transition: "The new economy demands new kinds of thinking," he says, "dispositions to flexibility and innovativeness, new kinds of hand/eye/brain co-ordination and visual analysis of quite extraordinary complexity; kinds of intelligence quite unlike those of the 'sedentary skills of reading and writing.' "[45] The postliterate world will revolutionize the way we learn, not just in formal education but as a lifelong activity in a world of continuous change.

The requirement for moral judgments. The new cultural landscapes of Cyberia will present their inhabitants with new and unfamiliar moral choices. Already electronic communications are bringing out both the worst and the best in human interaction. Relationships have grown from Internet contacts, leading to lifelong friendships and marriage. But the terrorist bomb attack in Oklahoma was also said to have been aided by bomb-making advice published on the Net. "Today the darkest of dark thoughts can be revealed anonymously in cyberspace," warns author and cyber commentator Patrick Dixon, "with pointers for people of like mind to get in touch via e-mail."[46] The challenge to create morally acceptable norms for cyberculture is immense. "The first step," according to Bill Buxton of the Toronto Telepresence Project, "is to recognize that this is not a story about technology, nor are the associated issues primarily ones for engineers, technologists or business. Rather it is a story about people and communities. The issues are inherently social, and must be discussed as such if we are to avoid having, yet again, the tail of technology wagging the dog of society."[47]

The postliterate future is a very different place to the world we have known. It will turn upside down the parts of our lives that touch on communications. For those whose lives revolve around communication, the turmoil will be considerable. This must include the church, whose activities include learning, interchange and the formation of community, and whose sense of mission drives its members to prioritize communication. It is imperative that we consider the impact of the postliterate revolution on the Christian faith community.

Screenagers in Love

Living with Postliterate Communication

The Word became flesh, said St. John, and the church has turned the flesh back into words.
TOM WRIGHT, *The Crown and the Fire*

It gets into your system. The music rushes round your head. The adrenaline courses through your body. Stopping is not an option. First you're racing to win, then you're fighting to survive. One moment you're marvelling at how real everything seems, the next you can't believe the sheer depth and scale of what you're getting into. No side effects are yet known but the potential is widespread. With over 300 different ways of getting the bug and 1 in 10 households already affected, no one is immune.
SONY PLAYSTATION, advertising copy

In the beginning was the web.
CHARLES HENDERSON

In 1993, European advertising executive Jim Carroll was involved in a research project testing reactions to a range of youth-oriented magazine titles among a select group of opinion-leading young people. "I threw about twenty magazines on the floor," he explains,

> and asked them to pick out any they might be interested in. Having allowed them to peruse the selection for a few minutes, I quizzed one woman as to the basis for selecting a particular title. She flicked through it in front of me and pointed out that it had a good feel; she remarked on the interesting type, the unconventional camera angles, the creative art direction. She really seemed to have bought into this magazine. And then suddenly she said "Oh no. Actually I wouldn't buy it. It's all about Indie music and I don't like that kind of stuff." The point of this story is that this young consumer had gone a long way down the road to reaching a verdict on the title before she even considered the nature of its verbal content.[1]

What is being described here is an encounter with a screenager,[2] a member of a new generation so impacted by the transition to postliteracy that image has already taken precedence over word. Raised on MTV, Windows, the Web and video rentals, screenagers are already making the journey away from the dominance of text. More concerned with their ZIPs than their zits, more interested in pixels than pimples, screenagers are redefining what it means to be young in terms of an information-rich, visual experience. Young people, Carroll claims, have become victims of the "treachery of the word." They "have not just been seduced away from the word and text by other forms of communication," he writes. "The word has actually betrayed them. Young people rarely even bother to raise a sneer any more at the political double talk of 'job seeking,' . . . corporate heads talking of 're-engineering the workforce' and 'rightsizing'; they discard unread the personalised direct mail letters with computer-drawn signatures—the letters that offer us the chance of a lifetime and present us with an alarm clock. . . . No wonder young people read less. What do words mean any more?"[3]

Screenagers are uncomfortable with the traditional authority of text but at home with the visual, stimulated by multimedia but bored by words on a page, alive to the interactive but dead to the passive. Clearly, if the church, whose history is so rich with words, is to engage this generation, it must break free from whatever captivity words, text and the age of print have imposed. "In recent years," writes leading cultural analyst John Drane, "I have gradually been moving towards the conclusion that our words are getting in the way of the gospel—that the church is somehow imprisoned in a kind of cognitive captivity which is inhibiting our mission."[4]

In conversations with the transitional generations we must understand that they do not *see* text the way that we have seen it. This will have a range of implications for the church's ministry to screenage culture:

☐ It will impact the ways in which screenagers *communicate,* touching on any aspect of the church's life that involves the transmission of a message, from posters advertising services to one-to-one counseling.

☐ It will deeply impact the way screenagers absorb information and *learn*—challenging the church's work in teaching and education.

☐ It will impact the way screenagers perceive and use *books*—challenging the central role of the Bible in church life.

So Long Scriptura?
For the Christian faith community, the last of these implications represents perhaps the most far-reaching challenge of the postliterate age. Already approaches to the Bible are among the hottest topics debated by those working at the frontiers of cultural change. The necessity of printing Bibles was mother to Gutenberg's invention, and the Bible has remained the most reproduced and bestselling book since. Well over five hundred years at number one is an impressive record—making the Bible the book of all books—but it also serves to confirm just how closely the Bible and the age of print are tied together. The challenge is particularly difficult for the Prot-

estant community—and within that sector, for those who hold to "a high view of Scripture." "Protestant interpretation of scripture has developed hermeneutical traditions that are well suited to the printed medium," David Lochhead explains. "Protestantism is not solely the creature of print. That would be to ignore the spiritual dynamics of the reformation period. Nevertheless, the print medium became a central factor in the shape that the Protestant Reformation eventually took. Classical Protestantism can aptly be described as the spirituality of print."[5]

How will screenagers, newly exiled from the Gutenberg galaxy, treat this "book of God" that has been so much a part of print culture? Does the end of the age of print signal the end of the Bible's authority? These are real and pertinent questions, which mark the boundaries of the debate raging among the church's own younger generations.

Scholarship and Pragmatism
Within this debate there are two distinct questions that need to be dealt with in different ways. The first is the "big question" of theology and hermeneutics: "How will the shift to postliteracy change *what we believe about* the Bible?" It is to this question that systematic theologians are turning—and their task is extraordinarily complex and delicate. An estimate in gallons of the blood spilled in Europe in the years of the Reformation and Counter-Reformation would be a useful reminder of just how painful such changes can be. My own stance is that I do not feel qualified even to enter the battle arena, let alone proffer conclusions. I am glad to know that this debate is taking place, and I dare to hope that it will come to a bloodless end. Print technology may have dominated the church for five centuries, but the narratives and texts of the faith have sustained its life for almost twenty. All the same, I would be cautious, here as anywhere, before wading in.

The second question, though, is more practical and invites us all—qualified or not—to join the debate: "How will the shift to postliteracy change the *way we engage with* the Bible?" If screen-agers struggle to engage with *text*, we must not allow this to stop them from engaging with *truth*. In our struggles to relate an age-old faith deep in tradition and history to generations raised on screenage postliteracy, we will need to rediscover the power of God's Word *outside of* the power of text. This will demand that the church recognize and embrace other forms of expression—not so much alternative truths as alternative means by which truth is accessed and understood. According to Amos Wilder, the church has always appropriated the communication methods of the culture in which it finds itself, beginning with the very basics of speech. "Every step of the way, beginning with Jesus himself, represents an identification with and renewal of existing idioms. In one sense, as language, the Gospel met every man and each people where they were—was 'all things to all men'—in another sense it spoke a new word to all."[6] Is it time for an "identification with and renewal of" the media and idioms of the screenage? If so, some of the places we might start are these:

1. Recovering the power of story. A capitalist was walking one afternoon on the beach at Naples, and he was shocked to find a fisherman sitting idly by his boat smoking his pipe.

"Why aren't you out fishing?" the capitalist asked.

"Why should I be?" said the fisherman.

"Well, if you fished all day instead of just the morning," the capitalist explained, "you would catch more. More fish would mean more profit. You could trade this old boat for something better, buy new nets for even more fish and even more profit. Very soon you could afford to employ a crew to do the work for you."

"And what would I do then?"

"Then," said the capitalist triumphantly, "you could afford to take it easy. You would have time to yourself; you could enjoy the fruits of your labors."

"And what," asked the patient old fisherman, "do you think I'm doing now?"[7]

There is power in story. New Zealander Mike Riddell, author of *Godzone, alt.spirit@metro.m3* and *Threshold of the Future,* has been a leading exponent of the value of story to the church. The Bible, he reminds us, is "the repository of stories . . . from generations of people who have tried to follow God. It is also the bearer of 'the story of all stories': the life and teaching of Jesus. . . . The Bible keeps alive for us 'the dangerous memory of Jesus.' "[8] There is wide support for a reemphasis at this time on story—a medium founded not in text but in the preliteracy of oral cultures. David Hillborn, theological secretary to the U.K. Evangelical Alliance, advises British churches: "If narrative is the way to communicate to an audience which no longer thinks rationalistically, then preaching will need to change."[9] Across the Atlantic, Brian Walsh and Richard Middleton insist, "It is imperative that the church unequivocally reclaim the Bible as narrative."[10]

The truth of story is arrived at in a very different way from that of print. "Listening to or reading stories is not primarily an application of intellect," Mike Riddell has said. "It is an act of shared imagination. In story, one is invited (not coerced) into a different world through the use of active imagining."[11] Lesslie Newbigin is careful to contrast the eternal significance of the story of God with the transient attempts we make to capture it in text.

> Our so-called eternal truths are the attempts we make at particular moments in the story to grasp and state how things are in terms of our experience at that point. They are all provisional and relative to time and place, as we recognise when as 20th Century people we read the seventeenth century language of the Westminster Confession. The reality with which we have to deal is the story—the story that begins before the creation of the world, ends beyond the end of the world, and leads through the narrow road that is marked by the names of Abraham, Isaac and Jacob, Moses, Amos, Paul, and, name above every name, Jesus.[12]

By retaining ambiguity, flexibility and nuance, story delivers us from at least some of the "cognitive captivity" of text and at the same time resonates with the newfound agility and interaction of hypertext. Story is fast becoming the common thread running through the many media of the our age. Video games are weak on text but strong on story; advertising increasingly sees its task as selling the product by telling the story; television, film and video are built on plot above all else; songwriting is in itself a form of storytelling; journalists "tell the story" where they used to "print the facts." In a silent revolution, narrative is replacing print as the unifying element of our culture. Leighton Ford has argued for a complete transformation of evangelism from outreach built on a rational defense of the gospel's credibility to "narrative evangelism"—the telling of God's story in its impact on our stories. There is something in the power of story that resonates deeply with a postliterate culture, freeing words to express the full range of their playfulness and charm. "What a story does is sneak up behind you and whisper something in your ear," says Brian McLaren, "and when you turn around to see what it is, it kicks you in the butt and runs and hides behind a bush."[13] The good news, for the Christian faith community, is that much of the Bible was story before it was anything else—and that the founder of the faith was without doubt one of history's best storytellers. Christian Scripture is rich with living, colorful, multi-layered stories to fund our culture's imagination. As Walter Brueggemann says, "Perhaps it will help if we give up thinking of it as a 'book' and regard it as a 'tradition' that continues to be alive and surging among us."[14]

2. *Recovering a symbolic and visual vocabulary.* A culture starved of the sensual in the realm of faith is rediscovering, in the screenage years, the potency of image and symbol. David Bosch explains: "Metaphor, symbol, ritual, sign and myth, long maligned by those interested only in 'exact' expressions of rationality, are today being rehabilitated; . . . they not only touch the mind and its conceptions, and evoke action with a purpose, but compel the heart."[15] From the physical presence of objects, through the sym-

bolic enactment of aspects of faith to the evident power of video and film, screenagers have a vocabulary of worship that takes in more by far than words. "In symbolic actions," writes Robert Webber, "we take the known and lift it to the unknown so that it is returned to us as the mystery of the transcendent."[16]

For some, the most potent contemporary use of this vocabulary has been seen in the concerts of rock band U2—the image-rich Zooropa tour and the more recent Popmart experience featuring the largest video screen ever constructed. Journalist Bobby Maddex wrote of the Zoo TV experience, "Trabant cars hung from the upper rafters of the stage, illuminating a bank of television sets and video screens which flashed random words and phrases (PANIC, SEX, NO ANSWERS, EVERYTHING YOU KNOW IS WRONG) at high speed intervals."[17] For U2, even text is just another image, ripped out of its context, stripped of linear meaning and thrown across a screen. Meanwhile, back at church, Zoo TV has proved an inspiration to a new generation of worshipers, who agree with record producer T Bone Burnett's assessment: "A U2 concert is what church should be."[18] Banked TV sets, video and slide projection, computer graphics and graffiti walls are taking the place of the pulpit as the places in which ideas about God are explored. For pioneers in this field, the management of a worship event is being superseded by the creation of a worship environment: a three-dimensional, multimedia sacred space, a temple made neither of stone nor of words but of sound and image. Guided by intuition and the deep longings of the soul, screenagers navigate the many signals of this print-free world, weaving truth from its many threads. "Everything in the service needs to preach," says Mark Driscoll, pastor of Mars Hill Fellowship in Seattle. "Architecture, lighting, songs, prayers, fellowship, the smell—it all preaches. All five senses must be engaged to experience God."[19]

Writing from the perspective of the denominational churches, Robert Webber makes the same claim. "The inquirer needs to be immersed within a space that bespeaks the Christian faith," he writes. "The very narrative of faith which we seek to know and to live is symbolically expressed in our space. We take the ordinary aspects of life—stone, wood, windows, tables and chairs—and form them into voices of the Christian mystery."[20] Communication, in this model, comes through "an immersed participation in the event."[21]

Even in print, the desire to explore the Bible as image and symbol rather than word alone is gaining ground. In the United Kingdom Jeff Anderson and Mike Maddox have worked for five years to create *The Lion Graphic Bible,*[22] presenting the whole span of biblical narrative in graphic novel form. Graphic novels—full-length comics to the uninitiated—are more usually the territory of Judge Dredd, Spawn and The Forever People. But the Bible, say the publishers, "is a unique tale of origins and cosmic powers; of the ageless battle between good and evil; of human potential and human treachery; and of a Messiah—a saviour for the world. This is indeed the stuff that graphic novels are made of."[23]

The power of a single painted image is explored in the late Henri Nouwen's remarkable book *The Return of the Prodigal Son.*[24] This extended meditation on the meaning of the famous parable was inspired not by the text itself but by Rembrandt's painting of the same name.[25] Nouwen describes how a chance encounter with this image spoke powerfully to him of God's love and of his own need for love and affirmation. He was later able to view the painting in St. Petersburg, and he stood for hours before it—transfixed by the picture and by the truth it carried. The result is a profound and moving exploration of the story of the prodigal son discovered in the detail of the Rembrandt masterpiece. Image is as varied and as valid a vehicle as text for communicating truth—and quite possibly a more useful one in the visual jungle of the screenage years. "MTV has captured the sight-and-sound generation," Leonard Sweet writes. "Has the church lost them?"[26]

3. Recovering the language of community. Lesslie Newbigin reminds us that the church "lives in the midst of history as a sign, instrument and foretaste of the reign of God."[27] Is there a language of community that can speak to young people resistant to the language of text? "Truth is not a product, to be processed and packaged and dispensed," says Mike Riddell. "It is an encounter which takes place when people share their stories in a place of safety and dignity."[28] There is mounting evidence that screenagers will be drawn to "the places of safety and dignity." In a world of dysfunctional relationships, a glimpse of true community will communicate more than volumes of static prose. "The emerging culture is more interested in reality than truth, . . . where there is consistency between word and action."[29] David Hillborn sees this as nothing more nor less than God's own preferred way of communicating: "Just as the divine Word was embodied in Jesus, so godly words are meant to be embodied—within relationships and communities of faith."[30] Community puts words into actions. In the postmodern condition, Robert Webber writes, "knowledge comes through participation in a community and in an immersion with the symbols and meaning of the community."[31] Are there actions we can take—for justice, for the poor, for our neighbors—that to screenagers will be more rich with meaning than the many words of the Westminster Confession?

4. Recovering the silence of contemplation. Is it possible that beyond the walls of words that we have built there lies the possibility of a richer experience of God? Maggie Dawn suggests that this is so. "My argument is that the heart of Christian experience is engagement not with words but with The Word—God as transcendent, but met in incarnation. . . . We are creatures for whom language is a necessary part of making real in our experience what we believe to exist in transcendence."[32] The screenage hunger for experience goes beyond the occasional, intense feelings aroused by acts of corporate worship. It is the longing for God day by day. Canadian theologian Ronald Rolheiser calls this "the eclipse of contemplation." He says, "Today we, the children of Western Culture . . . struggle with practical atheism. Our churches are slowly emptying and, more and more, the sense of God is slipping from our ordinary lives." The answer, he claims, is not connected to more words or a better grasp of textual truth. "The road back to a lively faith is not a question of finding the right answers, but of living in a certain way, contemplatively. The existence of God, like the air we breathe, need not be proven. It is more a question of developing good lungs to meet it correctly."[33] Contemplation taps into two sources of the richness of God—the power of silence to move us beyond words and the power of ordinary experience to enlighten us. In both, it is possible to hear God speak without text.

A new generation is rediscovering the insights of such spiritual giants as the eighteenth-century French writer Jean-Pierre de Caussade, who could say, even as print was charting its steady course to world domination: "It is right that we should worship and acknowledge the profound wisdom of God. But what is He telling us, in the words he pronounces moment by moment, whose substance is not ink and paper, but what we do and suffer from one moment to the next, do not these deserve our attention? . . . If we read the word of God in the Scriptures through the eyes of faith, it must be wrong to read his works with any other eyes."[34] Perhaps a generation struggling with text will be better able to read these "works of God" in the language of human experience. To do so would take God out of the box that we have called religion, and release him into the currency of everyday life—in the heart of a culture desperate for depth. This is the God who is, in the words of Dietrich Bonhoeffer, "the 'beyond' in the midst of our life." Might it not be in nonverbal experience that a generation disillusioned with text, jaded with too many words, will find fresh faith?

Pentecost in the Cacophony
Story, image, community and contemplation—these are four of the weapons in our armory as we live, pray, worship and communicate in a culture retreating from the high ground of literacy. Our prayer must be that postliteracy will not lead to a disengagement but to a reengagement with the truths that have brought the church to its two thousandth year. There is a harsh side to this transition—it will cost

the church the privileged status afforded to it in the Gutenberg galaxy. "For the first time in the history of Christianity," Colin Morris has said, "the Gospel will have to take its chance in the ultimate open society."[35] The task that faces us is to maintain a voice for the Christian community within the multiplicity and plurality of screenage culture. For David Lochhead, this redefines the priorities of Christian mission. "In a world of multiple voices," he asserts, "the Christian response of witness is one of pointing to and naming the signs of the Spirit in the multitude of voices. It is the task of discerning the Spirit, of locating Pentecost in the cacophony."[36]

Postliterate culture will present the church with both challenge and opportunity. The challenge: to extricate our faith from an overdependence on text—without killing the patient in the process. The opportunity: to reaccess, reexamine, rediscover and reexplore "the story" in new forms. Our success in facing these issues will be greatly significant to the church's engagement with screenage culture, and thereby to its fortunes in the century that lies beyond the end of print.

word.link: Famous Last Words
*Jesus did many other things as well. If every one of them were written down, I suppose that even the whole world would not have room for the books that would be written.—***John 21:25**

Those of us who love and value the Bible are used to quoting the things it says about itself. That it is "God-breathed" and "useful." That it is "a lamp to our feet."

The verse above is one we quote less often. It tells us that the Bible is incomplete. That it does not—that it *cannot*—tell the whole story. This is not a measure of the inadequacy of Scripture, nor a rejection of its authority. It is rather a measure of the adequacy, the hugeness and completeness of Christ. How could we have believed that a book could "contain" him? How could we have dreamed that ink and paper would be enough to describe him?

The place of the Bible in church life will be a hot topic in the years ahead—the end of the age of print will ensure this if nothing else does. Those of us who have loved and valued this depository of grace and wisdom over the years will have to work to keep it central. We will be called to be creative and innovative, to reimagine the place of God's story in our lives. To abandon, at this time of change, the cumulative treasure that is the Bible would be suicide. But we gain nothing by giving to the Bible the place of Christ. We are Christians, not Bibleians. It is Christ who is the final word. As Robert Webber asks, we must decide, "Do we believe in a book or a person?"[37]

"This Is My Truth, Tell Me Yours"

The Postmodern Worldview

An epoch approaches its end when its fundamental conviction begins to weaken and no longer inspires enthusiasm among its advocates.
ALBERT BORGMAN, *Crossing the Post-Modern Divide*

Postmodernism is a contemporary movement. It is strong and fashionable. Over and above this, it is not altogether clear what the devil it is.
ERNEST GELLNER, *Postmodernism, Reason and Religion*

In 1967 my family moved to a rented house in Paris.[1] The intention was that we stay for one academic year. My father had arranged a sabbatical and was to work on his Ph.D. thesis at the Sorbonne. Like the best-laid plans, our intentions went awry. Growing tension among both students and workers in France erupted in the riots of May 1968, in which thousands took to the streets and fought running battles with the police. We would be given a day off school if a march was planned in our quarter; we would walk past burned out cars in the street; my father would come home with his eyes streaming from the tear gas that had leaked from the Place Montparnasse to the Metro lines below. Eventually the Sorbonne was closed and a general strike gripped the country. Uncomfortable with the prospect either of prolonged chaos or of a communist government, my father packed us into the car and sped us north to the coast and to England—on the last ferry to leave before the strike shut the Channel ports down. As we drove across the Pas de Calais at dawn, smokeless factory chimneys could be seen adorned with the red flag of the hoped-for revolution. An eerie silence lay across the land as Europe held its breath and all eyes were on France. The skilled intervention of President De Gaulle broke the student-worker alliance, and order was restored. Neither my family nor the thousands of others caught in these events were aware of the significant role that this crisis would play in the philosophical history of France—and of the world.

To all those involved in them, *les événements* ("the events") of May 1968 remained a deeply etched experience. The revolution never came—in a sense, the dream was over—and the years following were marked in France by reflection and reevaluation by the radical left. If the 1960s "revolution" had ended in such disarray, if Marxism and modernism alike had failed, where was there to turn? Out of this disappointment—this search for a new, more permanent radical edge—a new philosophical movement was born. Disillusionment with the 1960s counterculture created a vacuum in philosophy, and a generation of young French philosophers, not unlike the postwar existentialists before them, stepped in with "the newest avant-garde in theory and politics, more radical than radical and newer than new; the hyperradical and hypernew."[2] This is the movement we now call postmodernism.

The Birth of an -ism
Much of the material from which these young writers constructed

their theories had been around for some time, not least in the work of the philosopher Nietzsche. The term *postmodern* had been in use in the art world from the early part of the century, and a range of ideas challenging the assumptions of modernity had been published over several decades. Many of the changes we now identify with the demise of modernity were well under way by the 1970s, but no one had constructed theories that tied all these things together. As Stephen Connor has said, the "concept of postmodernism cannot be said to have crystallized until about the mid 1970's."[3] From this point Jean-François Lyotard, Jaques Derrida, Jean Baudrillard and, in America, Richard Rorty published a series of works that have become the classic texts of postmodern theory. In the words of Best and Kellner, these theorists claim that "in the contemporary high-tech media society, emergent processes of change and transformation are producing a new post-modern society. . . . The era of post-modernity constitutes a novel state of history and novel socio-cultural formation which requires new concepts and theories."[4] Hundreds of other authors have now joined them with developments, rebuttals, applications and examinations of these theories, and the term *postmodern* is in everyday use.

Speaking in 1946 when existentialism was growing in popularity at a similar rate, Jean-Paul Sartre said, "Many of those who are making use of this word would be highly confused if required to explain its meaning. For since it has become fashionable, people cheerfully declare that this musician or that painter is 'existentialist.' . . . The word is now so loosely applied to so many things that it no longer means anything."[5] Much the same could be said of postmodernism, which has followed its parent to become a "flavor of the month" philosophy—used to describe an immense range of products and ideas from pop culture and fashion, through advertising campaigns to the highest realms of art and academia. *Postmodern* is becoming a catch-all adjective for anything that is different from the way it was last year. Even among those who use the term fluently, a coherent meaning has not yet emerged. "There is no unified post-modern theory," Best and Kellner inform us, "or even a coherent set of positions. Rather, one is struck by the diversities between theories often lumped together as 'post-modern' and the plurality—often conflictual—of post-modern positions."[6]

In this confusion, it is important to be aware that postmodern*ity* and postmodern*ism* are not entirely the same. Those who doubt that such similar words can have dissimilar meanings need only consider the significance of the words *spirituality* and *spiritualism*. The journey from an *-ity* to an *-ism* can be long and complex. Broadly, postmodernity is the condition in which we find ourselves as the "modern" era draws to a close. It is descriptive of a period in history, a cultural ethos at a given time. Postmodern*ism*, on the other hand, is a specific philosophical response to this condition. As Gene Veith has said, "If the modern era is over, we are all post-modern, even if we reject the tenets of postmodernism."[7]

This overlap of terminology creates an interplay between the actual (the things that are happening in our culture as modernity ends) and the uttered (the things that are being said about what is happening). Many of the traits of postmodernity that culture watchers are describing do not stem from the philosophy of postmodernism at all; they are symptomatic of wider historical and social change. At the same time, the speed with which this philosophy has become accepted in the West, especially among the young, demonstrates that for many people what is being said (the -ism) strongly resonates with what is happening (the -ity). To put it another way, postmodern*ism* is not the only possible response to postmodern*ity*, but it is a response that rings true for many people. As Leonard Sweet has said, "It is really true that today we are sitting on a demolition site—the modern world—while a new world—the postmodern world—is being constructed all around us."[8]

definition.link: *Postmodern*

The world of Generation X and beyond will be postmodern in the following senses:

1. The influence of "modernity" as a central fund of social and philosophical ideas will be greatly lessened.

2. A new group of ideas will come together to form the concepts of postmodernity.

3. Within this process, the theories of postmodernism will play a part as an influential voice in the new paradigm.

4. Evidence for the influences both of postmodernity and of postmodernism will be seen most clearly in the lives of the transitional generations.

As we consider the postmodern nature of the emerging culture, we need to ask ourselves four questions:

1. What is the nature of this modernity that is coming to an end?

2. What are the broad strokes of the emerging condition of postmodernity, influenced as it is by the philosophies of postmodernism?

3. What will the impact of these changes be on the transitional generations?

4. What challenges will this bring for the Christian faith community?

As before, the last of these questions will be dealt with in detail in a separate chapter—the first three will be our concern now. Because it is both a philosophical shift and a broad social movement, developing and unfolding even as we try to understand it, postmodernity is a moving target in a changing field. One way of beginning to understand it is to capture what it is that we are losing—what this "modernity" has been about.

Building Babel

A widely quoted measurement of the modern era is that given by theologian Thomas Oden, who claims that modernity was born in the storming of the Bastille in the French revolution of 1789 and lived exactly two hundred years to the fall of the Berlin Wall in 1989.[9] As Gene Veith explains, "The revolutionaries who installed the 'Goddess of Reason' in Notre Dame Cathedral ushered in an age of social engineering, culminating in the grandiose pretensions of Communism . . . with its totalitarian control of every facet of human life."[10]

The ideas central to the French Revolution—ideas that together we now know as the Enlightenment—grew through the eighteenth century and became the foundational creeds of modernity. Central to these ideas is the supremacy of reason, expressed in scientific inquiry and giving birth to technological progress. "Modernists genuinely believed that science would answer all questions," Veith says, "and that the application of scientific principles would solve all social problems. Through rational planning, applied technology and social manipulation, experts could engineer the perfect society."[11]

Walsh and Middleton compare this process to the building of a Babel-like tower. "The first or ground floor of the building of modernity was science," they explain. "Science has laid the foundations of modern progress." Onto that foundation was built an increasing faith in the products of science—the machines that began to fill our lives as the Industrial Revolution took hold. "Technology thus constitutes the second floor in the Western building of progress." But the building didn't stop with the machines—they were harnessed to produce wealth, so that "economic growth, seen as the purpose and raison d'être of industrial and scientific progress, became the third floor of the building of Western culture."[12] The supremacy of reason, the enterprise of science, the toys of technology and the dream of universal prosperity—these are the contours of the modernist worldview: in Bob Goudzwaard's memorable term, the "idols of our time."

What was envisioned by modernists, Walsh and Middleton explain, was "a veritable utopia of prosperity and progress in which the whole human race would be united. . . . Human progress is not only possible but inevitable, we have come to believe, if only we allow autonomous reason the freedom to investigate our world scientifically. By this free and open investigation, . . . humanity will be able to acquire the technological power necessary to control nature and bring about the ultimate human goal: increased economic consumption and affluence, with resulting peace, fulfillment and security."[13] The impact of this vision not only on our culture but on its churches is summed up by Tom Sine in the chilling words "We have sold our young the wrong dream."[14]

The Real World Strikes Back

So, what happened? How did the vision of the Enlightenment—which has given us so much in terms of technology, prosperity, leisure and progress—lose its magnetic force, its power to inspire our lives? The answer, simply put, is that reality stepped in. "After slavery, two world wars, communism, nazism and nuclear bombs," says D. Martin Fields, "people began to question the belief that the pursuit of reason, technology and science would make for a better world."[15] Walsh and Middleton see the genesis of this despair in the existentialism of postwar Europe, when "Existentialist writers, whether Christian or atheist, articulated in novels, plays, essays and assorted philosophical writings a profound loss of hope and sense of angst (undefined anxiety or dread) about the meaning and purpose of life in modern times. In this they became the precursors of our contemporary post-modern consciousness."[16]

Not long after this a countercultural movement exploded across the West, giving voice to this same existential angst. "The counterculture of the 1960's began looking for something different," says Veith, "and in many ways its advocates were the pioneers of postmodernism. As the student protestors grew up, they entered academia, the professions and the mainstream of the culture, bringing their 'new consciousness' with them." This brings us full circle to Paris in 1968 and the founding voices of postmodern theory. "Scholars began submitting scientific rationalism to a withering critique," Veith continues, "arguing that what is presented as objective truth is often a mask for personal bias, cultural prejudice and power politics."[17] If it is nothing else, then, postmodernity is a critical reaction to modernity. Christopher Jones, of St. Peters College, Oxford, has written, "It is perhaps best to see post-modernism as a corrective to the excesses of modernity, and a purgative to its pathologies."[18] Postmodernists are working hard to articulate a proactive philosophy, but there can be no doubt that postmodernity, at its root, is reactive. "First," Jones writes, "postmodernism defines itself negatively against the universal principles of knowledge and conduct characteristic of the period since the European enlightenment." Dave Tomlinson puts the same view in the form of a question. "What happens," he asks, "when the modern world loses its romance? When dreams of progress for the common good of humankind turn into nightmares like Bosnia and Rwanda?"[19] The answer is: postmodernity happens.

Into the Hall of Mirrors

What, then, is postmodernity? What are the contours of the culture that is emerging in place of the brash optimism of the modern progress myth? To answer this question is to piece together clues from a vast range of sources. It is like searching a crowd by the light of a mirror ball: fragmented spots of light are hitting disparate and unconnected corners of the culture. There are literally hundreds of writers and commentators working in this area, and each brings his or her own particular analysis. What follows is an amalgamation from several sources—some from within the church, some from without; some from published works, some from Internet papers—tempered by my own anecdotal experience of working with young people on the voyage to planet Postmodernity. Theirs is a complex, multiple journey. It is best described, I believe, as a series of transitions, in each of which there is an abandoning of the old and an embracing of the new. It is inevitable that any attempt to list these transitions will oversimplify, but it is my hope that the five "from X to Y" statements below will help those struggling to get a grip on these changes.

Transition 1: From Dogma to Deconstruction

The most famous attempt at self-definition made by a postmodernist is that of Jean-François Lyotard, "Simplifying in the extreme, I define post-modern as incredulity toward metanarratives."[20] The failure of modernity, Lyotard is saying, has left Western culture suspicious not only of the big story of the science-and-progress myth but of any big story that sets itself up as the answer to the whole of life. Metanarratives, according to postmodern scholar Patricia Waugh, are "large-scale theoretical interpretations purportedly of universal application."[21] Veith sees the failure of modernity as more than a simple questioning of science, "The bitterness of its critics suggests not mere disillusionment but, more deeply, loss of faith. Modernism, in effect, failed as a religion."[22] Burned by the betrayal of modernity, postmodernists are determined to reject every story that claims to be *the* story. Such claims, they say, become "totalizing" and inevitably lead to the marginalization and oppression of other stories. They want, in the words of Mike Riddell, "to throw the doors open and listen to all the stories,"[23] to bring the margins into the center. Thus truth is neither absolute nor abstract; it can exist only as the "indwelt truth" of local stories. There is no limit to the number of possible stories, and there is no basis on which to assign them anything but equal worth. As the College de France report on education summarized, "Today there is no more truth or falsehood, no stereotype or innovation, no beauty or ugliness, but only an infinite array of pleasures, all different and all equal."[24] Richard Rorty captures the scale of this climb down from metanarrative in his definition of objectivity as "agreement amongst everyone who is in the room at the time."[25]

History, for postmodernists, is a series of metaphors rather than an account of things that actually happened, and since every story carries the corrupting perspective of its author, all texts and truths must be "deconstructed." Deconstruction is "a mode of analysis that purports to take apart all expressions of objective meaning, showing that everything from a play by Shakespeare to the Declaration of Independence to a scientific experiment is actually unstable linguistic constructions, masks for cultural power and rationalizations for oppression."[26] These two factors—the rejection of metanarrative and the deconstruction of all truth claims—are the closest things post-modernists have to a core creed. They form a rock-solid floor to the new building of postmodernity. From them come some of the most significant characteristics of the emerging age, an age in which open-ended pluralism replaces the assumed superiority of any single idea or creed; ambiguity replaces certainty, and ambivalence takes the place of faith; and coherent systems of meaning are rejected, to be replaced by fragmented mosaic patterns.

Survival in this jungle depends on three simple rules: trust no one, suspect everyone, take nothing at face value. Above all, reject anyone who claims to bring you a truth that might claim to be *the* truth. Rejecting metanarrative presents the emerging culture with a significant dilemma. It is, quite rightly, antitotalizing, and it appeals to a generation "cynical of a concept of truth which has been defined by a small group of 'experts' (white, male, European academics), and used to dominate and silence any other voices in the community."[27] But it is also directionless, offering no framework to function "as a navigational guide throughout life."[28] If there is no moral order other than that which we each impose on our own "constructed" world, then the world "is devoid of meaning; it is a universe of nihilism where theories float in a void, unanchored in any secure harbour."[29] In such a universe, "the experience of the world as our 'home', in the sense of a place where we know the rules and responsibilities of the house, is lost and a nomadic homelessness dominates the ethical horizon."[30] A postmodern generation is a generation a long way from home, confused and wandering. A generation that has lost the map and is fast losing the will to look for it again.

Transition 2: From the Rational to the Irrational, and from Logic to Intuition

If the enthronement of Reason in 1789 was the central act of modernity's birth, then the shift to postmodernity will raise questions about the place of reason in our lives. And if reason and logic are no longer the doorkeepers of experience, a postmodern generation will want to open and explore other, neglected ways of knowing. "The post-modern framework," Kevin Ford says, "allows for the existence of realities that science cannot measure—the supernatural, the trans-rational, the spiritual, the eternal, the ineffable, the numinous."[31] Those growing up in this new postrational culture will show a greater openness to ideas presented in nonrational forms and to experiences rooted in nonempirical reality. The defined certainties of systematic thinking are thrown over for the ambiguity of story. Linear and rational argument gives way to juxtaposition, sampling and collage, allowing for "intuitive leaps of meaning."[32] A shift in music from melody to rhythm as the heart of the enterprise is indicative of this change. Feelings are back on the agenda; "dignity is granted to emotions and intuition."[33] The rational man of modernity who did not need to trust in anything beyond logic and sensory experience no longer dominates. The postmodern man is in the house. "With the demise of the absoluteness of human reason and science," D. Martin Fields has written, "the super-natural, that which is not empirical, is once again open to consideration."[34] The rejection of an unseen world beyond the seen is losing its strength in our culture; belief in spiritual forces is no longer considered antithetical to an intelligent worldview. As Walter James and Brian Russel have said, "The suspicion of and distaste for the exclusively rational leads in some measure to a re-enchantment of the world, reducing the tendency to treat wonders as commodities."[35] Postmodernity is reopening the doors that rationality and empiricism slammed shut. "The spiritual dimension is once again talked about with great ease."[36]

Transition 3: From Progress to Pessimism
The analysis offered by Middleton and Walsh among others is very clear in putting the "progress myth" at the heart of modernity: if the Enlightenment was about nothing else, it was about a better future for humanity. Postmodernity sweeps away any such notion. Without a unified vision of what is right or good, there can be no vision of the better future. Stanley J. Grenz writes, "In eschewing the enlight-

enment myth of inevitable progress, postmodernism replaces the optimism of the last century with a gnawing pessimism. Gone is the belief that every day and in every way, we are getting better and better. Members of the emerging generation are no longer confident that humanity will be able to solve the world's great problems."[37] No big story means no big finale: we are not heading anywhere in particular, and there is no great climax to look forward to. "The loss of a future which can be constructed and participated in has lasting effects on the way in which people structure their lives," says Mike Riddell. "The focus shifts very much to the present, with the emphasis on extracting as much enjoyment out of that sphere as possible, and damn the consequences."[38] Despair and hedonism, suicide and escape—in reality these are two sides of the same coin of angst, and postmodernity is providing more and more places to spend it.

Transition 4: From Creed to Community

If only local narratives have meaning, and if the only truth is indwelt truth, a new emphasis will be placed on the search for community. In the modern age, it was the abstract creeds, whether of science or of religion, that held people together; in the postmodern age it will be the interrelationships of networks, cells, friendships and communities that hold people together. Relationships are very important to postmodernity and are measured in organic rather than mechanistic terms. Philosopher Alasdair MacIntyre, though not himself a postmodernist, supports the view that truth and moral guidance can only be found in community. "I can only answer the question 'What am I to do?' " he says, "if I can answer the prior question 'Of what story or stories do I find myself a part?' "[39] Postmodernism's attack on the monolithic institutions of modernity opens the door for their breakup into smaller, more intimate communities, each living out its own "story."

Placed against the backdrop of the increasing dysfunctionality of the family in Western society, this search for authentic community will emerge as one of the primary drives and motivations of a postmodern generation.

Transition 5: From Commitment to Choice and Change

Ironically, the very philosophical shift that sends postmoderns off in search of community predisposes them *not* to commit once they get there. Removing the power of metanarrative opens the door to such a flood of choice and opportunity that long-term commitments seem unwise. What if something better were to come along tomorrow? "Experience is a series of unrelated 'presents,' divorced from ethics and dogma. Nomadic wanderings replace purposeful pilgrimage."[40] Life is about traveling, not about arriving—today's journey is good for today, but tomorrow another road beckons. If a lifetime's commitment is to emerge, it will do so not as the result of a once-for-all decision but because of the experiential quality and value of a whole series of decisions linked together. Loyalties are frequently reevaluated in the light of changing circumstances. Experience, like bread, quickly goes stale.

So powerful is the postmodern emphasis on choice and change that it attacks the one constant, unchanging element at the heart of modernity—the self. Central to the Enlightenment project was the autonomous self. For believers, the self is rooted in the existence of the God who has created it, hence John Calvin's words, "The true knowledge of ourselves is dependent on the true knowledge of God." For Enlightenment rationalists with no time for such superstitions, the self is *in itself* the center of the universe, hence Descartes's "I think, therefore I am." Either way, self-assurance, self-confidence, self-awareness have been strong elements in both belief and unbelief through the modern era. Postmodernism puts an end to such assurance. According to Kenneth Gergen, "Under post-modern conditions, persons exist in a state of continuous construction and reconstruction; it is a world where anything goes that can be negotiated."[41] If rationalism said, "Nothing is sure or certain except the self," postmodernism says, "Nothing is sure or certain, not even the self." The self-reinventions of Bono and Madonna are icons of this age, in which the dictum "If it feels good, do it" has become "If it feels good, *be* it." Richard Lints has written that "Madonna is in many ways a perfect personification of the post-modern reality: sensation without substance, motion without purpose, a self-centered persona undergoing perpetual change for its own sake."[42] No more able to look into the mirror of a knowable and coherent nature than into the mirror of a known God, we live instead in the hall of mirrors, presented with so many alternative selves that we become "paralyzed in the face of it all."[43] A postmodern generation will not only be in search of meaning and community; they will also be in search of some anchor, some solid point of reference from which they can answer the question "Who am I?"

These five conflicts—dogma versus deconstruction, reason versus intuition, progress versus pessimism, creed versus community, and commitment versus choice and change—mark out the key themes of the transition into postmodernity. For the Christian faith community, they identify a whole range of issues that the coming decades will present us with.

word.link: Get Up and Eat, Version 2

A voice told him, "Get up, Peter. Kill and eat."
"Surely not, Lord!" Peter replied. "I have never eaten anything impure or unclean." —Acts 10:13-14

Like Elijah, Peter was asleep in the heat of the day. Like Elijah, he woke to a vision of food—in this case a feast of every kind of "unclean" thing. Like Elijah, he heard a voice saying, "Get up and eat." And like Elijah, he was taken on a journey.

This is the incident described by Mike Riddell as "God telling Peter to do what God has told Peter not to do." It is perhaps the clearest example in the Bible of a paradigm shift at work. Before this vision, the gospel is for Jews; by the end, it is for the nations. Within days the fledgling church will be launching its global mission.

We are used to hearing that sin and disobedience will keep us from seeing the future God has for us. But it wasn't sin and disobedience that limited Peter's vision; it was holiness and obedience. It was Peter's very commitment to God, within the paradigms in which he had grown up, that held him captive. It's hard enough to change when we know we have been wrong; in times of shifting paradigms we are called to change where we have been right. How often through the centuries of the church has Peter's cry been echoed, "Surely not, Lord"? And how often has it been misplaced?

"Already, our cold logic—our 'absolute' truth—is surrendering to something new," writes Tom Hohstadt of the paradigm shifts happening in our time. "We are seeing with different eyes and hearing with different ears. Even reality itself is changing! It's not that two and two are no longer four, it's just that two and two are no longer the issue."[44]

Reimagineering the Church

Living with the Postmodern Worldview

How will you reach this post-modern generation—a generation that cannot conceive of objective truth, cannot follow your linear arguments, cannot tolerate anything (including evangelism) that smacks of religious intolerance?
KEVIN FORD, *Jesus for a New Generation*

The new generation is more interested in broad strokes than detail, more attracted to an inclusive view of faith than an exclusive view, more concerned with unity than diversity, more open to a dynamic, growing faith than to a static fixed system, and more visual than verbal with a high level of tolerance and ambiguity.
ROBERT WEBBER, *Ancient-Future Faith*

There is a memorable scene in the film *Hook* in which the adult Peter Pan, played by Robin Williams, tries to reenter the imaginary world seen as real by the lost boys. They sit down to a great feast together at which all the food is imaginary. At first Peter sees nothing, but as he slowly recovers the power of imagination, a tableful of rich and colorful dishes begins to appear, until the feast descends into the kind of food fight that only Hollywood can provide. At the crucial moment, when Peter is first able to imagine again, a wide-eyed lost boy looks to him with admiration and excitement. "You're doing it, Peter," he cries. "You're imagining."

For many of those struggling to relate the Christian faith to post-modernity, this is an apt image. The sense is that there is something to be recovered, a richness and color to the faith, that the rationalism and empiricism of modernity has taken from us. The task is not simply to rearrange the furniture in the church's shop window but to reimagine faith in a new context.

Nigel Wright is senior minister of Altrincham Baptist Church, one of Britain's fastest growing and most successful churches. For ABC, as it is known, growth and change have been synonymous. "Re-imagination should not be regarded as a superficial marketing ploy," Wright has said, "but as an intellectually serious act of self-definition."[1]

For the church, it is important to understand that engagement with postmoder*nity* is not the same as acceptance of postmodern*ism*. Our primary concern—a concern that none of us can afford to evade—must be to understand postmodernity as a description of the times in which we live. The task of reimagining faith in this new context is incumbent upon us for two reasons. The first, captured in the quote from Kevin Ford, is that only a reimagined church will *appeal* to the generations shaped by the emerging paradigms. The second is that only a reimagined church will *survive* in the West of the twenty-first century. As British academic and church leader Graham Cray has written, "If Christianity cannot be inculturated successfully within the post-modern context, there will be no Western church."[2]

Recognizing these twin goals, I propose to take each of the five tensions described in chapter eight and to look briefly at the issues these raise for the church. I will do this in the form of a brief list, under each, of suggested action points. As Graham Cray has said, "The central question to be faced is how should we respond to the emerging culture in a way which is true to the gospel. . . . It is through risk and experiment together with the making of mistakes that the future shape of the Church in mission will be established."[3] What, then, can the Christian community do to prepare itself for a postmodern culture and to embrace those shaped by it?

In the Tension Between Dogma and Deconstruction

Revisit the biblical metanarrative. For Middleton and Walsh, the answer lies in recovering the truth that the biblical metanarrative is "antitotalizing" in its impact. "The biblical metanarrative addresses our post-modern situation with both compassion and power," they write. "But does this metanarrative escape the post-modern charge of totalisation and violence? On our analysis, it does far more than that. Far from promoting violence, the story the Scriptures tell contains the resources to shatter totalising readings, to convert the reader, to align us with God's purposes of shalom, compassion and justice."[4] What this will mean in practice is a willingness to hear the multiple stories of postmodernity and to see the Christian metanarrative as the means by which God is able to indwell and transform each. "Postmodernists are right: the voices of the marginalised, of those who have been left outside the storyline that has been dominant in the West, need to be heard. . . . But we need to hear anew not so we can appropriate these voices for our own agenda, nor to conspire toward some sort of God's-eye view of the world. . . . Rather, we need to be able to hear each other and the whole creation that we might join together in fulfilling the story of redemption."[5] In this approach, "becoming a Christian" does not mean stepping out of our own local story into God's global epic; it means allowing God to walk with us in our story. God comes both in affirmation and in judgment of every culture—but he comes incarnate, in humility. Far from squashing every local story into one, he is, in his person, the fulfillment of each one.

Recover biblical humility. Anglican priest Nick Mercer sees the engagement with the postmodern as reminder of our own limitations and as an opportunity to recover humility. "There are no more certainties: only reasonable grounds for confidence," he says. "This must give us a degree of humility in our walk with others of differing theological positions, and in our dealings with those struggling with faith and practice."[6]

Don't mistake deconstruction for dismissal. Deconstruction is a way of dealing with knowledge and truth claims, a shift in emphasis from uncritical acceptance to critical engagement. For those raised on modernity, it feels more like rejection and dismissal. If I offer you a new Walkman and the first thing you do is open it up to check the works, I may find your suspicions offensive. But if that is how you have been taught to treat all truth claims, I may have to learn to live with it. Those who bring critical deconstruction to the faith are not always doing so in the hope of rejecting or destroying it; many are doing so in the hope that it will stand. As Walter James and Brian Russel urge, "The Church should welcome and embrace the less authoritarian and more learner-centred styles of education that the post-modern spirit exacts."[7]

In the Tension Between Reason and Intuition

Make room for nonlinear thinking. "Traditional, modernist-oriented, evidential apologetics relies on creating a sense of 'cognitive dissonance' within the other person—a sense that his or her own belief structure does not logically square with reality," Kevin Ford explains. "But [this] approach just doesn't cut it any more—not with Generation X. . . . With my generation you won't hear 'you're right.' You'll hear 'whatever.' "[8] While in some ways the church has been at odds with modernity from its inception, in others it has adapted all too well. One of these has been the tendency to present biblical truths in the systematic, linear, rationalistic forms picked up from the sciences. A postmodern generation rejects this approach and is looking for ambiguity, intuitive scope, emotional resonance. None of these is captured well in four spiritual laws.

Take emotion seriously. Much has been written—in dismissal as well as in support—about the "therapeutic age" in which we live. For good or ill, where modernity trusted facts and doubted feelings, postmodernity is switching the polarity. For the church, this is an opportunity to restore balance and to embrace the biblical wholism that views people—heart, soul, strength and mind—as a unity. The reimagining of our faith in the postmodern context may offer us the chance to heal old wounds, reuniting the wings of the church that have been forced by a false dilemma into two camps: those emphasizing intellectual truth at the expense of emotional experience, and those rejoicing in experience at the expense of the Christian mind. Their reunification is long overdue.

Open doors of spirituality. We will explore this whole area further in chapter twelve, when we look at the spirituality of a post-Christian society, but it is important in passing to note the relevance of this theme to a postmodern faith. Divorced as it may be from any definite sense of God, postmodern culture is nonetheless wide open to spiritual experience. Spirituality is seen not as belonging to "another realm" beyond some great divide but as being an aspect of human activity available to us—a muscle we may have forgotten how to use. "Ask an Eastern Guru to teach you how to pray, and he will say to you, 'Try this,' " a friend recently challenged me. "Ask a Christian the same question, and she will say, 'First you must believe.' " With more and more people asking the question, it is essential that we realign our answers.

Embrace technology. In modernity, technology is entirely wrapped up with the progress myth—it is one of the gods that will save us. To postmoderns, it has no such power and is associated, rather, with play. As Mike Riddell explains, "Postmodernists are children of technology. They embrace it enthusiastically for the enhancements it can bring to life . . . and especially for its ability to increase the scope of 'play.' There is no longer any expectation that technology is somehow going to solve existential angst, but it may

well provide better ways of escaping from it."[9] In the shift toward postmodernity, technology has "changed sides," from being the willing
slave of metanarrative to being the enabling force of deconstruction.
Digital technology is not associated with rationalism and empiricism,
even though it deals for the most part with logic and is built entirely on
the numbers one and zero! Postmoderns expect technology to be used to
explore the experiential, the emotional and the intuitive. In practical
terms, this may mean that it is as important to load the church computer
with a copy of Myst as with Microsoft Office.

In the Tension Between Progress and Pessimism
Rediscover the better future. "In a world drowning in cynicism,
nihilism and polarization," Tom Sine has said, "people are looking
for a reason for hope. And I am convinced that the people of God
have no higher calling than to offer hope to the world. The only
problem is that we cannot offer what we do not possess."[10] For Sine,
the recovery of hope demands the rediscovery of God's plans for the
human future—the biblical vision of a renewed cosmos and of the
"great homecoming" in which every tribe (and story) finds its place.
Missiologist David Bosch makes the same plea: "We should not
capitulate to pessimism and despair. All around us people are looking for new meaning in life. This is the moment where the Christian
church and the Christian mission may once again, humbly yet resolutely, present the vision of the reign of God not as pie in the sky but
as an eschatological reality which casts its rays into the dismal
present, illuminates it and confers meaning on it."[11]

The postmodern generations are reputed to have little sense of
either past or future and to live in a perpetual moment of "now." This
reputation is often based on a superficial and unfair judgment, but
even where it is true, there is an underlying need to be mobilized by
a substantive future vision. As long ago as 1969, theologian Jürgen
Moltmann spoke of the need to rediscover a Christianity with a
future tense. "Many abandon Christianity," he wrote, "because they
find in it no power of the future."[12] Robert Webber has argued more

recently that many streams of Christianity have lost their vision of *Christus Victor:* the Christ who not only has won salvation for individuals but has utterly disarmed and defeated every cosmic power of evil and is bringing fulfillment to the promise of God. This means "nothing less than the re-creation of the entire universe, including the structures of existence. . . . What is redeemed, restored and re-created is God's work of creation."[13] What might it mean for the postmodern Christian church to explore and celebrate once more both the *now* and the *not yet* of the kingdom of God?

Engage with despair. Kurt Cobain has become an icon of postmodern youth—hating himself, despising others, ultimately taking his own life. According to reports, in one of the last discussions he had with his record company, he asked that his song "I Hate Myself and I Want to Die" be used as the title track of the album Nirvana was working on.[14] They refused. He died. Youth suicide is growing throughout the West, as are the patterns of destructive behavior that fall just short of it. This is where the rubber of existential angst hits the road of real young lives, where individuals grow up under such a weight of confusion, pessimism and self-loathing that, in due course, it crushes them. Cobain was just one in a long line of artists whose careers are constructed on the power of self-destruction: from Iggy Pop via Sid Vicious to Marilyn Manson. If there is any gospel that is going to have nothing to say to such a culture, it is a triumphalistic, escapist easy-believism—the kind detractors call "happy-clappy."

London-based worship leader Jonny Baker, pioneer of the imaginative Grace services, argues that "pain and brokenness rather than success will connect with others."[15] It is not that the Christian story leaves us in our despair, but it begins by sharing the pain we feel. The irony of twenty-first-century apologetics is that Christians will be called at one and the same time to proclaim hope and to empathize with despair.

In the Tension Between Creed and Community
Live it out. In prioritizing abstract ideas, modernity allowed us to

divorce belief from action and lifestyle—to accept propositional truth without living it out. Postmodernity, by contrast, recognizes only indwelt truth. This is the "uniquely postmodern hermeneutic—there is no understanding without standing under—that insists that everything must be entered in order to be understood."[16] The emerging culture demands an "embodied apologetic—a flesh-and-blood, living and breathing argument for God."[17] Our culture is less and less interested in what the church *believes* and more and more concerned about the way it *behaves.* To the questions postmodernism is asking, Christopher Jones has said, "The Church's response must be to exhibit in concrete form the meaning of life lived in openness to the God of Jesus, the triune God who is Truth and Love and Goodness."[18] It is likely that the journey into postmodernity will produce new Christian projects and communities that are united not by a common creed but by a common lifestyle. The appeal of these communities to the wider culture will not so much be "join us if you believe these things" as "join us if you want to live this way." Once again this is a reversal of polarity, from churches in which dogma is essential and lifestyle optional, to churches built on lifestyle and leaving dogma to personal choice.

Build community. According to Jimmy Long, "Christians in the emerging post-modern era are beginning to see that they need to re-emphasize relational community."[19] Long quotes Gareth Icenogle as saying, "Jesus' mission was to demonstrate the nearness of God to alienated humanity. To do this he formed small group communities,"[20] and makes the claim that "tribalism, or community, is much more closely aligned than the autonomous self to God's intention."[21] The postmodern generation, then, will look for more than off-the-shelf truth, more even than truth embodied in an individual life. They will look for truth indwelt within a community or tribe. Like anthropologists breaking into the depths of the Amazon rain forest, they will ask themselves, *What makes this tribe tick? What are the norms of this community?* No amount of persuasive preaching will mend the damage if the lived-out answers to these questions are off-putting. The postmodern generation are looking for authenticity, reality, transparency and openness. To the extent that postmodernity is saying, "Don't talk to me about what you believe—show me how you live," it is entirely biblical—more so, at times, than the church it so savagely critiques.

Believe in friendship. Jimmy Long makes the observation that the postmodern generation are turning more and more to their friends as a new family. "Why is it," he asks, "that in the mid-1990's the most popular and copied TV program is *Friends*? In the 1950's we were immersed in family TV shows . . . today the themes of many shows center around friends, not family."[22] Mike Riddell supports this view, writing that "in the absence of transcendent values or meanings, participants in the new culture are finding significance in friendship. . . . Not just in sexual or romantic couplings, but in a lively sense of community expressed among groups of friends. It is a new social tribalism among those who recognise in others something of their own experience."[23] This shift is also evident in a new embracing of creative partnerships and collaborations. Many of the leading-edge media products of Gen X culture—*South Park* and *The Blair Witch Project* are good examples—were created by partnerships forged out of friendships. It is likely that these new dynamics of community flowing along the lines of friendship will become the natural seams of the emerging culture, so much so that church structures and plans that cut across them will be hotly challenged. The church has for many years understood the need to grow with, rather than against, the natural currents of family; now it must learn to respect, too, the lines of friendship. Small-group communities that build on the strengths of friendship will have a lasting quality far in excess of larger structures that ignore them.

In the Tension Between Commitment and Choice and Change

Embrace process and journey. If there is any one aspect of Christian practice that is roundly challenged by postmodernity, it is a turnstile understanding of conversion—the view that a single decision, made in a moment, is enough to secure lifelong commitment. The huge success of the Alpha course, which presses for commitment but does so in the context of process and journey, is indicative of this change. In postmodernity, the journey of faith is not a single crossroad at which both destiny and destination are sealed, but a series of junctions and forks in the road, at each of which choices must be made. Discipleship, in this context, is never about a short-term sales experience but is always about a long-term, ongoing relationship.

Revalidate faith experience. It follows that Christian experience, on this journey, requires frequent revalidation. No assumption can be made that a decision of last month or last year will still hold good next week. The newfound emphasis among young people on the experiential dimension of faith is a symptom of this need for revalidation, as is the revival in a sacramental view of the Eucharist, in which the Christian story is rehearsed, and the response of repentance relived, week by week. In one, postmodern young people want to check that God is still moving; in the other, they check that they are still moved. Repeated spiritual experiences confirm that God is still in business and that the magnetic power of the Christian story is still strong.

Celebrate diversity. Lack of choice is an abiding characteristic of modernity, offering one truth, one standard, one size that fits all. Postmodernity, by contrast, is extreme in its desire for choice. The church, says Nick Mercer, is in an ideal position to meet this change. "In a post-modern society where choice is of the essence of life," he writes, "the Church is in a strong position, with 57 varieties to suit most tastes and temperaments, all with one central, Christological and Trinitarian message. If only we could celebrate that diversity and love one another."[24] The church's calling "is not to monolithic unity but to reconciled diversity."[25] To borrow a phrase from D. Martin Fields, a church expressing the true richness of Christian diversity will be "not a melting pot but a salad bowl."[26]

Emphasize homecoming. Postmoderns are not looking for a set of propositions to assent to; they are looking for a place to live. If

Christianity is to work for them, it must become their home—the place of security from which the world is explored and understood. They will bring not only their "souls" or brains into the household but indeed the whole of their lives—the good, the bad and the ugly. An invitation to this generation that is founded on anything other than unconditional love will fall on deaf ears.

This is by no means a comprehensive strategy for engaging the postmodern generations. But it is a series of starting points—doorways into a reimagined church. Like many others, I have struggled to come to terms with some of the changes implied here. There are many issues in which conclusions remain unclear, but I do sense a growing momentum in the church's desire to truly engage the emerging culture. I share with Ian Cundy, bishop of Lewes, both the sense of postmodernity as a mixed blessing and the urgency of the task of engagement. The bishop writes:

> It is not surprising . . . that our view of the post-modern is mixed. Caution and excitement, criticism and enthusiasm are all present in some measure. But one thing remains our common concern. The task of understanding our context, however difficult, cannot be avoided if we are to be faithful to our mission. It is in and to this context that the gospel is addressed.[27]

word.link: A Mars a Day

God did this so that men would seek him and perhaps reach out for him and find him, though he is not far from each one of us. "For in him we live and move and have our being." As some of your own poets have said, "We are his offspring."—Acts 17:27-28

Paul's encounter with Athenian pop culture in the debating arena of Mars Hill is emerging as a key text among many postmodern Christians. One reason for this is that it shows a genuine, investigative interest in culture. Paul has combed the city; he has read the inscriptions on shrines and statues; he knows the poets. By the time he stands to engage these people, he has already put himself inside their spiritual journey. His quoting of Greek poetry is the first-century equivalent of an MTV clip or a review of *Eyes Wide Shut* or *The Matrix*. "Would the apostle Paul go to the movies?" is not the question. "Would he ever have time for anything else?" might be more apposite!

But there is something more here, something deeper. What Paul does on Mars Hill is demolish the invisible barrier that might be thought to exist between Christian and non-Christian—between insider and outsider, "saved" and "unsaved." In the twentieth century, a great deal of the church's mission took an approach to culture that said, "We are different from you—and you can be like us." Evangelists drew a line in the sand and invited others to cross. Paul draws no such a line. "I am just like you," he says. "I am exactly like you. I have the same questions; I face the same dilemmas. Like you, I search for something to make sense of my life." In so doing, Paul releases the immense power of authentic evangelism, because it is only when I am the same as you and share your questions that the answers I have found can be relevant to you.

If cultural engagement is to become a plank in the church's missional strategy for the twenty-first century, then it must be engagement on this basis: not "us and them" but just "us."

The Power of Globfrag
The Postimperial World Order

*Mickey is universal. He's just as popular in Moscow and Leningrad—
these places where he's never been. There's all these rip-offs in
copyright terms all over the world. He's on every T-shirt in the world—I
saw him in the wilds of New Guinea five years ago.*
ROY DISNEY

*Sadly, what is happening around us today, this horror, this chaos on our
soil, in the heart of Europe, at the beginning of the twenty-first century,
this destruction, this killing, this hatred—this, alas, is no dream but a
living nightmare.*
BORO TODOROVIC

For generations the Bosnian city of Mostar—economic, industrial and cultural center of the province of Herzegovina—was the "jewel of the south," a popular and renowned tourist destination. "On the banks of the playful Neretva," intones a brochure from the days of Tito, "lies a town of unequalled beauty—a harmonious link between oriental and western architecture. . . . Nature divided this town with water, man linked it with bridges." A remarkable gateway between East and West, where ancient empires met and Christian and Muslim civilizations merged, Mostar's centerpiece was the ancient Stari Most (Old Bridge), a high-arched, graceful stone structure recognized as one of the architectural treasures of the Balkans. Centuries ago, it was the *Mostari*—the bridge keepers who patrolled this and other crossings of the steep and winding Neretva Valley—who gave to this city its name. But the Stari Most was more than a stone span stretched across a river valley; it was a bridge across cultures, a visible symbol of a city in which people groups with very different histories worked together for a common future.

Today the Stari Most, like much of Mostar, has been reduced to dust and rubble. April 1992 marked the beginning of thirty-two months of shelling, sniper fire and house-to-house fighting that left Mostar as a city with its heart torn out. Death, injury, bereavement, hunger, displacement, anger and destruction became the bitter daily fare of those of the population who stayed. Thousands more left; many will never return. The evil that convulsed the body of the former Yugoslavia like a territorial fit found its epicenter in Bosnia, and Mostar, the former "jewel," was shaken to its core. This was not a war waged against a powerful invader; it was a war of neighbor against neighbor, a virulent, stupefying violence that turned ordinary men and women into killers, and the streets of the city into an apocalyptic nightmare. It will take years—generations even—for Mostar to recover.

Mostar is one city among many in the former Yugoslavia, one battle zone among many the world over. Its shelled-out ruins stand as a

symbol of one of the most powerful and dangerous currents of the closing years of the twentieth century and opening years of the twenty-first.
The breakup of empires, the redrawing of borders, the sudden prolifera-
tion, across the planet, of ethnic and territorial conflict—these are the
symptoms of a process so powerful that it leaves hardly a corner of the
earth untouched: the unfolding of a postimperial world order. The 1990s
were a decade in which bridges were both built and destroyed.

In its simplest form, postimperialism has meant that the huge
colonial empires that dominated the world at the birth of the twentieth century were broken up in time for its demise. The film *Titanic*,
with its strong subtheme of class differentiation, is a timely
reminder to contemporary generations of just how strong the imperial spirit was—even as recently as 1912. The Great War was perhaps the last stand of colonial assumptions, and the decades that
followed it saw the slow unraveling of imperial powers—a process
that continues to this day. At one end of the transaction, the former
colonies have sought independence and self-rule, while at the other,
their former colonial powers are coming to terms with the imperial
legacy as they evolve into multicultural, multiethnic societies.

Even before the dust had settled on the collapse of the once-
mighty colonialism, the final decade of the twentieth century
brought the astounding news of the end both of Soviet Communism
and of the South African system of apartheid. If there was any doubt
that the monolithic empires were breaking up, it was swept away in
1989 when the falling masonry of the Berlin Wall signaled the crum-
bling of the political system it had so darkly symbolized.[1] The Eastern bloc disintegrated and the hundreds of ethnolinguistic groups
under its control began to rediscover self-identity and the hunger for
self-rule. "From Azerbaijan to the Baltic," writes Marcus Tanner,
"nations long buried under the rubble of empire have risen to claim a
place in the sun."[2] Who could have believed that the generation that
witnessed these historic changes would also see the inauguration of
President Nelson Mandela, perhaps the world's most potent living
symbol of the end of the imperial age?

Not One Force but Two

If imperialism was characterized by the subjugation of small nations
and people groups into monolithic empires—whether colonial or
communist—and by the forced abandonment of cultural identity, the
postimperial age will be marked by the self-identification of an ever
more complex kaleidoscope of ethnic and social groups. The key to
understanding this process is the recognition that its momentum is
derived not from one force but from two. The twin but opposing
forces of *globalization* and *fragmentation*—the one drawing the
world together, the other tearing it apart—form the horrific double
act at the heart of a whole range of contemporary conflicts. This is
the power of globfrag—the most significant force at work in contemporary global politics. Philosopher Michael Ignatieff[3] dramatically captures the counteraction of these forces. "The more evident
our common needs as a species become," he writes, "the more brutal
becomes the human insistence on the claims of difference. The cen-
tripetal forces of need, labour and science which are pulling us
together as a species are counter-balanced by centrifugal forces, the
claims of tribe, race, class, section, region and nation, pulling us
apart."[4]

The postimperialism of the coming decades will be the child of
these mismatched parents. This is the reality described by Benjamin
Barber as "Jihad vs. McWorld." "McDonald's in Moscow and Coke
in China will do more to create a global culture than military coloni-
zation ever could," he writes.[5] But at the same time, "There were
more than thirty wars in progress last year, most of them ethnic,
racial, tribal or religious in character, and the list of unsafe regions
doesn't seem to be getting any shorter. Some new world order!"[6]

Somewhere in the mysterious interplay of globalization and fragmentation—in the crosscurrents of human identity and aspiration—
lies the dynamic tension that will characterize not only nations but
neighborhoods in the early twenty-first century. This is a tension that
surfaces not only in the planet's ethnic hot spots but also on the
streets of cities the world over, as young people ask, "Who am I?"

The youth of Beirut holding high a Kalashnikov and wearing chest bands of bullets may be a symbol of the struggle for identity, but so is the child of East L.A. and the Bronx, armed only with a can of spray paint, out to make a mark on the world.

definition.link: *Postimperial*

The world of Generation X and beyond will be postimperial in the following senses:

1. The old global context built on the assumptions of empires, colonies and monocultural rule will have finally given way.

2. In its place, a new world order will emerge founded on the competitive multiplicity of the planetary marketplace.

3. The twin forces by which this new order is shaped will be those of globalization and fragmentation.

4. The tension of these forces will be felt not only among nations but within nations, as the nation-state itself is shaken by cultural fragmentation.

The purpose of this chapter will be to explore the broad contours of this postimperial world and the implications of globfrag. For the Western church, these implications will surface in two distinct areas:

1. The implications of globfrag will surface in the church's understanding of mission—the global dynamic of the church's identity and task. If mission in the past has carried with it imperial values, what values will carry mission into the future?

2. The implications of globfrag will surface also in the church's engagement with the generations impacted "at home" by the power of globfrag—generations swept up in globalization, torn apart by fragmentation and struggling for identity.

Not surprisingly, there is a significant overlap between the historical progress of postimperialism and the philosophical development of postmodernism, which speaks of "hearing all the stories" and "bringing the margins into the center." What the philosophy asks us *in theory* to consider, world history is asking us *in practice* to embrace. To some extent, this overlap explains the remarkable speed at which postmodern theory has gripped the hearts and minds of our culture, because it speaks into a context already taken up with the questions it addresses. The pragmatic, hands-on, people-centered, real-world questions of globfrag will put arms and legs on the church's response to its postmodern context. Our exploration of these themes will first examine the nature and interplay of globalization and fragmentation, before going on to consider their implications.

You and Your Mall Corner

Globalization is a real and powerful force. It shaped the world in the closing years of the twentieth century and it will go on doing so in the early decades of the twenty-first. At the heart of globalization lie the new possibilities of commerce, travel and communication opened up by the technologies of our time. Commerce delivers more products than ever on a global scale; travel carries individuals to diverse and far-flung destinations; and communication brings the cultures of the world onto screens, speakers and telephone receivers in the intimacy of our own homes. The fuel that has enabled us to exploit these possibilities at such an alarming speed is the fuel of consumerism—the drive to deliver more goods to more people in more places than ever before.

The growth of the literal McWorld[7] is a measure of this. In 1966 McDonald's operated fast-food outlets in one nation: the United States. By 1976, they were represented in twenty-one countries, and by 1986, in forty-five. By the late 1990s, the chain included eighteen thousand restaurants in ninety-four countries on five continents—a growth rate to rival that of any religion the world has ever known. "I am open to any course that helps McDonald's dominate every market," says chairman of the board Michael Quinlan.[8] Add to McWorld the names of Coke, MTV, Disney, Dreamworks, Michael Jordan, Madonna, Microsoft, Nintendo and the hundreds like them, and the scale of global culture begins to become clear.

Never before have the diverse cultures of the world been exposed to so many common products. The rising generations of the coming decades will reap the fruit of a world remolded by these forces, recognizing no community but the market and no authority but the customer who pays, as they deliver unprecedented levels of globalism in the twenty-first century. *Time* magazine's special report in November 1997 contrasted this upbeat future promised by the global mall with the realities of life as experienced by so many: "The children of the 21st century will inherit a world in many ways beguiling. For everyone but the poorest, it beckons as a magical empire of Mammon, a madcap consumer's paradise of immediate gratification and express delivery, of hot images and cool gadgets, of designer jeans and designer genes."[9] But this is not the only story. "Beneath the surface," the report goes on, "all is not well. . . . The modern economy masks a disfigured planet."[10] While much is positive in the rise of globalism—not least the breaking down of barriers—there is also much to be wary of.

Are You Being Serfed?

Tom Sine is in no doubt of the role of commercial interests in the drive toward a global culture, nor of the challenge that this represents for the Christian faith community. "Economic globalisation is being advanced by powerful financiers, influential CEOs of transnational corporations and international political brokers," he writes.

> None of us were given an opportunity to vote whether we or our respective countries wanted to be part of a one world economic order. . . . It's like going to sleep in your bed in your own home and waking up jammed into a gigantic global rocket ship with 6 billion others all hurtling through space at fantastic speeds with absolutely no notion of the destination.[11]

Sine characterizes God's plan for the human future as a different kind of globalism, the "mustard seed" variety that has "more to do with making a difference than with making a dollar, . . . more to do

with creating a new reconciled global community of justice and cele-
bration than with the production of a new global community of consumption, . . . more to do with coming home to Jerusalem than
Babylon."[12] He poses the question that must be at the heart of the
Christian church's agenda in the years that lie ahead: Which will
prove stronger, mustard seed or McWorld?

The Coca-Colonization of Youth

As targets in an increasing proportion of planetwide marketing,
young people are at the epicenter of this globalization storm. One of
the most telling side effects of transnational consumerism is that it
gives young people more commonality with their global peers than
with the former generations of their own home cultures.

Journalist Colin Morris explored this new dimension of culture in
his study of the impact of broadcasting on young people. "Since all
cultures have to locate themselves in time and space," he wrote,

> oral societies had a sense of continuity over time, but were spatially
> discontinuous. Things were reasonably harmonious between genera-
> tions within the same society, but there were vast differences and
> often conflicts with other societies a hundred miles or so apart. Time
> bound oral societies together, space separated them. When oral cul-
> tures gave place first to print and then to the electronic media, . . . the
> relationship between time and space was reversed. . . . It was space
> which became continuous because the airwaves could annihilate dis-
> tance.[13]

This is the origin of the generation gap, described by communications theorist James W. Carey in 1969 as the process by which "the
axis of diversity shifts from a spatial . . . to a temporal or generational dimension."[14] While the opening of this gap was first seen in
the 1960s, the transitional generations of more recent decades are
the first to be fully formed in its context—young people shaped
more than ever in history by an awareness of the planetary scale of
their own generation.

This was a key theme of the report I coauthored in 1996 for Youth for Christ International:

> Young people around the world are not suddenly the members of one homogenous people group—but they operate more and more in one market-place. More and more they seek points of reference among their generational peers rather than their geographical elders. More and more they are shaped by the same global forces, many of them commercial, despite the great distances that separate them. For some the need to belong, the longing for roots and tribe, has been transferred entirely to generational peers. . . . They no longer want to belong to anyone but each other.[15]

This radical shift represents a huge challenge to the Christian faith community, which for the most part still assumes time to be continuous and space discontinuous. No indigenous church can assume any longer that the passing of the faith to the new generation will be an easy, natural process. Nor can any one culture assume that its chosen "flavor of faith" will be attractive to its young. Communicating faith across the generational divide is fast becoming as significant a cross-cultural challenge as communicating across oceans and language barriers once were.

Balkanization Bites Back

If evidence for the progress of globalization is overwhelming, so is that for the pain of fragmentation, and the rising generations of young people and children are, once again, caught in the crossfire. "The dropping of the atom bomb on Hiroshima in 1945 sent a chilling message to an entire generation, and led to the superpower deadlock that became known as the Cold War. Somehow this deadlock averted global war. But at the same time, small-scale wars using conventional weapons reached epidemic proportions, with over 200 wars world-wide since 1945. Globalisation has kept a kind of peace, but fragmentation has let loose a different kind of war."[16] This is the greatest irony of the late twentieth century, that an era of peace was

also an era of war. There are no signs that this violent fragmentation—nations literally tearing themselves apart—is abating, and the
world enters its third millennium with an unprecedented number and
range of actual and potential conflicts. "The Leviathan seems to
have seized the global village and taken its inhabitants hostage,"
writes Felix 'Machi Njoku of the situation facing Africa. "Hence-
forth, the law of the jungle reigns supreme and only the strong can
escape from its clutches."[17]

Even contained at current levels, the degree of violence attributed
around the world to ethnic breakup is sufficient to render fragmentation one of the primary driving forces of the new century.

Patchwork Populations

Within nations, not least in the vast sprawl of multicultural cities,
the same fault lines are being projected from the global to the local
scale. The world's megacities are growing as patchwork quilts of
diverse and varied cultures. In many ways a city is a microcosm of
the planet, playing out on its own scale the warring forces of globfrag. "Here is the multiplex, morphed world in which we live,"
writes Leonard Sweet. "Temple Methodist Church in San Francisco
befriended a Ukrainian refugee woman who works in San Francisco's most traditional German restaurant, which is owned by an
Arab who is married to a Chinese woman who runs a pizza restaurant managed by a Russian."[18]

Globalization is present in the melting-pot effect, as diverse ethnic groups living in close proximity lose some of their distinctives.
But fragmentation is also present as many members of those same
groups, lost in the urban vastness, struggle with issues of identity. It
is no longer possible to identify a people group primarily in terms of
their geographical location. Patrick Johnstone's *Operation World*
defines a "people group" as "a significantly large sociological
grouping of individuals who perceive themselves to have a common
affinity."[19] Johnstone recognizes three types of group: *ethnolinguistic*—defined primarily by language and ethnicity; *sociological*—

defined by a long-term relation to the wider society, such as a traditional occupation or class, and *incidental*—defined by temporary or circumstantial factors, such as high-rise dwellers, drug users or commuters. Explaining the counting of such groups, Johnstone says, "The Tamil are counted 23 times in the global totals because Tamil communities exist in at least 23 countries, likewise the Kurds 20 times, the Sininke of West Africa 6 times."[20]

Nations, cities and neighborhoods may contain dozens of subcultural groups, each participating in the unity of civic life but each retaining in some measure its own identity. The coming century will present us with an overabundance of threatened peoples retreating into old and new tribal shells, in societies shattered like a broken mirror into thousands of pieces. An approach that assumes one dominant cultural identity for a given city or region will run counter to the whole flow of history, and the Christian church will face the challenges of cross-cultural mission as much "on home turf" as abroad. This is the case already in significant sectors of inner-city populations, but as globalization and fragmentation increase in power and play out their deadly game, it will become the case for every church in every sector.

Picking Up the Pieces

Living in the Postimperial World

Take a look at the Brooklyn Tabernacle Choir. It is the face of the future.
LEONARD SWEET, *SoulTsunami*

No country can build an unbreachable wall around itself. The image of vast armies of wretched poor, surging around the globe and clamoring at the borders of the more fortunate nations, may finally awaken the world to the kind of future that today's leaders may be foisting on the next generation.
EUGENE LINDEN, "Legions of the Dispossessed"

If these two forces of globalization and fragmentation are set to shape not only the "world order" of international relations but also the domestic order of Western, urban culture, what challenges do they present to the church's response to the transitional generations? What can we expect the impact of globfrag to be?

The Cry of Unheard Voices

The challenge to engage at a deep level with an increasingly multicultural society, both at home and abroad, brings with it the challenge to renounce once and for all the limited and limiting paradigms of a Eurocentric theology. Three examples of this process at work—the first from Europe, the second from North America and the third from Asia—serve to illustrate not only the necessity but also the cost of such a renunciation, along with the fruitfulness it can bring.

Robert Beckford is a black Pentecostal theologian who has extensively researched Christian thought and practice in Britain's postcolonial context. Engagement with such a context requires us, he says, to change the way we "do" theology. "The white academic establishment's monopoly in defining, doing and validating theology in Britain," he says, "renders Black Christianity and its theologies invisible."[1] It is not that theology necessarily bars participation on the basis of skin color but that it makes cultural assumptions that, by default, exclude ethnic diversity. "Black Christian theological thought is difficult to express using traditional Western categories," Beckford writes, ". . . because, in most white-led denominations, professional theologians, primarily white, male and elitist, 'do theology' on behalf of their churches. In the main they use methods, concepts and resources which have emerged from European history, thought and experience."[2] His responses include evaluating the "Dread" culture of young Caribbean immigrants to Britain, exploring black images of Jesus and using the lyrics of Bob Marley as a source for theological reflection[3]—all of which produce new and fresh insights into key aspects of the Christian faith.

H. P. Spees is a Youth for Christ area director who has been heavily involved in programs of urban renewal in Fresno, California. Exploring the North American context, he contends that without reconciliation across the races, neither social renewal nor Christian revival are possible. "To see ethnocentrism in the church," he writes, "one need look no further than the Christian bookstore, Sunday

School material and the offerings of seminars in the United States. Within the Evangelical Christian community, alternatives other than those shaped by the values of the white dominant culture are by far the exception rather than the rule."[4] The postimperial world will demand not only that we embrace the work of such theologians as Robert Beckford but that we extend and encourage the spread of a similar theological process into other ethnic and cultural groups.

A third, and perhaps more widely known, example of postimperialism at work in the church is that of Japanese theologian Kosuke Koyama. A gifted and able scholar, Koyama became a missionary to Thailand, where "he decided that he must subordinate great theological thoughts, like those of Thomas Aquinas and Karl Barth, to the needs of the farmers. He gave priority to the farmers over Aquinas and Barth because he was preaching in Thailand, not in Italy or Switzerland."[5] Koyama's willingness to uproot theology from its cultural setting and reroot it in a local community produced a rich vein of insight and achievement—better theology, in effect, than that which he might have attained had he kept within safe boundaries. An example of the fruitfulness of this expressly non-Western approach was his book *Three Mile an Hour God.* The book emerged from Koyama's recognition that the people he was working with in Thailand had a very different pace to their lives than that of modern, Western (or for that matter, Japanese) culture. When he began to explore this slower, more reflective timestyle, he found in it a resonance with much of the Bible, not least with the lives of the ancient Hebrews. *What was God's pace,* Koyama asked himself, *as he lead the Israelites, on foot, through the desert?* "God walks 'slowly,' " he writes, "because he is love. . . . Love has its speed. It is an inner speed. It is a spiritual speed. It is a different kind of speed from the technological speed to which we are accustomed. . . . It goes on in the depth of our life, whether we notice or not, whether we are currently hit by storm or not, at three miles an hour. It is the speed we walk and therefore it is the speed the love of God walks."[6]

What the theological reflections of both Koyama and Beckford illustrate is just how much Western thinking might gain from the renunciation of its white, male, European exclusivity. But this is not a preoccupation only for theologians; it must be allowed to spill over into the everyday world of church culture. How much of the cultural exclusivity of our faith is invested not in our belief structures but in seemingly innocent, ground-level practice—the music we listen to and use, the language we adopt, the clothes we wear, the images and illustrations with which we choose to explain our faith? These different factors add up to a corporate body language, sending out messages whether we know it or not. As does the visible mix and makeup of our leadership and staff—those we allow to exercise public authority. It is also at this highly practical level, as well as in our theology, that we must change. "Do we . . . suffer from the blindness of mono-cultural leadership?" asks H. P. Spees. "We must hire, partner with, pray with, shape our organization(s) to make room for, support, serve, raise money for existing leaders from disenfranchised cultures, and include them in whatever way possible at the highest levels of our organization(s)."[7]

More and more, the twin forces of globalization and fragmentation are throwing a spotlight onto the cultural bias in our churches and giving a voice to those long silenced. To the extent that postimperialism leads us to listen to the powerless, to give voice to the marginalized, to see through the eyes of the poor, it is a thoroughly biblical process. If the twenty-first century demands of us that we embrace cultural diversity and renounce the power structures that prosperity and good fortune have enabled us to build, then it is doing no less than calling us back to the foundations of our faith.

Advertainment and Alienation

If the forces of globalization and fragmentation produce anything "on the street," it is a crisis of identity. Young people cut off from the fading appeal of their tribal roots, but unable to find their place in the new global village, come to live in an emotional and cultural no man's land best captured in the term *alienation*. The groundbreaking

1985 report "Faith in the City," commissioned by the Church of England, explored economic deprivation in the United Kingdom and dramatically described the lives of such young people.

> The overall impression is clear. It is that there are sizeable groups of young people who are trapped in Urban Priority Areas, who only gain attention when they become a threat, who are denied equality of life chances, and with whom the churches have little or no contact. It is difficult to exaggerate how alienated these people are: from adult ideas of how young people should behave; from their peers of different social classes; from agencies they think of as acting on adults' behalf and not in the interests of young people, e.g. from the police; from school; and from the church.[8]

This deep sense of rootlessness and loss of purpose was captured, with the insight and passion of a prophet, by the French artist Paul Gauguin in 1897. Painting what he thought would be his last painting before he attempted to take his own life—his visual suicide note to the world—Gauguin chose as his title three questions, scratched into the oils of the painting itself: *"D'où venons nous? Qui sommes nous? Où allons nous?"* ("Where do we come from? What are we? Where are we going?"). Since discovering this picture over twenty years ago in the Boston Museum of Fine Arts, I have been haunted by these words, which seemed to hover over the century whose birth Gauguin witnessed. Of all the common threads that weave through the tapestry that is global youth culture in our day, there is none that is more common or stronger than the thread of alienation.

This is the "vacuum in orientation" that theologian Hans Küng cites as one of the major issues facing the twenty-first-century world. "In the United States," Küng writes, ". . . the population has increased by 41% since 1960 but violent crimes have increased by 560%, single mothers by 419%, divorces by 300%, children growing up in one-parent families by 300%, and shootings are the second most frequent cause of death after accidents (in 1990 4,200 teenagers were shot)."[9] At the heart of these tragic figures, Küng insists, lies a simple truth. "People normally feel an unquenchable desire to hold on to something, to rely on something," he writes. "In our technological world which has become so complex, and in the confusion of their private lives, they would like to have somewhere to stand, a line to follow; they would like to have criteria; a goal. In short, people feel an unquenchable desire to have something like a basic ethical orientation."[10]

In American culture, nothing has brought home the reality of youth alienation more powerfully than the recent spate of teen killings, tragically typified in events at Columbine High School. Speaking of the young men caught up in such acts, Professor James Garbarino of Cornell University, author of *The Lost Boys,* has said, "These boys fall victim to an unfortunate synchronicity between the demons inhabiting their own internal world and the corrupting influences of modern American culture: vicarious violence, crude sexuality, shallow materialism, mean-spirited competitiveness and spiritual emptiness."[11] The mother of a nineteen-year-old shot dead in Los Angeles put the fears of many into words when she said, "What's been real for those of us in the inner city is now real in the suburbs. Violence is like a movie: it's coming to a theater near you."[12] The irony of the new "global youth club" is that the one thing young people most share the world over is this sense of lostness. Who could fail to be moved by the desperate cry of Thomas Solomon Jr., who after shooting and injuring six fellow students at his high school surrendered his gun to a vice principal, saying, "Oh my God. I'm so scared."[13]

If alienation is our culture's bitter fruit, then advertisement is the tree on which it grows. The glittering appeal of global culture draws the young away from any sense of tribal or family rootedness but offers nothing of substance in its place. Aimed at stimulating the needs of the marketplace, at locating dissatisfaction and driving it home, advertisement is, by definition, designed to disappoint— MTVessels make the most noise.

Psychologist Oliver James has completed a major study in Britain of the impact of such alienation on measures of mental health. He is in no doubt that there is a link between personal alienation and social fragmentation and that both in turn are linked to the immense power of the consumer machine. "The collapse of marriage and of the close social networks that characterised our ancestors is a major cause of . . . depression, aggression, compulsions," he says.[14] Looking at the lives of those—often men—in whom such alienation is expressed in violent behavior, he adds, "They contrast the consumer goods, the permissive lifestyle and the self-focussed opportunism of the media role models offered on film and television with the reality of their own lives."[15]

If the Christian church is unable to confront this lostness in the new generations—if it fails to confront the power of advertainment and the wild aspirations it brings, and to deal with the core issues of identity, status, attachment and community—then it will lose its foothold in the cultures of the twenty-first century. The challenge is to provide both roots and wings—to bring young people into a sense of connectedness with the past that doesn't rob them of their vision for the future.

Tony Campolo[16] explains this "roots and wings" philosophy in the context in which it is most easily applied—the family. "Roots. The parent must communicate to the child a sense of stability, of security; a sense of belonging," he says, " . . . so that who I am is firmly established and what our family stands for is firmly defined. The family must also provide wings. That is, it must create in children a sense of imagination. . . . To imagine what they could be, . . . what the future might be. . . . To dream dreams—to help a child believe in herself."[17] In some cases this requires the validation of a person's known roots—affirming the strength and dignity of the tribe and history from which they come even when this falls outside of the church's dominant norms. In others, it requires the provision of a new history—a foster tribe able to give identity to those so cut off from their past that no personal history remains. In both cases, and all between, it requires the recognition, in a world cut loose from its moorings, that roots and relationships matter, that the need for love is the one need that our culture most stimulates and least meets.

Catching the cry of those lost in the headlong rush to the global mall, Mike Riddell writes, "The trendy word for being lost is alienation. . . . It is an ache in the deepest part of you, a longing which nothing in the world ever quite touches . . . the sense of being lost comes like a fragment of a song. Finding the way is all about coming home."[18]

New Tribes Born

Oliver James goes on to explore the relationship of cultural alienation to gang culture, in which those under pressure "create alternative sub-cultures in which their attributes—impulsiveness, aggression, nothing to lose—are valuable. . . . In the wider society's terms they may be losers but in their subculture, they can be on top of the world."[19] Walsh and Middleton write that "the escalation of fascist ideology among teens in Europe and the multiplication of inner-city gangs in North America, often with a narrowly conceived ethnic identity, is further evidence of the desperate need to belong to a group and inhabit a meaningful story, even a narrow and violent one, so long as it gives identity and purpose."[20] Gang culture is the urban expression of the same destructive forces that, on a global scale, produce ethnic and genocidal conflicts.

Ironically, gang culture has itself become a favored brand image of the global youth club, with music and fashions forged in the street battles of Chicago and L.A. transformed into cultural products for export to the world. In a watered-down form, gang culture becomes the new tribalism of youth, with millions of young people the world over seeking identity in coded signs of commonality. New tribes spring up with unprecedented speed as subcultures give birth to sub-subcultures, groups within groups gathering around ever more complex and specific distinctions—and often replicated in mirror-image groups thousands of miles and several continents away. The drive among the young to seek identity and status in the external signs of tribalism is probably one of the strongest and deepest currents in our present situation. The evident truth that "culture has meaning precisely because it differs from other cultures"[21] pushes young people not only to choose an identity but to express it in divisive or hostile terms. Even if the powerful forces of globalization and fragmentation were to stabilize tomorrow, millions of young people would still be dealing, for years to come, with the effects of gang culture.

Ancient Tribes Born Again

August 9, 1998, was officially designated "Indigenous Peoples Day," and the United Nations has declared a "Decade of Indigenous Peoples." While urban gangs carve out new tribes for themselves, there are old tribes—some as old as human civilization itself—restating their claim to self-rule. "The cause of the planet's myriad indigenous populations is gaining ground," writes journalist Rupert Cornwell. "In the last 20 years, the total number of tribal peoples has risen, Survival International (the largest campaigning group for indigenous peoples) estimates, from 200m to 300m."[22] At the heart of the struggle of indigenous peoples are the questions of land and culture. In cases such as those of Australian and North American native peoples, the conflict is over land taken from them in the past. In cases such as those of the Amazon rain forests or of Irian Jaya, the Indonesian half of New Guinea, it is land being taken even now. Usually at the center of such a conflict there is a question of profit, most often from mining and forestry rights, but there are other, less measurable factors: the submerging of a culture; the refusal to acknowledge traditional views of nature, land and ownership; the loss of a way of life. "And so it goes the world over," Rupert Cornwell says,

> You can see it in the clusters of dispossessed, drink-ravaged aborigines at encampments in the dried out watercourse of the Todd River at Alice Springs. You see it in the mosquito-ridden swamps of northwest Siberia where the local Khanty and Mansi hunters and herders

lament a way of life submerged beneath the foul lakes of crude oil spewed forth by the Soviet-era rigs. The Khanty do not want the full proceeds of what is among the richest oilfields on earth, . . . merely their land as they once knew it.[23]

There can be no doubt that the crisis of identity of the world's indigenous peoples—and the echoes of guilt among those who have wronged them—will continue well into the twenty-first century. The rediscovery of the rights of such peoples, the questioning of the imperial and industrial assumptions that sought to blot them out, the reevaluation of the contributions of native peoples to human art and civilization—these will be significant strands in the twenty-first-century worldview, and a shaping influence on its young generations.

Lazarus and Dives: A Game of Two Halves

Not only does advertainment accentuate and fuel divisions within cultures; it is increasingly seeping across international borders to accent the growing gap between rich and poor, empowered and powerless, propertied and dispossessed. *Time* magazine, in October 1995, published new figures that estimated the per capita wealth of the world's nations, taking account not only of hard cash but also of human resources, produced assets and natural capital. On this basis, the top five nations of the world each held over $500,000 (U.S. dollars) per person, led by Australia at $835,000, while the bottom eleven all held less than $3,000 per person, with Ethiopia the lowest at $1,400. If these figures are accurate, the average Australian is six hundred times richer than the average Ethiopian—a rich-poor divide on the scale of the Grand Canyon. "The world has 358 billionaires." reported the *Financial Times* in 1996, "and their combined assets exceed the total annual income of nearly half the global population. . . . If it continues, the rich-poor divide—at individual and country level—will produce a world 'gargantuan' in its excesses and grotesque in its economic inequalities."[24] In America, a recent study by the Center on Budget and Policy Priorities revealed similar trends on the domestic scene. "The 2.7 million people who comprise the richest 1% of American households," the report states, "this year will receive in total as much after-tax income as the 100 million people with the lowest incomes combined. . . . Wealth is now more concentrated among the top 1% and top 20% of American households than at any time since the Depression."[25]

This growing gap between the haves and the have-nots is about more than paper wealth; for the world's children it is a matter of life and death. According to a 1993 World Bank report on global healthcare, "In the Irish Republic only 10 children per 1,000 live births die before the age of five. . . . In South America the average equivalent figure is 54, in East Asia 57, in South Asia 131 and in sub Saharan Africa 183. In some African countries almost one third of all children die before they are five."[26] The difference is not always about physical distance—one of the features of globalization and fragmentation is that the geographical gap between rich and poor is often less pronounced than the economic gap seems to imply. "A child born in 1991 in Romania, or even in Turkey, on the borders of the European Union is five times more likely to die in the first year of life than a child born in Switzerland," says the same World Bank report.[27]

As the consumer markets of the developed world expand and accelerate, the gap between the haves and the have-nots is growing, with little real prospect of significant change. As Matthew Connelly and Paul Kennedy have written, "We are heading into the twenty-first century in a world consisting for the most part of a relatively small number of rich, satiated, demographically stagnant societies and a large number of poverty-stricken, resource-depleted nations whose populations are doubling every twenty-five years or less. The demographic imbalances are exacerbated by grotesque disparities of wealth between rich and poor countries."[28]

It is a bitter irony of this two-speed race that the consumer lifestyle, with its rapid-fire images of success, prosperity and the satisfied life, is more widely broadcast than ever. Not only are millions denied a place at the feast, but they are reminded, day in and day out, of just what they are missing. In the 1997 crisis in Albania, as thousands crowded onto small boats to cross the narrow ocean gap to Italy, observers commented that for months many had been watching the commercial excess of Italian television. When there was no bread in the shops of Albania, its people were watching ads in which cat food was served on silver trays.[29]

Whether through such close media links or through the explosive growth of the world's megacities, the poor are increasingly shown, close-up, the lifestyles of the rich. In world-class cities, the haves and the have-nots share the same streets, living in daily proximity but rarely having any meaningful contact. Like Lazarus and Dives, they are close neighbors with entirely different lives.

For the church, the challenge is to choose which neighbor—Lazarus or Dives—we most identify with. When Mahatma Gandhi traveled to Buckingham Palace to meet King George V, he did so wearing only his habitual loincloth. Asked afterward if he had thus felt at a disadvantage, he replied cheerfully, "Oh no, His Majesty was wearing enough for both of us."[30] We would do well to consider which of these two leaders our own church most resembles—the king decked out in enough finery for two or the diminutive figure wearing only a simple cloth.

The Age of the Unclear Family

Running in parallel with the forces of cultural fragmentation, Western culture is living through a significant decline in the status of the family. If the twentieth century was, perhaps unwisely, the era of the *nuclear* family, the twenty-first will be the age of the *unclear* family. More and more young people are living through adolescence without the support of a secure family environment. Writing from the perspective of church-based youth ministry, Mark DeVries has pointed out that "even in the most conservative churches, youth leaders deal with teens whose parents are alcoholics, sexaholicis, workaholics and drug addicts. Bankruptcy, embezzlement, court battles and custody disputes are terms that are becoming more and more familiar to those called to Christian ministry with teenagers."[31]

This is not merely a question of "broken homes"—though these are an increasing element in the lives of young people, and it is predicted that there will be more children in stepfamilies than in nuclear families by 2010—but also of an apparent loss of confidence among parents themselves. According to John Balding, director of the Schools Health Education Unit, based at Exeter University in the U.K., parents often appear "frightened of their children. They don't know how to give them adequate direction. In order to escape from this, they try to make their children grow up too quickly, and put the responsibility for their actions into the child's hands."[32]

Many commentators note the destructive role of advertainment in this process. Lynne Monck, a high school principal in Britain, commented that media images "raise expectations about how they should be looking, about the interests that they should be having and what they should be doing. Students are under pressure to match up to the images."[33] "TV inflates our sense of what's normal," says Juliet Schor in *The Overspent American.*[34] In one study, Schor's team discovered that every hour of television watched per week raised consumption by an additional $208 per year.[35]

For some, the resultant tension spills over into violence and drug and alcohol abuse. "Things such as joy-riding and ram-raiding [using a stolen vehicle to ram and subsequently loot a store] . . . are just the tip of the iceberg of youth alienation and insecurity," writes Professor Richard Whitfield. "Children are expected to achieve more—yet many are not getting the parental support they need."[36]

It is clear that many of the young people caught up in the whirlwind of globalization and fragmentation in the coming decades will not have a strong, supporting family to turn to. In their struggle for identity—their cry of "Who am I?" so often couched in violent and antisocial terms—they will be thrown alone and unsupported on the mercy of a wider society. All too often it will be a society with neither the will nor the means to answer.

The Reinvention of World Mission

One final area in which the forces of globalization and fragmentation will exert significant influence is that of Christian mission. Not only does postimperialism challenge the link between Christian mission and cultural paternalism, but cross-cultural mission as it has been practiced is failing, for a range of reasons, to engage the commitment of the emerging generations. Some of the ways in which the transitional generations are challenging traditional views of mission are the following:

1. The new generations have a different view of "lostness." Western imperialism saw white European culture as essentially redeemed and redeeming, and non-Western cultures as lost and in need of saving. Postimperial young people are switching this polarity. They have a deep awareness of the lostness of their own culture and an increasing appreciation of the redeeming qualities in non-Western cultures, particular those of premodern and indigenous religions. Coupled with this, many young people are questioning traditional Christian theologies of judgment and "lostness." They are not entirely convinced that every person "outside of the church" is condemned to damnation, and they are increasingly immune to mission motivated by this concern.

In the Peregrine model of mission developed in Europe through Café.net, we have emphasized the mutuality of the mission enterprise.[37] Drawing inspiration from the Celtic church, which sought to "wander with God" in journeys that combined elements both of mission and of pilgrimage,[38] we have encouraged those engaging in cross-cultural mission to "take something with you: bring something back."

2. The new generations are more drawn to physical service than to evangelism. Just as symbol and community are languages more readily understood by young people than print and text, so action is a more fluent tongue to them than belief. Where Billy Graham might have been the Christian icon of their parents, they are more likely to honor Mother Teresa or Princess Diana as she embraced the HIV-positive child and talked with land-mine victims. Touch is a strong dynamic among the new generations: there is no mission without real, substantial human contact.

3. The new generations will respond differently to the structures and institutions of mission. In a paper given at the Missions Interlink Forum in Australia in July 1998, Kath Donavan and Ruth Myors note some of the key factors missions agencies need to take into account in working with Generation X and beyond. They note that Gen Xers are not particularly comfortable in traditionally structured mission organizations because of the following:

a. Gen Xers are misunderstood—assumed to lack commitment but in fact capable of very deep friendships and commitments.

b. They need emotional and spiritual support, carrying a strong awareness of their own vulnerabilities.

c. Their view of leadership is egalitarian—they want to be committed not *to* an organization but *with* it.

d. They are experiential, with a longing for deeper spirituality often unmet in traditional models.

e. They look for participatory leadership and are empowered by being given scope to run with their vision.[39]

In the comprehensive reevaluation of church that the coming decades will bring, it seems unlikely that the traditional view of mission will remain unchallenged. Rather, the postimperial context of globalization and fragmentation and the emerging consciousness of Generation X and beyond will combine to redefine and reorder the church's understanding of its global task. In the transition from Generation X to the Millennials, many of these changes will be accentuated by a shift in historical context. Where Gen X have lived with the pessimism of being a premillennial generation (a generation born too late to alter history's record of the century in which it has lived), the Millennials will be postmillennial (a generation presented with a new and unformed century on which to make its mark).

word.link: Fridge Words
If you spend yourselves on behalf of the hungry and satisfy the needs of the

oppressed, then your light will rise in the darkness, and your night will become like the noonday. The LORD will guide you always; he will satisfy your needs in a sun-scorched land and will strengthen your frame. You will be like a well-watered garden, like a spring whose waters never fail.—Isaiah 58:10-11

A prophet was visiting the home of a wealthy and successful advertising executive. In the kitchen he found on the door of the refrigerator a collection of magnetized words, arranged into random sentences. With these words the ad man had expressed the essential philosophy of his life. "Satisfy your needs at all costs," he had written. "Spend all you have on yourself."

Alone in the kitchen for a few moments, the prophet went to work. Much later, when he had gone, the merchant found a very different message displayed at the heart of his kitchen—the words of Isaiah 58:10.

This encounter never happened, but it might as well have. It is as if Isaiah has read the slogans of Western culture's advertising boom, and from the same words built a radically different message. He takes the core words of the consumer creed—*needs, self* and *satisfaction*—and turns them around. We are challenged not to spend until we have satisfied ourselves but to *spend ourselves* until the needs of the poor are satisfied.

This remarkable passage, and the chapter in which it comes, have become in recent years a rallying cry to Christians seeking an authentic gospel for tomorrow. This is a gospel that rejects the marrying of faith to an individualized, feed-me, consumerist culture, calling instead for service and sacrifice. It is a perception of biblical faith that brings the poor and the oppressed from the margins of our field of vision to the very center.

1 2

Gods R Us
Post-Christian Spirituality

Just look around! In urbane, urban centers like New York City, more
spiritually sensitive seekers go to the Metropolitan Museum of Art on
Sundays than to cathedrals.
THOMAS HOHSTADT, *Dying to Live*

Is there any truth in the cliché that today's youth is fearfully searching
for signs and portents, miracles, gurus and the big idea? Even the most
ungodly clubbers now chill out to the sound of Gregorian chants and
wear magic rune symbols on their chests.
HELEN CHAPPELL, "It's Hip to Be Holy"

With a long history of radical humanism and a public
school system built exclusively and deliberately on the values of
laïcité (secularism), France might well be described as one of the
world's least believing nations. It's all the more surprising, then, that
belief in God and in the nonmaterial realm remains a strong and per-
sistent feature in the lives of French young people. In a nation in

which weekly church attendance since 1945 has plunged in some areas from a level close to 80 percent of the population to less than 14 percent, young people cling all the same to a sense of God and an interest in spirituality.

Phosphore[1] is a French magazine specializing in issues relevant to junior high and high school students. In 1994 *Phosphore* interviewed a representative national sample of fifteen- to twenty-year-olds to find out just how deep such beliefs run. Their findings confirm that, while the church may be outmoded, God is popular. As many as 55 percent thought the existence of God certain or likely, compared to just 38 percent unlikely or impossible. Meanwhile, 40 percent attributed the creation of the world to "a greater power." Asked what they expected to experience after death, only 16 percent believed that there was nothing. Among the rest, there was belief in eternal life, reincarnation and bodily resurrection, but a full 50 percent expressed the view that "there is something but we don't know what."[2]

The *Phosphore* survey gave a clear signal that while belief persists, it is less and less connected to traditional, established or orthodox creeds. Of the 55 percent who rated the existence of God as certain or likely, 31 percent qualified this God as "present within each one of us," while only 19 percent could believe in God as "a being who has spoken to mankind in history."

Commenting on these outcomes, sociologist Françoise Champion linked the preference for an "inner God" to deep cultural changes amounting to a new spirit of the age. "What we look for today is personal experience," she says. "What counts is to feel something. This new way of dealing with faith is not restricted to the young."[3] Nor is it restricted to France. These findings resonate with parallel evidence right across Western culture. There is a blossoming of spirituality among the young people of Generation X and beyond, but for many this goes hand in hand with a rejection of the creeds of the established church. It is in this sense that the newly formed cultures of the twenty-first century are post-Christian.

definition.link: *Post-Christian*

The world of Generation X and beyond will be post-Christian in the following senses:

1. The primary influence on popular spirituality is no longer orthodox Christianity.

2. In its place, new generic spiritualities are emerging that prioritize personal experience, pluralism and self-made creeds.

3. The influence of these perspectives is pervasive, touching many who would not call themselves religious and sparking a revival in spirituality.

4. The new emphasis on spirituality will shape the way individuals choose and express a faith but will also impact the ways in which popular culture perceives and judges the Christian church.

Before we look at some of the implications of the post-Christian spirituality of youth, it is important that we understand more fully where this influence has come from. We will do this by examining three separate strands in our recent cultural history—each representing an area of search and exploration, and each, in its way, giving rise to new spiritual life.

New Gods

Post-Christian spirituality is above all else a symptom of the wide and long-established decline of the church's influence in the West. For centuries the term *Christendom* described the "forms of Christian civilization which have given Western peoples their spiritual values, their moral standards, and their conception of a divine law from which all human laws ultimately derive their validity and their sanction."[4] But such a close connection of faith and culture is a thing of the past. David Bjork is an American missionary resident long-term in France. He has recently completed a Ph.D. program exploring mission to post-Christian Europe, which he describes as standing in the wake of "two hundred years of progressive secularization

during which the distinctively Christian institutions and social standards have been gradually eliminated. Many contemporary missiologists and sociologists have used the term post-Christian to identify
this trend in contemporary Western European culture."[5] This decline
flies in the face of the global picture, in which the Christian faith is
still in the ascendant. "While continuing to flourish in the fertile cultural fields to which the faith was exported," says Mike Riddell,
"Christianity has steadily diminished in those lands which were the
'sending nations.' . . . The one massive gap in the church's expertise
is how to do mission in the post-Christian West."[6]

In one sense, none of this is news. The decline of Christendom
was observed and commented on for much of the twentieth century.
What is newer, and to many a surprise, is the blossoming, in this
context, of popular spirituality. Where the harsh, dry conditions and
hard ground of secularization might have been expected to produce
little in terms of spiritual growth, they have seen a remarkable flower-
ing of personal faith.

Jacob Needleman and David Applebaum, professors of philosophy at San Francisco State University and State University College,
New Paltz respectively, are in no doubt as to the origin of this spiritual awakening. "In almost every area of our culture," they write,

> the realisation is dawning that material progress and scientific
> achievement cannot of themselves lead us towards an understanding
> of the meaning of our lives. . . . Our modern contemporary civilisa-
> tion is characterised by its fascination with the technological applica-
> tion of scientific discovery and its neglect of those aspects of our
> nature that require other kinds of perceptions, other kinds of "food."
> These parts of our mind, these aspects of ourselves, are starving, and
> if they die, we will die with them. This is not speculation: it is an
> obvious truth that we are all beginning to sense.[7]

Writing from a Christian perspective, John Drane makes the same
observation, "Rapidly increasing numbers are finding it possible to
believe in reincarnation, spirit guides and extra-terrestrials and all

sorts of other esoteric ideas," he says. "It certainly means that these people are spiritually open as no other generation in living memory has been."[8] In the ruins of modernity, with the dream of a scientific utopia in tatters, spiritual shoots are growing with unexpected strength.

New Science

A second source of inspiration for the post-Christian spiritual rebirth comes, ironically, from science itself. Even as millions of young people have questioned the scientific account of life and meaning, scientists have been exploring the boundaries of belief and truth. Research in quantum physics and related fields has undermined confidence in the materialist-empirical worldview, and scientists working at the very limits of human knowledge have found themselves standing on common ground with those holding a more spiritual, pre-Enlightenment view. "It has taken scientists until the second half of the 20th century to prove what we have known all along," writes one Native American commentator, "we are all related. Not just human beings, but four-legged and winged brothers and sisters, as well as those who crawl."[9]

While general science has opened the door, if tentatively, to the possibility of faith, there are specific scientists moving much faster to embrace a spiritual worldview. Biologist Rupert Sheldrake, who has held senior posts at both Harvard and Cambridge universities, is just one of the many scientists who is forging a path away from the mechanistic worldview toward more traditional, spiritual concepts. "A lot of harm was done in the West by splitting apart science and religion in the seventeenth century," he says.

> Science became very limited in its focus to mechanical, material things, and religion became very introverted; it became very concerned just with the human spirit and with morality. . . . In most traditional cultures, these are not separated in that way. . . . I think that as science emerges from this narrow, mechanistic phase that it has been

in and we move to a broader vision, a new kind of connection between the realms of science and spirituality becomes possible.[10]

Sheldrake's personal journey takes in a fascination with Eastern mysticism, and his work lays foundations for the "New Science"— an approach that, far from rejecting spiritual experience, provides it with a context and rationale. His theories of *morphic resonance* represent an exploration of the connectedness of all nature and an objective apologetic for monism, the belief that "all is one."

Through the work of scientists such as Sheldrake, and notably the physicist Fritjof Capra, the deadlock between science and faith is being broken. Spiritual searchers are being encouraged to believe that science may not have written the gods out of history after all.[11]

New Age

Many of those embracing new expressions of spirituality have done so under the umbrella of the New Age movement. Born in the late 1960s as the "Age of Aquarius," the New Age movement peaked in the mid 1980s as thousands of young and not-so-young Westerners signed up for courses in spirituality and self-actualization. The spark that ignited this movement, at first in America and later throughout Western culture, was the belief that the planet was moving from the age of Pisces (marked by the dualities of good versus evil, male versus female, spirit versus body, humanity versus nature, and so on) to the age of Aquarius (marked by harmony in these and all other matters). A long-held view among astrologers, the division of human history into astrological ages of approximately two thousand years, was promoted by psychologist Carl Jung and became a popular view in the 1960s. The Age of Pisces, in this view, began in the year A.D. 1 and would give way to Aquarius sometime in 1997.

The Aquarian Age used the language of astrology—and the fast-approaching end of the millennium—to give voice to a "cosmic evolutionary optimism"[12] that had begun to surface in the 1960s, not least in the writings of Pierre Teilhard de Chardin. A priest, scientist and philosopher, Teilhard de Chardin plowed what was then a lone furrow in bringing these disparate fields together. The closing words of his *The Future of Man* now read like a classic New Age text, but in the 1960s they were a radical new faith looking for a name and a home: "And then will be the end. Like a vast tide the Being will have dominated the trembling of all beings. The extraordinary adventure of the world will have ended in the bosom of a tranquil ocean, of which however each drop will still be conscious of being itself."[13]

By giving this optimism a name and a focus, the Age of Aquarius created a platform of credibility for all things alternative, and at breakneck speed a movement grew up in which the only thing you couldn't do was stay the same. The watershed publication in this explosion of new thinking was Marilyn Ferguson's *The Aquarian Conspiracy* in 1980. Ferguson used the term *conspiracy* in a loose and positive sense to describe her feeling that there was an unspoken connectedness among a whole range of new groups, communities, therapies and theories emerging in America. It was essentially after her book was published that the term "New Age movement" became current.

Across the Atlantic, author Jean-Luc Porquet observed the early growth of this same movement in the French context. "Suddenly, we saw dynamic young executives walking on hot coals," he writes, "and gurus affirming that they were the reincarnated inhabitants of the lost island of Atlantis."[14] Porquet is quick to point out that in France, as elsewhere, this first New Age movement has now given way to a second, looser, more diverse period. "All this quickly went out of fashion," he continues, "but a second, more discreet New Age arose in its place. . . . With neither a leader nor single organisation, this New Age is a kind of network of networks in which you find journals, conferences, publications, specialist bookshops, music and, most of all—in this ideal promotional environment—a vast array of training courses."[15] This second-wave New Age movement has grown away from a specific belief in a new astrological age to embrace a more general commitment to spirituality, personal fulfillment and self-actualization.

In this sense, the New Age movement has become part of the wider shift in our culture toward a post-Christian spirituality. New Age thinking has contributed to this shift—and many people remain committed to core New Age ideas—but it is a mistake to see post-Christian spirituality as purely a product of the New Age movement. While the movement itself will continue to influence thousands, the wider cultural shift toward exploratory and experiential spirituality will impact millions and will be a key factor in shaping Western culture in the coming decades. Post-Christian spirituality will be a factor in the lives of young people long after the term "New Age" has dropped out of our speech and thousands have deserted the movement in bitter disappointment at an age of harmony that never arrived.

Unconnectable Jesus

These three factors, then—the West's search for new gods, new science and a new age—have been primary influences on the wave of post-Christian spirituality we are now seeing. At the heart of this spiritual renaissance there is a cruel irony for the Christian church. On the one hand, it heralds the return to spiritual pursuits that the church, in the face of growing secularization, materialism and humanism, has longed for. At its heart is the recognition that there is reality beyond the material, that empiricism is not the final answer, that the soul is as real as the body. It represents, in essence, a recovery of the supernatural. But on the other hand, this newfound desire for faith among the young sees the Christian church as an integral part of the very modernity it rejects. "Before Christians get too excited about the renewed interest in religion," writes Mike Riddell, "it is well to note that the emerging culture's exploration of spirituality is in many ways a reaction against institutional Christianity as it has been experienced in the West."[16] John Drane sounds much the same warning. "Christianity is very firmly perceived as part of the old order," he writes, "and therefore something to be discarded rather than trusted for the future."[17]

This is not to say that there is no scope for Christian growth in such a context. A spirituality that is post-Christian is not by definition anti-Christian—it is "post" in the sense of "going beyond." Post-Christian young people are not dismissing any possibility of encounter with the Christian God, but they are rejecting the forms and formulas in which they have seen faith in that God expressed. This ambivalence is captured by Douglas Coupland in his reaction to the output of American Christian radio stations. "I did not deny the existence of Jesus was real to these people," he says, "it was merely that I was cut off from their experience in a way that was never connectable."[18]

Whatever the future holds for Christian mission in Western culture, it will require of us that we overcome, for millions of young people, this perception of an "unconnectable Jesus." This will mean making connections with the very spirituality that has, in its post-Christian pilgrimage, rejected what it knows of Christ. A starting point for this process lies in a fuller exploration of the nature and key themes of popular spirituality among young people. The five themes outlined below by no means exhaust the exploration of post-Christian spirituality, but they each provide a starting point for a fuller understanding of it.

Theme 1: I Can't Believe It's Not Buddha—The Exploration of Non-Western Faiths

There are clear parallels between the dynamics of the emerging spirituality and the central ideas of Eastern faiths—Buddhism, Hinduism and their many, many mystical spinoffs. Westerners disillusioned with their own society—and unconvinced of Christianity's capacity to heal it—have taken their search for enlightenment eastward. Film director Martin Scorsese, responsible for the 1998 film biography of the Dalai Lama *Kundun,* explains this attraction. "I can't talk about the nature of man because I'm not a philosopher," he says. "I just know that what I was taught in church and what I was taught on the street are two different things. Somehow one has to win out. That's the same thing the Tibetans are talking about: compassion, love, kindness and tolerance. Ultimately, this film is about non-violence, and I've seen too much that was the other way."[19] Scorsese is not alone in failing to see "compassion, love, kindness and tolerance" in the dealings of the Christian church. Throughout the West, young people are finding in the Eastern tradition a purity and detachment that they believe Christianity to have lost. The faith of the West, by contrast, they view as complicit in the very violence from which they seek release.

Among the heroes and role models finding favor in a new generation are monks like Shi Yanzzi, a master of Shaolin Kung Fu[20] recently dispatched from deepest China to set up a Shaolin temple in London. Shi Yanzzi and his colleagues have been featured in glossy fashion magazines such as *The Face* and *Esquire*, as well as drawing huge crowds to martial arts displays demonstrating both physical and spiritual excellence. Journalist Grace Bradberry, writing for *The Times* in London, describes the lifestyle that appears so attractive to a young, Western audience: "In a typical day he spends two hours meditating and three hours studying the Buddhist scripture, as well as devoting six hours to kung fu training." Of the resultant martial arts displays, she writes, "The aura of spiritual calm is what makes the performance so remarkable."[21]

When the Dalai Lama visited New York in August 1999, his popularity was such that FBI and NYPD agents upgraded his security coding to category one—reserved for the most significant of dignitaries. When he stood to give a long session of religious teaching in Central Park, it was to a crowd of ninety thousand. "Despite the crowds and the heat," reported journalist Isabel Hilton, "you could have heard a pin drop. In New York the Dalai Lama is a hot ticket."[22] Just what is it, Hilton went on to ask, that makes the Dalai Lama such a hit? "This amalgam of political refugee, religious teacher and moral exemplar—the whole wrapped in the garb of a Central Asian

monk—has never, it seems, been more appealing to Westerners
trapped in a culture that regards their primary role as that of consumer."[23]

Somehow disillusionment with the West has become disillusionment with the faith from which it grew, and only the non-Western
offers hope. As John Drane points out, "One of the key things that I
hear people saying is that they think the church is irrelevant—they
actually say it is unspiritual, that if you want spirituality, the last
place to go to is the church. . . . Many people seem to believe that the
Church is not a place where you find spirituality anyway. It's a place
where you'll find hair-splitting theology."[24]

Theme 2: Wanting to Be Indian—The Embracing of
Pre-Western Faiths

Alongside contemporary non-Western expressions of faith, the richest source of inspiration for the emerging post-Christian spirituality
has been the pre-Western faith of indigenous peoples. The motivation is the same—a genuine disillusionment with the Western
"project"—but the prescription is different. Instead of looking
beyond their own borders to faiths expressed in other regions of the
world, Western young people are looking to their own roots and asking what expressions of faith existed in their own lands before the
arrival of Christianity, science and the modern worldview. "Many
people are searching for a deeper spiritual engagement with the
world and feel a hunger unmet by the teachings and services of traditional religious institutions," writes Myke Johnson. "Some have
begun to take an interest in Native American spiritual practices, and
one can easily find workshops and lectures offering Indian rituals
and ceremonies to non-Indian people."[25] A similar assessment could
be made in other parts of the world—whether the "first peoples"
tribes of North, Central and South America, the aboriginal peoples
of Australia and New Zealand, or the pagan Celts of Europe, the religions of first peoples are experiencing a remarkable worldwide
revival.

Lecturer John Barry Ryan suggests some of the elements of native spirituality that appeal to the postmodern mind. "These rituals are communal, earthy and experiential, with group involvement in rites that appeal to the senses," he writes. "This contrasts strongly with an individualistic approach to overly intellectualized worship forms that leaves the participant alienated."[26]

Canadian artist Dale Stonechild describes the very personal way in which he is rediscovering the power and value of his own native background. "When I was a boy," he says,

> whenever I asked "Why?", my grandmother and the old people would answer by telling stories. These stories related the marvellous exploits of many wondrous creatures and beings. All the stories had a moral lesson. They taught me how to behave, and they taught me about nature and life on Mother Earth. . . . After my old people died, I forgot these stories. Now, I am returning to them . . . re-connecting with the teachings of these stories.[27]

Native religions did not rely on propositional truth, theology or preaching but rather on community, ritual and story—strong themes in the postmodern worldview. Neither could they be approached from an individualized position. "Indian religions are not something one can convert to, as one might to Christianity, by adopting a set of beliefs or principles," writes Myke Johnson. "Indian religions are built upon systems of relationships."[28]

Looking to the past is one very clear way in which Western people disillusioned with the present and nervous of the future are seeking inspiration. Young people at odds with modernity and unsure of just what postmodernity will bring look to premodernity for clues. There are many questions to be asked about just what they find in their search, about just how transferable and adaptable these religions are, about whether it is even possible for Western, predominantly white young people to indwell these ancient stories in any meaningful way. But even acknowledging such questions, we would be fools to ignore the deeply felt needs that this resurgence of native faiths reveals. Whatever the future holds, there is something in these stories and rituals, in this simpler more reverential worldview, that is deeply appealing to the young of the twenty-first-century West. A church that ignores their voice is a church trapped in the twentieth century and destined for the dustbin of history.

Theme 3: The Eco-Puritans of Wandsworth—The Recovering of Reverence for the Earth

A third significant theme in the post-Christian spirituality of our age, and one that overlaps considerably with the appeal of native religions, is that of sacred ecology. So great is the swing toward environmental awareness among the young that it has ceased to be simply a matter of lifestyle and sustainability but has spilled over into spirituality and become an issue of faith.

Journalist Paul Vallely has written movingly of a visit in 1995 to the site of an antidevelopment protest at Gargoyle Wharf in London. Protesters had illegally occupied the site to bring building works to a halt. Vallely found a temporary community bound together not only by an immediate sense of purpose—to stop a planned shops, apartments and gas station development—but by a long-term, underlying commitment to the integrity of the environment. "In a post-Christian age, where ecology has become the nearest thing we have to a shared religion," he wrote, "the Eco-Puritans of Wandsworth are not so far removed from the Christian Puritans of the 17th. century as might be imagined."[29]

If there is any one theme that runs through most contemporary expressions of post-Christian spirituality, whether inspired by Buddhism, Celtic paganism or New Age eclecticism, it is this theme of the sacredness of nature. Reverence for the earth—respect for non-human creatures, for the natural world, for the elements of fire, water, earth and air—is a strand so woven into these new faith expressions that it would be all but impossible to imagine them without it. The Western way is rejected because of its destruction of the earth. Christianity is rejected because of its traditional interpretation of the Genesis mandate—"to rule and subdue"—as a license to dominate, exploit and destroy. To the new Eco-Puritans, the church, for the most part, is the enemy.

One powerful expression of this theme, particularly strong among those whose roots, if not their current practice, are in orthodox Christianity, is the creation-centered spirituality associated with former Dominican priest Matthew Fox. From being a radical voice on the fringes of Catholic theology, Fox, now expelled from the Dominican order, has moved in recent years to being probably *the* voice at the heart of the new eco-orthodoxy. He rejects the notion of the fallenness of the natural world and speaks instead of "original blessing"—the essential goodness of the creation. His Jesus is the "Cosmic Christ," identified with and at times inseparable from Mother Earth. "Though Fox affirms belief in the historical Jesus," writes Mitchell Pacwa, "he considers the Cosmic Christ to be a 'third nature' in addition to the divine and human nature. By saying it is the 'I am' in every creature, the Cosmic Christ is identified with creation. The earth is called the Cosmic Christ."[30] Ritual is of great importance, and centers on the Cosmic Mass, when the Christian Eucharist is reimagined in terms of the salvation of Mother Earth. Communion itself, in this context, becomes "the eating and drinking of the wounded earth."[31] Fox has recently dialogued with Rupert Sheldrake to produce a book, *Natural Grace: Dialogues on Science and Spirituality.* "Essentially he is trying to recover a sense of spirituality in nature," Sheldrake explains; "that it's not just something inside, or to do with morality and sin. It's to do with the whole of nature. The divine presence in the sky, in the earth, in our experience of nature all around us."[32]

Fox and Sheldrake cohabit the overlap between Christianity and a post-Christian approach, but they are not alone in their embracing of creation-centered spirituality. There are those who have retained stronger links with Christian orthodoxy but are nonetheless working to recover a more reverential view of the created order, while others whose roots are entirely outside the Christian faith community share the same goal. For some, sacred ecology is the very heart and soul of their faith; for others, it is a low-profile element, pervading belief but never quite breaking the surface. In either case, and for millions of young people the world over, a faith that does not deal in respectful terms with the nonhuman creation and look in some measure to the healing of the earth will have no place in the twenty-first-century worldview.

Theme 4: I Have to *Feel* It—The Primacy of Personal Experience
A fourth theme that emerges as a common thread in post-Christian spirituality, despite the variance and diversity of its expressions, is that of the *personalization* of religious experience. Just as Teilhard de Chardin anticipated much that was to come in terms of New Age optimism, so the psychologist Carl Jung, who died in 1961, foresaw the radical shifting of faith from the public, corporate, institutional and communal domains to the realm of personal experience. Jung's thought was widely popularized in the 1960s and became foundational to the notion that spirituality was primarily about *personal experience,* measured not in terms of adherence to given rules of belief or behavior but subjectively, in terms of the depth of the experience itself. "The seat of faith," he wrote in 1957, "is not consciousness but spontaneous religious experience. . . . It will always remain doubtful whether what metaphysics and theology call God and the gods is the real ground of these experiences. The question is idle, actually, and answers itself by reason of the subjectively overwhelming numinosity of the experience."[33]

For Jung—and for the generations who have followed him, many knowing neither his name nor his ideas—spiritual experience is not the *means* by which faith achieves its end; it is *an end in itself.* The God we reach out for does not exist objectively, separate from us and outside of our experience, but is contained, somehow, in the great ocean of the unconscious mind. Thus post-Christian spirituality is predominantly inward-looking. Where there is a focus on healing and harmony, on justice and compassion, this is the outworking of the inner experience. The healing of the cosmos begins with the healing of the person.

Theme 5: I Have to *Use* It—The Necessity of a Practicable Spirituality

One final area in which post-Christian spirituality marks a departure from contemporary Christian experience is in its practicability. Whether in the rituals of native faith, in the techniques of Eastern mysticism or in the diverse experiences of the New Age, there is in popular spirituality an increasing focus on *doing*. Techniques of meditation, prayer beads and wheels, repeated individual and corporate rituals, breathing exercises, Tai Chi, inversion therapy, chanting, silent sitting—these and thousands of other techniques invite spiritual devotees not to *believe* something but to *do* something. Many post-Christian spiritualities do not revolve around regular attendance at some public assembly or act of worship, but around a regular—often daily—cycle of personal spiritual exercises. More often than not, this will be a cycle or pattern that can be woven unobtrusively into the busy patterns of contemporary urban life—bite-sized chunks of spiritual experience to offer brief pools of stillness in the frenetic rush, moments of sanity in a world gone mad, oases of refreshment for the urban desert. The practitioner of such exercises becomes responsible for her own spirituality, sensitive to the inner rhythms of her own experience, the arbiter of her own spiritual journey.

"One of the major reasons for the rapid growth of the New Age in recent years," writes John Drane, "is the need felt by many people for some kind of hands-on symbols, rituals and experiences that will hold out the promise of putting them in tune with the mystery that is God."[34] Christianity, by contrast, even though it has examples of many of these techniques in its own long and diverse history, tended in the twentieth century to focus on belief, to be a religion of propositional truth. This has been especially true of the Protestant denominations, but it is often also true of Catholics, who experience the rituals and routines of their church not as dynamic personal exercises but as the mumbled, all-too-familiar patterns of spiritual wallpaper. Spiritual seekers visiting a Christian church may be offered the opportunity to observe and to listen, and may be invited at some stage to give assent, but they are unlikely to be given new techniques to "try out." Nor will there be a take-away bag of faith and practice to sustain them through the ensuing days. There may be sound theological reasons for this; the church may wish to hold on to the notion that belief, in some form, must precede experience. But while it is doing so, the spiritual searcher will simply go elsewhere—and who knows how many might *come into* belief, given a practicable and personal entry point?

creative.link
Communion Liturgy
from Graceway Church

This contemporary Eucharistic liturgy comes from Graceway Church in New Zealand. It is written for two leaders, one male and one female. I have retained the names of the two team members who were originally used to lead this act of worship.

Jan: Waitangi Day,[35]
where Maori and Pakeha[36] wanted to be one,
hoping for security,
dreaming of biculturalism.

Jan: We who are many are one body.
Tony: *Ka whatiia e tatou tenei taro.*[37]

Tony: Communion,
where God wants us to be one,
hoping for restitution,
dreaming of full and final settlement.

Jan: We who are many are one body.
Tony: *Ka whatiia e tatou tenei taro.*

Jan: Communion. [RAISE BREAD]
Take this and eat it. This is my body.
Jesus, broken, that we might be one.

Tony: Communion. [RAISE CUP]
Take this and drink it. This is my blood.
Jesus, broken, that we might be one.

Jan: We who are many are one body.

Tony: *Ka whatiia e tatou tenei taro.*

Jan: Waitangi Day—Divided Day.
We hear the protest from our margins.
We hear the rage of the disillusioned.

Tony: Communion.
And so we are God's body,
caught in the projection of bread and wine.
We are bringers of peace. We are messengers of hope.

Jan: Communion—brokenness that we might be one.
Take this and eat.
Take this and bring peace.

Tony: Communion—brokenness that we might be one.
Take this and drink.
Take this and live hope.

Together (Tony and Jan):
We who are many are one body.[38]

Karmageddon

Living with Post-Christian
Spirituality

We are a diverse group, with influences from Creation Spirituality,
Evangelicalism, Charismatics, Celtic culture, high and low church
culture, dance music culture, anglo-catholics, liberation theology and
liberal theology. We have no party line, no gurus, no simple solutions
and use meditation, candles, slides, rituals and music in services.
THE NINE O'CLOCK COMMUNITY, Sheffield, U.K.

This hunger for spirituality does not today, perhaps for the first time in
many centuries, cause people to come to the churches. If . . . we live in
the midst of a time of genuine spiritual search analogous to the Great
Awakening, how do we communicate the riches of our spiritual heritage
to a generation not interested in being in communication with what
churches do?
LOREN MEAD, foreword to *An 8-Track Church in a CD World*

n 1835 a seventeen-year-old in Germany included the following words in a school essay: "Union with Christ consists in the most intimate communion with Him, in having Him before our eyes and in our hearts, and being so filled with the highest love for Him, that at the same time we turn our hearts to our brothers whom He has closely bound to us, and for whom He also sacrificed Himself."[1] Tame words—standard fare from a young Christian with a passionate faith and a good handle on religious jargon. But hollow words, when you realize that they were written by Karl Marx.

For those concerned with the discipling of young lives in the building of the "once and future church,"[2] Marx's words stand as an urgent reminder that the stakes are high. The task of passing on the Christian witness amounts to more than teaching the young a few religious words and eliciting a programmed response. Marx may well have been happy at seventeen to "talk the talk" of religious faith, but the experiences that shaped his life and the deep truths that motivated him were drawn from other fountains—and bore a very different fruit. Faith that lasts is about more than superficial belief; it is about deep experiences, significant relationships, strong convictions, the shaping of a worldview. Unless faith is deeply rooted in the lives of the young, they will not carry it with them into their later adult years—and the church will not be rerooted in the cultures they create. The crisis of the Western church at the turn of the millennium could be summed up in this one failing: it has not engaged deeply enough with the cultures of the young. The need to embrace change, to create structures and models of church and community that resonate with the transitional generations, is urgent.

The post-Christian spiritualities evident in the transitional generations threaten many strongly held views of the twentieth-century church. But equally, many of the themes and nuances of these spiritualities are present in that same church's history. After two thousand years of growth, diversity, experimentation, discovery and experience, the Christian church has a vast store of spiritual expression available to it. The problem has been that much of this expression remains locked in the storeroom, and little of it has been on display of late in the church's shop windows. The issue is not that the church has no future but that it has no future without change.

Among missiologists and cultural analysts across the denominational spectrum, a consensus is emerging that significant engagement with the emerging twenty-first-century cultures will take the church on a journey well beyond the boundaries of its present experience—and certainly beyond its comfort zones. Writing in 1998, George Barna expressed this consensus in stark terms. "At the risk of sounding like an alarmist," he says, "I believe the church in America has no more than five years—perhaps even less—to turn itself around and begin to affect the culture, rather than be affected by it. . . . We have no more than a half-decade to turn things around."[3] The church we have known stands on the threshold of the future much as a grain of wheat might stand before a plowed field— it has within itself the genetic riches necessary for a bumper crop. But in the final words of Oscar Romero, "If it did not die, it would remain alone. Only in undoing itself does it produce the harvest."[4]

It is appropriate to remind ourselves, at this point, of the huge significance of the transitional generations—Generation X and beyond—to this crisis. These generations represent the last young adult generation of the twentieth century and the first of the twenty-first. By the year 2020, they will constitute the entire working population of the Western world. Everyone under sixty who might or might not join your church at that date will be shaped by the Generation X and Millennial experience—in varying degrees postindustri ., postliterate, postmodern, postimperial and post-Christian. Thus, to begin now to consider how the church might adapt to this experience is not to enter into a peripheral concern for youth ministry but to weigh up the very future of the church. There is no response to the future that is not a response to Gen Xers and the Millennials.

Where the church is responding—where it is recognizing and engaging with the post-Christian spiritualities of our times—it is sowing seeds of hope for the years ahead. Not only is there a very real possibility that the church will discover, in the coming decades, new ways of expressing its life and faith that will appeal to post-Christian young people, but there are signs even now of such expressions emerging. These do not come from any one denomination, theology or stream but are emerging in many branches of the Christian family as young leaders respond to the post-Christian spiritualities we have identified, exploring those aspects of their faith that are non-Western, pre-Western, ecological, experiential and practicable. Many of these new expressions are small and faltering, and some will peter out before they have had time to amount to anything. But others will gain strength and grow to become, for thousands, new points of entry into Christian faith and practice. Only time will prove which are, in embryonic form, the mainstream Christian expressions of the twenty-first century.

Alternative Worship: A Grassroots Movement

Across Great Britain, in Australia and New Zealand, and in certain parts of Europe, a loose network of experimental worship communities is emerging, with a very real commitment to embrace the post-Christian generations. Often highly technological, these groups create worship that is visual and participatory, that creates and discovers new Christian rituals and that recaptures something of the ecological commitment inherent in the biblical narrative. The most widely known of these experiments was the Nine O'Clock Service in Sheffield— the subject of much press attention around the "fall" of its leader, Chris Brain. Before sinking into a mire of sexual intrigue and manipulative leadership, the Nine O'Clock Service was a remarkable experiment in post-Christian spirituality, encompassing sound and vision, ritual, community and an overarching ecological reverence. A remnant from this group still meet, under the name Nine O'Clock Community. Other groups with a mercifully lower profile—such as the Late Late Service in Glasgow, Grace in London and Parallel Universe and Graceway in New Zealand[5]—have been able to continue these explorations, and are creating a diverse range of models for worship, community and teaching. New Zealand pastor Chris Chamberlain comments, "The most exciting part of my ministry is in sharing the dreams and struggles of my people who are bored, tired, sick or confused with the current ways we 'do' church—and together dreaming and experimenting with new ideas."[6] Embody <www.embody.co.uk/emberdays.html> is a recent U.K.-based attempt to transfer this spirit of experiment to the Internet, offering an online worship experience through Shockwave technology.

In the U.S. context, an equally wide range of projects is emerging, with young leaders experimenting, exploring, and planting churches. Mars Hill Fellowship in Seattle <www.marshillchurch.org> is perhaps the best known of these experiments, but founder Mark Driscoll estimates that there are in excess of fifteen hundred linked or similar projects emerging nationwide.[7] Andrew Jones, also associated with the Younger Leaders Network, sees this emerging edge of creativity in three distinct arenas:

☐ First, among the Gen X church plants—some independent, some sponsored by parent churches. These are groups whose primary motivation is missional in the sense that they have been created to reach Gen X. They have a wide diversity of purpose and practice: from those who are updating music styles and incorporating home-grown video to those who are establishing community, growing social-action projects or moving quickly away from modernity in the reinvention of worship.

☐ Second, in a more diverse array of "organic, backyard groups: small, meeting in coffee shops or clubs or living rooms." Many of these are peopled by church members disillusioned with both traditional and contemporary forms of worship and searching for something more authentic in the postmodern context.

☐ Third, and further still from the existing paradigms, "a scattering of 'wildflower' projects—more random than an English country garden and camouflaged deeply within the underground." These are artist's colonies, intentional communities and creative believers, many of whom travel widely and most of whom use cyberspace as their arena for connection and interchange. They are more at home in rave and street culture than in church, and will often resist the label Christian, preferring "follower of Jesus."[8]

Their number growing fast, these various groups are exploring the forms of postliterate learning described in chapter seven and appealing directly to the concerns of a post-Christian spirituality. Often they are "fringe" or "sister" groups to an established congregation or parish. For the most part they are small projects, learning as they go, making mistakes and struggling to stay on track. Some are dipping their toes into postmodern waters, others wading waist-deep, others still diving deep and staying under. Their shared commitment is to ask what it will mean for the Christian faith to be rerooted in the emerging cultures of the transitional generations. As such they are a measure of the Western church's potential for rebirth.

Experimental groups seeking to engage the Christian faith in a postmodern context will often lack the resources, profile or success record of the Boomer congregations. By definition, they are new, untried, relatively disorganized and fearful of self-promotion. They reject the corporate model of church so beloved of their Boomer forebears, and thus do not appear, according to existing paradigms, to be significant. But don't be fooled. Somewhere in the genesis and genius of these diverse groups is hidden the future of Western Christianity. To dismiss them is to throw away the seeds of our survival. "Our rebellious youth and advanced technologies are not the enemies of the church," writes Thomas Hohstadt. "At this moment, in fact, they are our only hope."[9]

Ancient Paths: The Rediscovery of Celtic Faith

A much wider movement touching both Catholic and Protestant denominations and appealing to both old and young is the reemergence of Celtic spirituality. Championed by such writers as Ian Bradley, Michael Mitton, Esther de Waal and David Adam, and popularized through monastic and lay groups such as the Iona and

Northumbria communities, the Celtic worldview strikes a resonant chord with the concerns of post-Christian spirituality. It embraces a love of nature and a passion for its wild and elemental forces, a love of art and poetry, a love of story as the primary means of learning, respect for the role and ministry of women, a rejection of any supposed boundary between the sacred and the secular, a place both for personal devotion and its communal expression, and an emphasis on the dynamic experience of intimacy with God. Esther de Waal says of these ancient ways,

> The Celtic journey I am describing . . . is unlike any other journey that I know. Its shape and its end are different, as are the songs I sing while I journey, the company I keep on the road. I have been brought into contact with the visual and the non-verbal, confronted by the power of image and symbol. I have found myself thinking about God as a poet, an artist, drawing us all into his great work of art. I have been taken beyond the rational and intellectual and cerebral for this world touches the springs of my imagination.[10]

For many, the rediscovery of the Celtic way represents the return to an authentic, ancient faith. In the same way that many first-peoples spiritualities are seen as immune from the corruption of the West, so Celtic Christianity, as a premodern form, is ascribed a certain purity. Ian Bradley, for instance, disassociates the Celtic church from the "evangelism as conquest" style so often associated with modernity. "The approach of the Celtic missionaries was essentially gentle and sensitive," writes Ian Bradley. "They sought to live alongside the people with whom they wanted to share the good news of Christ, to understand and respect their beliefs and not to dominate or culturally condition them."[11]

The rebirth of the Celtic church is attributed by many commentators to the close parallels between premodern and postmodern Britain. "Looking back at the Celtic church gives me great heart and vision for the future," writes Michael Mitton. "It is as though God is alerting us to the fact that he has done the impossible before in these lands. He has broken into a society that was culturally confused and riddled with spiritual uncertainty and superstition."[12]

Inculturation and Contextualization

If the Celtic revival represents an engagement of the church with its own history, there are also those working more directly with indigenous, pre-Christian spiritualities in an attempt to bring the best of them into a Christian framework—or to see the Christian faith incarnated in the native context. These theologians and worship practitioners are engaging directly with the postimperial, post-Christian fascination with first-peoples cultures. The collapse of modernity has brought the opportunity to reevaluate the church's historic rejection of these cultures, not just their beliefs but their lifestyles, social structures, technologies and insights. If it has been possible for the church to be incarnated for so long, and so deeply, in the modern "story" of Western progress, then surely it can equally be incarnated into other, premodern cultures?

At the extreme end of this movement are those who seek to immerse themselves entirely within the cultures and rituals of pre-Christianity, even at the risk of losing Christian identity. Michael Shirres, who died in 1997, was a Dominican priest who worked for twenty years among the Maori people indigenous to New Zealand. His life's work was to find points of connection between Maori culture, traditions and spirituality on the one hand and the Christian gospel on the other. He called this process inculturation:

> Inculturation is a theological term which embraces two rich and seminal ideas, enculturation and incarnation. Enculturation involves growing into a culture which is a process which is continuous right through life. Incarnation is a theological term that expresses God's becoming a human being. . . . Inculturation is a made-up word which signifies the process where Jesus, as a human, took on the culture of a particular people. Just as he became a Jew so he becomes a member of other communities, taking on their particular culture. As the Word is made flesh becoming a Jew, so "the Word is made flesh", becoming a member of each human family.[13]

Part of the process of inculturation, for Shirres, lay in the creation of prayers and liturgies that were thoroughly Christian and yet drew on the imagery, traditions and writings of the ancient Maori nation. This lifelong quest took on new poignancy when, in 1994, Shirres was diagnosed with a form of motor neurone disease and was told that he was dying. Throughout his final years, at various stages of incapacity, he spoke of "the experience of the love of Jesus" brought to him by the words of a Maori chant for the person dying: "Your heart. My heart. You give me your dying heart. Let me give you my living heart. Cross over to life. Rise up above!"[14] By taking this prayer out of its pagan context and into his knowledge of Christ, Shirres found strength, encouragement and comfort.

Others working in the field of contextualization would shy away from Shirres's wholesale embracing of native faith and would seek to maintain some sense of distinctive, Christian identity within the ancient context. This is more accurately described as contextualization than inculturation. Steve Taylor, also a New Zealander, is pastor of Graceway Church in Auckland. Much of what happens at Graceway is geared to a postmodern generation, and running through the church's approach is the thread of contextualization: seeking to live authentically in a nation that is at once both ancient and postmodern. Graceway services are "strongly aware of the contemporary culture and the need to contextualise: TV advertisements, video and slides are used to introduce worship, as 'worship wallpaper' and as sites for prayer."[15] And many aspects of Maori culture—indigenous to New Zealand since the Stone Age—are explored and honored. The heart of the church's mission is expressed in the ancient Maori cry *"He tangata, He tangata, He tangata"* ("the people, the people, the people").

The transitional generations have grown up with an inquisitive respect for premodern cultures—the stories that inspired us before the Western dream took center stage and pushed them to the margins. For the many who struggle with issues of origin, ethnicity, roots and identity, the recovery of these stories and the worship of a nonwhite Jesus go together. For these generations, a church that honors and embraces the very best in all cultures will be a church worth knowing.

The Postcharismatics: To Pentecost and Beyond

A fourth area in which young people are exploring the possibilities of adapting to a post-Christian context, particularly in Europe, is among a new generation of charismatics. These are young people who are embracing the emotional dimension of faith, very often making use of dance music and video technology and creating a worship experience built around the dynamic experience of the presence of God. Intuitive, creative, holistic, relational, these young people are rejecting the notion of the church as an institution and working instead through cells and small congregations, deeply committed to peer relationships and to an indwelt, 24/7 spirituality. "How can you get excited about God in an old-style church, sitting in a row of pews?" asks Russ Oliver, founder of the Interface events in southern England. "At our events we shout if we feel angry and cry if we feel sad. It's more like a pop concert or a football match."[16]

As well as prioritizing the experience of faith, these groups are exploring new models of community, reclaiming a Christian commitment to social justice, celebrating the whole spectrum of the arts and creativity and gleefully sending missionaries into the postmodern subcultures of dance clubs, skate parks, fashion houses and the music industry.

Breaking the Power of the Old

What these four strands or developments—alternative worship, ancient paths, contextualization and postcharismatism—have in common, alongside their willingness to explore new ways of expressing the Christian faith in a postmodern culture, is a willingness, more crucially, to abandon some of the ways in which the faith has been expressed in modernity. Unless young people are allowed to take hold of faith for themselves—to test its durability, to explore its boundaries, to deconstruct and reconstruct its style, to reroot it in the soil of their own lives—they will neither embrace nor uphold Christianity in the cultures of the coming century. As long as the structures and styles of our faith are too precious and untouchable to be released into the hands of the young, we are doomed to a "rapidly expiring shelf-life."[17]

As the post-Christian era takes firm hold of our spirituality, more and more young people from the transitional generations will seek expressions of worship and entry points to faith which are new and different. As George Barna expresses it, "As we introduce new approaches to ministry, many of the fundamental elements of the church will undoubtedly be redefined."[18]

Those more established in the existing expressions of church, who might find aspects of these new models by turns frightening, disturbing, exhilarating and bizarre, will need to make space for young people, to encourage and support experimentation, to offer support in both success and failure—in the words of Martin Scott to "bless the strange ways of God."[19] Studies in "paradigm shifts" (a concept developed by scientist Thomas Kuhn) reveal that "paradigm shifters are usually found at the edge, not the center of the existing paradigm."[20] What new expressions of the Christian faith are growing already on the fringes of the current church—ready to offer spiritual experience, direction, fulfillment and purpose to the post-Christian generations? Whatever they are, they are our hope. "The mystery of the gospel," Lesslie Newbigin has said, "is not entrusted to the church to be buried in the ground. It is entrusted to the church to be risked in the change and interchange of the spiritual commerce of humanity."[21] The question we must ask is not, dare we change? but rather, dare we not? "We cannot be born anew," Paul Tillich has written, "if the power of the old is not broken within us."[22]

Let those who find such a challenge too frightening to even think about take time to consider, by way of a parable, the legend of the unbreakable coffeepot.

creative.link
The Unbreakable Coffeepot

The precise origins of the unbreakable coffeepot were buried in time. It had come into the family when great-grandfather Joe, wandering the muddy trenches of Ypres at the height of the 1914–1918 war, found it in a bombed-out farmhouse. Certain no one would return to claim it, he kept it for his own.

By the time Joe returned, war-weary, to marriage and industry in Oregon, the coffeepot had become a legend. Through torrents of shelling and sniper fire, through trench maneuvers and interminable route marches across the burned and scarred French fields, through nine months of warfare on an apocalyptic scale, Joe had carried his coffeepot, and his coffeepot had remained unbroken. Even its spout, that most fragile of coffeepot appendages, was intact.

"It's a miracle!" Joe's platoon had declared.

"It's an omen," Joe had answered, clinging to the hope of survival.

Somewhere along the way—and forever after—the enameled tin pot became known as "the unbreakable coffeepot." Back home it was given pride of place on the kitchen stove. It was a talking point, an excuse to reminisce about the war. When Joe's kids came along, the coffeepot was the focus of a hundred stories to enthrall them—stories they would later tell to their own children. The darkness and horror, the friends won and lost, and always the unbreakable coffeepot, surviving at the heart of it all like the miracle of life itself.

Until Joe passed it on to his eldest, Tom, the coffeepot was in daily use on the family stove, earning its keep, providing for the family's needs. "This is not to be an idle curiosity," Joe told the family. "It's a working pot, and as long as I drink coffee, it will be."

Tom's eldest, Roger, grew up with the coffeepot on the shelf. Year by year its legend grew even as its usefulness diminished. New stories were added—"It's been dropped, three times, on the concrete pantry floor," they would say, "and never a scratch to show for it."

"It saved my granddad's life," Roger would add apocryphally. "Blocked a bullet heading right for his heart."

Margaret, Roger's wife, took care to dust and clean the coffeepot once a week. It even began to shine from her repeated administrations of polish and elbow grease. She had been fond of Joe and enjoyed the memory of him. But she had her own tastes in kitchenware and could easily afford a better-quality pot. Besides, who could say when a handle might get broken or the seams begin to leak? Better to keep it safe than risk its loss. And slowly the kitchen filled with more up-to-date appliances: first an electric kettle; then a drip-filter coffee machine; and finally an all-singing cappuccino affair, built into the kitchen like a personal Starbucks. Apart from the weekly dusting, the unbreakable coffeepot was rarely off the shelf.

The crisis came when young Joe, named after his great-grandfather, was just ten. Like his sisters and cousins, he had grown up knowing all about the coffeepot. Rarely had he been in the company of Grandfather Tom without the stories being told. Tom would conjure up, through the magic of words, the very presence of his long-dead father, as he sat, turning the coffeepot in his hand, speaking with reverence and awe of what it meant to him, and how nothing—not war, nor water, nor a drop on the floor—could break it. Young Joe, whose own hands had never touched the precious pot, would listen wide-eyed.

"Why not?" he would ask his mother, when she told him for the millionth time that the pot was out of bounds to him on its high shelf, that he was never—not ever—to touch it.

"Because it's precious," she would say with genuine awe. "It's been in our family for three generations already, and one day it will be yours—but it's not for a child to touch."

Sometimes, when he was alone in the kitchen, Joe would look up to the high shelf, stretched like a skyscraper above him. He would examine the cold hardness of the pantry floor, kicking his toes against it until it hurt, and wonder at the things he had been told. And much as he loved Grandfather Tom and the stories of Great-Grandfather Joe, and much as he trusted his parents and believed what they told him, and much as he wanted the stories to be true, he couldn't help wondering if, after all, in the real world, they were not.

It was Grandfather Tom's seventy-fifth birthday. Relatives had come out of the woodwork to gather at Joe's house to celebrate. Grandfather Tom, happy at the heart of it all, spent much of the afternoon with assorted combinations of grandchildren on his knee or at his feet, repeating once more the legends of the unbreakable coffeepot, conjuring up again the presence of old Joe.

Young Joe, meanwhile, was shocked by the irreverence of his own thoughts. *If it's unbreakable, why can't I touch it?* he asked himself in silence. *If the stories are true, why keep it on the shelf?*

The relatives were gathered on the front drive, making their fare-wells and extracting cars from the sardine parking. Grandfather Tom, in his wheelchair, was positioned to the left of the front porch, in the shadow of a rhododendron bush, from where he could watch them all leave. Roger and Margaret were at either side of the front gate waving their final goodbyes. It was Joe's Aunt Peggy—Roger's sister—who noticed first.

"What the . . . ?!" she cried as her arm shot upward to point out the horror, and every eye followed its line. Four generations gasped and held their breath.

At the very top of the house, where the dormer window of the attic bedroom reached almost to the edge of the roof, young Joe was leaning out. One foot set on the window ledge, he held with one hand to the frame—his body swinging out over the drive. In his free hand, its spout to the wind, he held the unbreakable coffeepot.

From opposite sides of the drive, Roger and Margaret realized at
the same moment what it was that their son was about to do. The
screamed words left their mouths in unrehearsed unison, "No,
Joe, don't . . ."

Too late. Their heads held in horror, the assembled relatives saw
the coffeepot slip from young Joe's hand, beginning its graceful
fall to the ground. Every face was contorted with horror. Every
face, that is, except that of Grandfather Tom. Alone in his chair,
he looked up at Joe. He could see the concentration on the boy's
face. He could see the pot falling like a stone toward the concrete.
And as he saw it, he thought of old Joe, his father. And he smiled.

PART 3

Root Growth

*Resources for
the Management of Change*

Pillar to Post

The Impact of Change on the Church

If you are among those who are experiencing a ride on the wild side, if you are feeling out of control, let me whisper an important word in your ear. All appearances to the contrary, the Creator God is quietly transforming our "future shocked" world. While we may feel out of control, our God isn't.

TOM SINE, *Mustard Seed Versus McWorld*

Within the Christian community, two dangers which hinder God-initiated growth lurk below the surface: building on the glory of an irrelevant past and star-gazing into a fantasy future that will never be. To be able to avoid both of these pitfalls we will need to be sensitive and responsive to what is happening around us.

VIV THOMAS, *Future Leader*

aking an overview of the "five 'posts' of Generation X and beyond," it is not hard to see why some in the Christian faith community feel threatened by these waves of social change. These are not peripheral areas of faith and practice undergoing minor alterations; these are core areas, for some the very pillars of the faith, being deconstructed and reformed. Both literally and figuratively, we are being driven from pillar to post. Even a cursory glance at the kinds of questions our journey through the culture junction has raised will reveal the breadth and depth of these changes—questions of the nature and structure of the church, and of what it means to belong; of the place and treatment of the Bible in nonbook culture; of the place of evangelism and conversion in pick-and-mix times; of the future of mission on a changing planet; of the style and content of Christian worship. It is hardly surprising that for many, especially those who have invested most heavily in the existing models and structures, change is a demanding and difficult journey.

This chapter suggests six steps in the management of personal and corporate change that might contribute to an easier ride and give confidence to those just setting out. The six steps do not necessarily function in a set order and are not set out as any kind of program. Rather, they are six suggestions to explore, six gateways into change. They are intended to help those faced with change to make a real and considered IMPACT (investigate social change, make space for personal change, prioritize the young, accept what you find, champion hinge leaders, take the plunge) on the future we all face.

Gateway 1: Investigate Social Change

It is not that those deep things of the faith have changed. Rather, the structures in which we have housed them and the thought-forms with which we explained them have grown archaic. New languages and new structures will be needed for the gospel truth to be articulated in this world of postmodernity.
—LOREN MEAD, foreword to *An 8-Track Church in a CD World*, by Robert N. Nash

One of the great enemies of constructive change is apathy—we don't change because we are simply not interested in changing. We have our own small world well ordered and complete; what goes on outside the windows is of little value to us. If this book has achieved anything, I hope it has proved the inadequacy of such an attitude and, for some, burst the bubble of virtual reality. The world is changing, and the changes it brings can be merciless. Our engagement with change begins with the simple act of being interested. For some, this will mean exploring areas they have previously chosen to ignore—changes in technology or philosophy or popular spirituality. For others it will mean listening afresh to those immersed in change, not least the younger generations. Only if we will begin with investigating, exploring, examining, gathering data—with throwing the net wide and letting the catch inform us—will we be able to negotiate and manage the changes demanded of us.

Five key suggestions for getting through gateway one are the following:

1. Buy or subscribe to a magazine covering an area about which you know little but which is on the leading edge of change—computer technology, rave culture, the youth underground, management, commerce. Read it with two questions foremost in your thinking: "What does this tell me the future might be like?" and "Where does it lead me for further exploration?" Cut and keep helpful articles on key areas, then add others from newspapers, other magazines and the Internet.

2. Identify individuals who have recently made big changes in their lives—those who have moved from employment to self-employment, those adopting a new faith, those working in new industries, those returning to study after a long period in work—and ask them how and why they made the changes they have made. Ask yourself how much of their experience relates to wider cultural changes.

3. Get involved with the Internet, if you aren't already. Search and surf, using key words and site recommendations. Join a future-focused chat group, or create your own with half a dozen friends or colleagues on e-mail. Set aside specific times to surf with a purpose, using time to learn about the new environment that is the World Wide Web.

4. Talk to people younger than yourself, especially those by whose lifestyles you are most challenged. Ask them why they live as they do—not so that you can judge but so that you can *know.* Why body piercing? Why the Marilyn Manson look? Why choose tantric Buddhism over Christianity? Start with those known to you before you graduate to strangers!

5. Look into a field parallel to your own but with a different emphasis. Protestants, for instance, have much to learn from the ways in which the Catholic Church deals with change, and vice versa. Leaders in business and the nonprofit sector can learn from one another. Christian foundations can learn from the experience of those of a different faith confession or none. Many of the changes we are facing come into focus only when we can see the big picture—like the earth viewed from space. Often this view will emerge only through interdisciplinary thinking.

Gateway 2: Make Space for Personal Change
Not only does he bring about change, but in a significant sense God himself experiences change. After God acts, the universe is different and God's experience of the universe is different.
—**Richard Rice,** quoted in Clark Pinnock et al., *The Openness of God*

A second great enemy of change is overcommitment. The overcommitted are often pursuing the most noble and high-minded of motivations, but they are so tied up in maintaining the status quo that they haven't the time nor the energy to even contemplate change, let alone deliver it. Business and career, church and faith, family and home—all are capable of submerging us in such a weight of important tasks that we forget what made them important in the first place. But none of us is so well established, so fully formed that we can afford to dismiss personal change. Few will have the luxury of calling "Halt!" to everything, but most can call halt to something and create space on the margins in which new ideas can form. The irony of overcommitment is that it is often focused on the very structures and programs that need to change. We have spent so long cultivating our personal portfolio of causes, committees and conflicts that it is unthinkable to abandon unfinished tasks and battles, even though the significance of victory would fade if only we allowed new paradigms to emerge. To change direction requires more space and time than to go on without changing.

Here are five suggestions for approaching gateway two:

1. Set future-focused priorities and purposes for your life, whether in terms of career, family, leisure or faith. Reexamine your many goals in the light of the emerging culture. How many of them make good sense in this changing context? How many contribute, rather, to a status quo that will be gone by the time you achieve them? Take time to create a genuine and balanced future focus, then look for activities you are engaged in that do not contribute to its fulfillment. Plan your withdrawal from these activities.

2. Commit one regular slice of your time—an evening each week, a morning once a month, two full days a year—to focusing on new areas of thinking, learning, exploration and prayer. This might be through additional reading, through a short course, through a prayer retreat alone or with others. Whatever it is, the key is that it should be focused on listening and learning rather than on activity, and that the commitment, once made, should be kept. Even if all you can redeem is one hour each week, redeem it, and use it as space for change.

3. Rediscover walking, whether it is in the open countryside on the weekends or in the city during a lunch break. Reembrace the slower pace of the pedestrian and open your eyes to what is around you. Use regular walking time to observe, reflect, think and pray.

4. Invest in relationships—as a couple, as parents and children, as colleagues and friends, as strangers on a bus. Reinvent the lost art of conversation. Learn to ask open-ended questions and to listen to replies. Recover a passionate interest in people—in their motivations, their struggles, their hopes and dreams. The questions in your own life that never get answered are the ones you never ask. Where the relationship is secure, be ready to be vulnerable about your own struggles—you are more likely than not to find them common.

5. *Think seriously about potential big changes.* Job, location, income, lifestyle, timestyle, friendships, leisure patterns, possessions, ambitions—these are the building-block decisions from which our lives are constructed. They do not change easily, and as a general rule, the longer it is since the choice was made, the harder it is to change it. But it *may be* that time taken to reflect, pray and invest in relationships will highlight a need for change on such a scale. Sometimes it is only when we stop that we see how far off course we are.

Gateway 3: Prioritize the Young

We will tell the next generation the praiseworthy deeds of the LORD, his power, and the wonders he has done.
—Psalm 78:4

That the future belongs to those who are presently young is the truism to end all truisms. Strange, then, that so little of our thinking reflects this. When we think about the future, we often fall into the trap of projecting our own experience forward and of assuming that the concerns of our own day and generation will remain the concerns of tomorrow. The reality couldn't be more different, and it is essential that our focus shift to those who will both shape and inherit tomorrow: the "next" generations. In Psalm 78:6, this includes two generations—our children and our children's children. If our thinking is to genuinely focus on these generations (for our purposes, these fall somewhere within Generation X, the Millennial generation and whatever comes next), then so must other considerations. We will not embrace gateway three without reevaluating some things.

1. *Reevaluating our budgets.* How much of the money we allocate

in churches, communities and projects actually meets the needs and aspirations of the rising generations? Do our financial decisions genuinely reflect the disproportionate stake they have in the future?

2. *Reevaluating our strategies.* How many of our strategic decisions (think of planning, buildings, activities, events, training, purchases, literature, decor, facilities) are targeted toward these needs? How many of our decisions would be different if we said at every stage, "The future is youth, and youth are the future"? When was the last time we asked them about anything?

3. *Reevaluating our use of time.* Might it be possible to audit our own timestyle—in terms of thinking time, activity time, study time, work time and so on—and ask how much of it deals with the needs of the rising generations? Even if we are employed in an old people's home, might we make a 5 percent time investment in future generations?

4. *Reevaluating our trust.* When was the last time we took the risk of trusting a younger person with a task we might otherwise place in "safe hands"? In the case of the church, it is the safe hands that have strangled us. Why not give the risky hands a try?

Gateway 4: Accept What You Find

The crucial issue for Christians is the extent to which we are prepared to accept the integrity of those adopting a different approach from ours. If we insist that any approach other than ours signifies lack of integrity and lack of true faith, fragmentation of the body of Christ is inevitable.
—**D. Gareth Jones**, *Coping with Controversy*

A significant block to creative change is the rush to form premature judgments—literally, *prejudices.* Before our brains can fully assess the implications of a new idea, our mouths have already formed the words "It'll never work." This is a particular problem for those in the Christian faith community, who have become so adept at defending the truth from error that they stop every new suggestion at the door and body-search it. Pouring the cold water of judgment on every creative idea, we stunt growth, inhibit exploration and, by implication, block change. In a time of transition, this is death. When a community has lost its source of food, it is not wise to lynch every hunter who suggests where new food might be found. Transition demands that we allow the new to emerge and show itself, and that we allow the young the freedom to explore.

This is not to suggest that we abandon all judgment and embrace the new for its own sake. It may be necessary to keep a critical and analytical faculty loaded and ready to use, but it may serve us well to take our finger off the trigger. When we are faced with the new, the extreme, the bizarre, the challenging, our first thought should not be "burn the heretic!" but "hold your fire!" Who knows when what seems at first bizarre might not prove, at closer quarters, to be your salvation.

Author D. Gareth Jones, in exploring the very specific field of controversy in the church, has suggested five questions as the basis for a group discussion. All five—and the suggestion that you discuss them with your peers—will help significantly toward achieving gateway four:

1. What do you consider as central and peripheral issues for Christians? How do you distinguish between the two?

2. To what extent do you think evangelical Christians have freedom to explore new areas of thought or practice? Give examples of what you think might or might not be acceptable.

3. What measures do you think should be taken to avoid confrontation within churches?

4. *Compromise* is often regarded as a dirty word, since it stands for accepting second best. Do you agree with this, or is it sometimes the path to be followed by Christians? Try and think of specific examples.

5. If you are faced with a novel way of doing something, how do you react? Discuss the various reactions within the group. Think of ways we can build on these initial reactions and make them more Christian.[1]

Gateway 5: Champion Hinge Leaders

The mainline denominations are bleeding. Their churches have more pew than flock, and unless they change, they have more history than future.
—**Charles Trueheart,** *Welcome to the Next Church*

One of the reasons many people find it hard to embrace change is that they genuinely and honestly don't understand what is happening. We struggle, as Loren Mead has written, "to make sense out of the changes that seem to sweep over our culture and threaten to make many things we do obsolete."[2] We know how to construct good decisions from good *understanding,* but we don't have good understanding, and we don't know where to get it. Such is the speed of change that everything about the challenge we face—the people involved, their language codes, their identity and aspirations—are alien to us. We are from Venus, they are from Mars. It is for this reason that we stand urgently in need of a generation of "hinge leaders," that is, people sufficiently at home in the new to understand it, and sufficiently at home in the old to help *us* understand it. Hinge leaders have attachments in both cultures (in our current situation they are drawn for the most part from Gen X); they have the capacity to hold in tension the best of both old and new and to broker communication across the culture gap. Churches, communities, businesses, families, nations can all benefit from the go-between services of hinge leaders. Theirs is the voice that will open up the future for us, and theirs is the vision that will first bring the new into the old. But they themselves need support and nurture. Living in two worlds is a tough call, and they are as likely to be rejected by both as accepted by either.

Here are six steps you can take to get through gateway five by nurturing, supporting and championing hinge leaders:

1. Find out who they are. Who are the Gen X leaders on the fringe of existing communities and structures who have an intuitive grasp on the future? Chances are, they will be found among those who struggle with existing paradigms and don't fit easily into existing plans. They may be the very people you almost banned from the church last week for being too rebellious and troublesome!

2. Give them time and attention. Let them know that you are there to support them. Ask them what their needs are. Provide friendship, training, resources, inspiration. Become allies in bringing the future to birth.

3. Listen to their vision. Ask them what the priorities should be, what changes they are looking for and why, what they see and hear from their standpoint on the margins. Trust them to tell you where your own direction could change.

4. Find room for them in the structures. This might be on the fringe of things, in a quiet corner, but it must be room in which they are empowered to pursue their vision. Putting hinge leaders onto committees to give the *appearance* of sharing power is pointless and unjust. Find them a space, no matter how small, where they have real power.

5. Get behind them—emotionally, financially, structurally. Become known for your support of them. Defend their record; tell their story; validate their experiments. Put your trust of them into action. Share with them the joys and pains of success and failure. Coach them; encourage them; resource them.

6. Stay close to them. There is nothing more dangerous than an experiment left to run on remote control. A relationship of accountability has to be just that—a relationship. You are not a champion of innovation in which you have no stake or involvement and of which you have no understanding. Risk allows for the possibility both of triumph and of disaster, and your presence will be needed to manage either.

Gateway 6: Take the Plunge!
Change is the angel of a changeless God.
—**Archbishop William Temple,** quoted in Graham Cray et al., *The Post-Evangelical Debate*

Imagine yourself climbing the steps to a high diving board. Proud of your courage, you ascend to the highest platform. You share with fellow divers the joy of being numbered among the brave. You step forward to the very edge of the board, which trembles under you. You have mentally rehearsed the move a thousand times; you have overcome all the early anxieties and exaggerated fears. But there is one final barrier—a new and unimagined terror that doesn't grip you until your toes are wrapped over the very end of the board and the pool below appears as a tiny patch of water in the far distance. You haven't yet won the battle—you have to jump.

Dramatic imagery for some, but for others, an accurate picture. It's all very well to investigate change, to make time and space for it, to think *The future is youth, and youth are the future.* It's all very well to suspend your judgment of others, even to identify and champion hinge leaders. But there comes a time when it is right to make real changes for yourself, and it is costly. To be aware of change, to broadly welcome it is one thing—to cut right into core activities and make significant changes is another. It can cost in terms of power relinquished, ambitions abandoned, support sacrificed. It can mean surrendering competence, becoming a novice again. It can mean relinquishing known success to embrace the possibility of failure. The new, by definition, begins smaller than the old and runs the risk of infant death. But the new, very often, is where God is. As you consider gateway six, ask yourself the following questions:

1. Is there a key area in which I could soon "take the plunge" and change my life?

2. What is there in my current work, home or lifestyle that I love very much but might well have to abandon as I embrace change? What does the diving board represent for me?

3. As I have examined the "five posts" analysis, what areas have been highlighted for me as personal hot zones?

4. How does my imagined "church of tomorrow" differ from my experience of the "church of today"? What steps lead from one to the other? What is the first of these steps?

5. Who do I most admire for their capacity to embrace and manage change? What would it take for me to emulate them?

6. What new dreams and visions have surfaced in me as I have considered the challenge of change in this chapter?

7. If all of my current commitments were miraculously canceled as of tomorrow, what would I spend the next five years doing?

8. What three things could I do within the next two weeks to get through one of the six gateways described in this chapter?

Retrenchment or Rebirth?

The great drama teacher Konstantin Stanislavsky would occasionally insist that his students, before being allowed to leave the room, should say "Goodnight" to him in fifty different tones of voice.[3] His point was that creativity—the capacity to think beyond the box, to explore new avenues, to be original, to find diversity, variety and freshness in the everyday—must be worked at and fought for. It is easier to say goodnight the way we've always said it than it is to find fifty new ways, but the actor who takes the easy option will achieve all but nothing. In so doing Stanislavsky shaped and inspired some of the greatest actors of stage and screen in our century, and his legacy holds power to this day. Creativity takes work; new thinking can be exhausting, even painful; but without it we are doomed to stay within existing paradigms, saying goodnight forever in the same, dull voice and losing contact, bit by bit, with our audience.

And those who find it hardest to embrace change, very often, are those who have known the most success within the status quo.

Two small boys were playing on their bikes on the street outside their house. One had a beat-up old thing. It had lost most of its paint; rust was taking over; parts were loose. Even when it was new, it hadn't been up to much. The other boy had a much better bike—the newest model, with all the latest gadgets. He was proud of it, and on it he felt invincible. In terms of boys and bikes, he was light-years ahead of his friend.

But a steamroller came around the corner and began heading for the very stretch of asphalt the boys were playing on. Both boys immediately jumped from their bikes and scrambled to the sidewalk.

The differences between their bikes seemed suddenly less relevant. In terms of steamrollers, they were pretty much the same.

You might be involved in a small, struggling neighborhood church with scant resources, few programs and very little scope for change. Or you might belong to the biggest megachurch on the planet, with a staff team of fourteen thousand, a seven-figure budget and an interplanetary satellite network. In terms of Christians and churches, you may be light-years ahead. But in terms of steamrollers, and of the future, we are all pretty much the same.

word.link: Inherit the Wind

Jesus declared, "I tell you the truth, no one can see the kingdom of God unless he is born again."
"How can a man be born when he is old?" Nicodemus asked.—**John 3:3-4**

Nicodemus might well ask. He was not only old; he was also educated, wise and wealthy. He was powerful, significant, competent and respected. He was everything a religious leader of his generation might want to be—a prominent elder on the eve of a satisfied retirement. And he was everything a newborn baby is not. Jesus issued a direct challenge to this wise old man so scared of change that he crept to the appointment under cover of darkness. He called him to swap his competence for newness; his knowledge for ignorance; his certainties for mysteries; his faith in a static, unchanging God for a living relationship with the wind that "blows wherever it pleases."

To give up religion and inherit the wind. How many of us who fill the pews of today's religious institutions, who are as sure of our faith as Nicodemus was of his until he met Christ, who even call ourselves "born again," stand in need, as much as Nicodemus did, of such a change?

The twentieth century was not always kind to the church, but all the same, there are those who have learned how to be Christians within it. We are, like Nicodemus, competent. To change now might mean abandoning all this, giving up the very things that have made us strong to become, once again, dependent infants. But there are times in all our histories, just as there were for the Jewish leaders, when God calls us on. To the extent that we have become like Nicodemus—educated, established, in control, ready to retire—God calls us to become the newborn, that is, bloody, crying, confused, weak and vulnerable—but alive! New birth is painful, disruptive, difficult, demanding, inconvenient. But without new birth, all we're doing is dying. To use Mike Riddell's chilling words: "I think this is the call of God to the Western church at the end of the second millennium: to change or to die."[4] Unless a church is born again . . .

Tsar Wars
New Models of Leadership

Good leaders grow people, bad leaders stunt them; good leaders serve their followers, bad leaders enslave them.
SIR ADRIAN CADBURY

Go to the people. Live amongst them. Start with what they have. Build on what they know. And when the deed is done, the mission accomplished, of the best leaders the people will say, "We have done it ourselves."
LAO TZU

In his exploration of the island of Lindisfarne,[1] Magnus Magnusson describes some of the cultural distinctions between the Celtic and Roman approaches to the Christian faith. "Celtic monks lived in conspicuous poverty," he writes, "Roman monks lived well. . . . Celtic bishops practised humility, Roman bishops paraded pomp.

Celtic bishops were ministers of their flocks, Roman bishops were monarchs of their dioceses. Celtic clergymen said 'Do as I do', and hoped to be followed; Roman clergymen said 'Do as I say', and expected to be obeyed."[2] In citing these examples, Magnusson is touching on one of the key reasons for the renewed interest in all things Celtic, and one of the core arenas in which our culture is in crisis—the arena of leadership. Shaped by the uncertainties of post-modernity, and schooled in its ambivalence toward authority, the emerging generations are seeking out models of leadership far removed from the control-and-command approach characteristic of the twentieth century. The future is a challenging road for all of us, but the climb is steepest, and the way most difficult, for those called upon to lead.

Remote Controllers: The New Leadership List

Of all the charges laid at the door of the church by many disaffected young people who in recent years have made the choice to leave, the most frequent and damning is the charge of *controlling leadership*. Styles of leadership forged in the certainties of modernity, fitted to the assembly-line routines of industrialism and built on the linear and literate thought processes of print technology, are increasingly alien to a generation in search of new models. Gen Xers, according to Kevin Ford, have been "burned by pathological models of author-ity."[3] In the home and workplace, in communities and organizations, the massive changes shaking the foundations of our culture are call-ing for a new understanding and practice of the skills of leadership. For too many young people, there has been no distinction made between leading and controlling; to accept leadership and authority has been to accept control. Stifling creativity, stunting innovation and imagination, forcing uniformity, silencing dissent—controlling leadership acts like a blanket thrown over a crowd, subjugating the needs of the many who follow to the needs of the few who lead. "The remarkable thing," writes Viv Thomas, "is that many leaders feel they can change things which are beyond their control. With this fantasy in place, they lead people towards an initially exciting world of control and power. In the process these same leaders become gods of the naïve, giving the people they lead a simplicity which in the end is deceptive and damaging. Believing the world is a certain way will not help you when you meet the truth that it is not."[4] The claustrophobia this produces is pushing many people to seek fresh air and freedom outside the confines of the church—not because they hate the gospel but because they hate the bondage that the gospel has been made to bring. As Meic Pearse of London Bible College asks, "Are we equipping the saints or fostering their dependency on us? Can we let go of our scarcely admitted itch to control or bolster our positions? Pastors and preachers, house-group leaders, Sunday school teachers, worship leaders, youth workers: we all want our egos fed. It's time to start asking, 'Who's feeding whom?'"[5] Whatever else the current wave of social change calls for, it calls for a reformation in the church's understanding of leadership.

Jim Partridge is a young leader in his twenties who has observed leadership at close hand in a range of church and parachurch organizations in the United Kingdom. Professionally, he is a middle manager for a major Christian organization, with a job description that includes the oversight of an "emerging leaders" process. He has also recently joined the leadership team of his own local church. Like many younger and emerging leaders, he is convinced that the new situation into which we are moving will require new models of effective leadership, and a new attitude in those who exercise it. Surveying the current church scene, he has identified four key demands that the twenty-first century will place on its leaders: (1) a willingness to listen and change, (2) a willingness to take risks and move forward, (3) a willingness to serve and obey, and (4) a willingness to trust and delegate.[6]

Together, these four will form a matrix of priorities for those exercising leadership in church and society: the essential leader's checklist for the early decades of millennium three.

Priority 1: Check That You're Looking, Listening and Learning

Leadership was once about hard skills such as planning, finance and business analysis. When command and control ruled the corporate world, the leaders were heroic rationalists who moved people around like pawns and fought like stags. . . . Now, if the gurus and experts are right, leadership is increasingly concerned with soft skills—teamwork, communication and motivation.

—**Stuart Crainer,** "The Era of the Hard Man Is Over"

The shift in industry from "hard" to "soft" skills is now well documented. At its heart is the drive for cooperation, for leadership built on negotiation, motivation and mutual benefit rather than coercion, control and fear. The Industrial Society,[7] a nonprofit foundation, is one of the leading organizations in Britain in the arena of leadership, management and employment issues. In 1999 they commissioned a survey of three thousand people from businesses across the United Kingdom to determine what they saw as the best and worst traits of leaders. The five weakest areas of less successful leaders were cited as the following:

☐ They fail to be sensitive to people's feelings.

☐ They fail to recognize other people's stress.

☐ They fail to develop and guide their staff.

☐ They fail to encourage feedback on their own performance.

☐ They fail to consult those affected before making decisions.

Parallel research has not been carried out among those attending (or leaving) churches. But can we really believe that, if it were carried out, it would not produce very similar results?

Viv Thomas, an international leadership consultant with Operation Mobilization, insists that "leaders are measured by their influence on people. This is the only way in which it is possible to sort out the Hitlers from the Teresas. Charisma, skill, education, background are all neutral in assessing a leader's potential. . . . The measure of how well the job is done will be the effect it has on people."[8]

Beyond the immediate "soft" skills of listening for the sake of cooperation and motivation, twenty-first-century leaders will also be called upon to look, listen and learn for their own survival in a changing environment. In a static culture it is enough to learn skills once, perhaps in college, and to dedicate a life to practicing them. In a culture reinventing itself every five to seven years, this is untenable. "A new paradigm means that everyone goes back to zero," advises the Dallas-based Leadership Network, the fast-growing network developed by Bob Buford to link and resource new churches. "You lose any leverage you had in the old paradigm. Anticipatory, not reactive leadership is required."[9] To be a leader in the coming decades will mean, by definition, to be a lifelong learner—not only gaining new skills, but being able to adapt existing skills to new situations with dramatic frequency: with one eye on the task in hand and one eye on the horizon. "We need to become experts at reading and understanding cultural maps," author David Fisher has advised.[10] The shifting sands of our cultural environment are not only the context in which we must work; they are also our most potent source of up-to-the-minute learning. Twenty-first-century leaders will find themselves asking constantly, *What have I learned today? This week? This year?* Those unable to listen and to learn will soon find that they are unable to lead.

Priority 2: Check Out Your Imagination, Inspiration and Innovation

Christ came as a liberator. Christ understood that we as humans were forever held to the ground by the pull of gravity—our ordinariness, our mediocrity—and it was through his example that he gave our imaginations the freedom to rise and fly.
—**Nick Cave**, introduction to *Mark's Gospel*, Pocket Canon

Leadership that doesn't inspire the imaginations of those who choose to follow is little more than cleverly disguised bureaucracy. "The greatest leaders are those who explain the world," leading British politician Tony Benn writes, "and thus help us to gain control of our destiny."[11] If human beings did not need help in understanding their times and inspiration to overcome fear and inertia, they would not need leaders. It is crucial that leaders see this and take seriously their responsibility to inspire—to switch on the imaginative functions of those they lead. This is just the opposite of closing down creativity because it is too much of a threat.

The capacity to inspire courage, to give vision against the odds, to create dreams out of the raw materials of fear and uncertainty is more needed than ever in a context of fluidity and change. "Leading people (as opposed to simply managing them) in a new direction," writes David Nadler, "means reshaping their view of the world. It means shattering their sense of stability, tossing out their old standards of success, and prying them loose from the status quo. And then it means replacing what you've wiped out with a new, coherent and energizing vision of what you believe the future can and should be."[12] Every institution in our culture, not least its churches, is crying out for the kinds of leaders who will take risks and foster innovation, finding new solutions to old problems and meeting new problems head-on.

Steve Taylor recently surveyed around one hundred younger leaders in New Zealand, asking them to identify their most pressing needs. Among these, there was a clear identification of the need for skills in innovation. "The most highly sought-after ministry skill among young leaders is that of innovation," Taylor writes. "40% of the responses spoke of needing to be open to change, to stay abreast of new technology, to find new ways of working, seeing, being. Aware of a rapidly changing culture, flexibility and adaptability are prized ministry skills. Young leaders want to dream, to think outside the box."[13]

Priority 3: Check Up on Your Servanthood, Sacrifice and Self-giving

The best kind of leaders serve the people they are leading. A servant leader needs to know what people need in order to help them to lead themselves. Jesus Christ was a prime example—it is all about empowering, not dominating.

—**Sir Clive Thompson,** president of the Confederation of British Industry

Over the generations, many different symbols have come to represent the power and role of leadership—the five stars on a general's uniform, the huge executive office and chauffeured limousine, the bishop's miter, the short words *Senator* and *Congressman*. Yet the only symbol that could be said to capture the essence of Christian leadership is one that rarely arises—that of the towel. Jesus' act of washing feet is the fountain from which the resources of Christian leadership arise and flow. There is no New Testament model of leadership that is not servanthood.

As the new generations struggle to come to terms with their own brokenness, their disillusionment with authority, the dysfunctionality of their home experience, they stand more than ever in need of the kind of leaders more attuned to washing feet than making speeches. "To build something enduring," writes George Bullard, "you have to think beyond yourself. To help your congregation succeed 50 years from now, you have to have a servant-leadership mentality that focuses on the congregation succeeding, not just yourself."[14] This may well be the greatest contribution that the church can make to the whole arena of leadership development, that it has a framework that makes sense of the very acts of service and love the culture is looking for. The mysterious balance of power and powerlessness evident in the life of Jesus, his capacity to be single-minded yet open, to move resolutely forward in the pursuit of his destiny and yet not violate the destiny of others, to hold to nonviolence and yet be strong, even strident, when needed—in short, to serve and yet lead—these are the very qualities twenty-first-century leadership calls for.

Priority 4: Check If You're Trusting in Talent and Team
Most delight and pain in our communities and organisations can be traced back to some leader or other who shaped us, either directly or indirectly.
—**Viv Thomas,** introduction to *Future Leader*

It is ironic that some of the leaders who ask most insistently that those who follow should trust their vision without questions struggle themselves to trust those around them. But trust is a leadership commodity increasing in value by the day. Leaders who are unwilling to trust those they lead will never see them break out of low-skill patterns of dependency: growth comes through being given something to achieve. "Hire talent!" is one of Tom Peters's key principles for new-paradigm leadership.[15] Leaders need to see themselves increasingly as those who recruit, resource and release the gifted people who are going to get the job done, rather than as the lone heroes who are out to achieve. Overly complex control systems, micromanagement of tasks and an atomistic approach to delegation will all serve to stifle initiative and suffocate talent. Charles Handy speaks of the creation of a "culture of consent." "Whereas the heroic manager of the past knew all, could do all and could solve every problem, the post-heroic manager asks how every problem can be solved in such a way that develops other people's capacity to handle it. It is not virtuous to do it this way, it is essential."[16] How might the culture of our organizations change if every leader were asked to walk, each day, through a doorway over which is written the words "I am not the answer"?

If these four challenges offer a framework within which to reevaluate the approach to leadership in the light of a culture in transition, there are two further attributes essential to the effective leader: an embracing of gender balance and a focus on the future.

The Tender Gender

God was not the issue. I still believe in him. But the church was all about the power of a few men. It's a man's church and some of the ways that women and young girls are treated are disgusting.
—**Sarah,** quoted in *Author,* "Christian Soldiers"

For many observers of the current scene, the changes demanded by our shifting culture add up to the leadership equivalent of gender reassignment, with the primarily male skills of command and control being replaced by the gentler, female skills of encouragement and nurture. Sarah, an ex-member of a British church with a particularly strident view of male leadership, shows us just how important such a transformation can be. Many both within and outside the Christian community see this as a key issue. To many commentators, this is seen as *the* defining characteristic of the transition through which we are moving. When economist James Robertson wrote the influential book *The Sane Alternative* in 1983, he chose to express the paradigm shift through which our culture is moving as a shift from the HE (hyper-expansionist) to the SHE (sane, humane, ecological) future.[17] This is not simply a neat semantic device, nor an isolated case. Among many younger and emerging leaders, there is no issue more urgently in need of attention in the church than the male monopoly on leadership.

In business circles, too, there is an increasing appreciation of the gifts and distinctives that women bring to leadership roles. According to Susan Cuff, CEO of recruitment consulting agency Best International, women are better than men at today's style of leadership because "women tend to create harmony, and we see situations in the round and not straight up and down."[18] Amin Rajan, CEO of CREATE, the Centre for Research in Employment and Technology in Europe, supports this view. "Women cope better. They have empathy and good listening skills, even if they are outwardly aggressive."[19] If the twenty-first century is to have the leaders it is crying out for, then more leaders must be women, and male leaders must adopt a more gender-balanced approach. This is an insight recognized and welcomed by many in the rising generations, with a growing commitment to see a more balanced view of leadership, both in terms of the skills employed and of the gender of those employing them. If roughly half the population of the world is female, why aren't half its leaders?

word.link: Auto Pilate
That day Herod and Pilate became friends—before this they had been enemies.—Luke 23:12

There is no more stark or compelling image of biblical leadership than that of Jesus before Pilate and, in turn, Herod. Pilate: the

Roman governor representing an oppressive military regime, a five-star general steeped in the world of battle and commands, a manipulator seeking above all a trouble-free tenure in this volatile province. Herod: the enemy of Rome and yet its puppet, last in a long and glorious line of Hebrew kings, standing in the heritage of David and Solomon and yet a decadent ruler, more concerned with his own power and pleasure than the fate of his people, a man willing to see infants slaughtered at the mere whisper of a rival for the throne.

Until this day these two had been sworn enemies—pushed back behind the lines of race, language, culture and aspiration that marked out the differences between them. What happened to change this? What was it that set enmity aside and brought the two together?

It was this: in the course of one day they were each confronted by a man, Jesus, who was called the Christ. He was sweating, dirty. His clothes were torn. He came from the lower echelons of Hebrew culture—he was neither Roman nor royal. He had no earthly power to call upon for rescue; he had no friends at court; he was neither feared nor favored in high places. He was powerless, penniless, naked, weak, alone and unarmed.

And yet he possessed a strength, an inner certainty, that unnerved. He was known to have mobilized the poor. He had stirred up the religious leaders of the Jews to the point of hysteria. Crowds of ordinary people had followed him gladly.

Here was a picture of leadership that undermined every rule by which these men had ruled. Here was a leader so different from any they had encountered that they were reminded of how much they are alike. By contrast with this Christ, they had everything in common. As, so often, do we.

Focus on the Future

Living in the great turbulence of El Salvador of the 1970s, Archbishop Oscar Romero was a man who knew what it was to witness sweeping social change—and to undergo dramatic personal change.

His "conversion to the poor" is one of the most celebrated Christian transformations since that of the apostle Paul. He was a leader of quite astounding personal courage who ultimately paid with his life for his determination to speak the truth on behalf of his people. In a sermon given to a group of priests in his care, he touched on the very essence of effective leadership. "It helps, now and then, to step back and take the long view," he said.

> The Kingdom is not only beyond our efforts, it is even beyond our vision. We accomplish in our lifetime only a tiny fraction of the magnificent enterprise that is God's work. Nothing we do is complete, which is another way of saying that the Kingdom always lies beyond us. No statement says all that can be said. . . . No set of goals and objectives accomplishes the Church's mission. This is what we are about. We plant seeds that one day will grow. We water seeds already planted, knowing that they hold future promise. We lay foundations that will need further development. We provide yeast that produces effects far beyond our capabilities. We cannot do everything, and there is a sense of liberation in realising that. This enables us to do something, and to do it very well. It may not be complete, but it is a beginning, a step along the way, an opportunity for the Lord's grace to enter and do the rest. We may never see the end results, but that is the difference between the master builder and the worker. We are workers, not master builders; ministers not messiahs. We are prophets of a future not our own.[20]

If leadership is not about a focus on the future, what is it about? In a culture in transition, leaders are by definition those who see the future first—and those who are prepared to work for deferred rewards. Our culture is crying out for leaders, regardless of gender, age and social background, who are ready to look ahead, to grasp intuitively the outlines of an emerging landscape and to chart a course that they and those who travel with them can follow. To chart such a course will mean, very often, to miss out on the rewards of staying put. There will be many in leadership who are just not ready for a frontier-town culture, who have invested too heavily in the acquired status of a settled life. These are leaders of whom Loren Mead says, "Our difficulty in responding to the need to change comes from our love of the familiar and our desire to protect valued practices and structures from the past."[21] But there will be others— some thrown into leadership for the first time—who thrive on the gold-rush mentality of social change and bring a flood of new thinking to their responsibilities. These are the leaders who will break the cultural ice and blaze a trail into the future. Given the choice, which leaders would you follow?

If this book is nothing else, it is a call for the Christian faith community to focus on a future not our own, to invest our emotions, our intellect, our strength and our resources in the lives of the rising generations. They and only they have the right and responsibility to bring to birth a church for the twenty-first century. They do so in the sure knowledge that the God they worship is out there already walking the planet, tasting its cultures, swimming in its streams. Our strategy must not be for survival but for rebirth. Not the church we know today protected into its old age, but a new church born in the fields of tomorrow—a church that springs up from the ground on which, unknowing, we have thrown seeds. The church of the future will arise not where the pillars of our certainties are grounded but where the seeds of an ancient gospel reroot.

Notes

Introduction

[1]The emerging spirituality might equally be described as "postestablishment" or "postorthodox." I have used the term *post-Christian* in an effort to remind my own faith community of the fragility of our hold on Western culture.

[2]Tom Sine, introduction to *Wild Hope* (Crowborough, England: Monarch, 1992).

Chapter 1: No Small Change

[1]Michael Resnick, "Changing the Centralized Mind," *Technology Review* (July 1994), quoted in John M. McCann, "Digital Dawn Cyber Trends," <www.duke.edu/~mccann/q-ddawn.htm>.

[2]Paul Tillich, *The Shaking of the Foundations* (London: Penguin, 1963).

[3]Quoted in John Abbott, "Education 2000," September 1997, The Twenty-First Century Learning Initiative, <www.21learn.org>.

[4]Peter Drucker, *Post-Capitalist Society* (New York: Harper Business, 1993), p. 1.

[5]Quoted in John Abbot, "What Kind of Education for What Kind of World" (paper presented at the North of England Education Conference, Sunderland, U.K., January 1999).

[6]Alvin Toffler, *Future Shock* (New York: Pan, 1970). The Tofflers have recently acknowledged that both husband and wife were involved as partners in the early research and publications, even though these appeared under Alvin Toffler's name only. The partnership is acknowledged in later books. I have therefore referred to both authors throughout this book.

[7]Ibid.

[8]Ibid.

[9]Lynda Marshall, "john one" (unpublished article, 1996).

Chapter 2: Homo Xapiens

[1]The Coupland File, <www.geocities.com/SoHo/gallery/5560/coupbiog.html>.

[2]National Library of Canada, <www.nlc-bnc.ca/events/readings/coupland.htm>.

[3]Douglas Coupland, *Generation X: Tales for an Accelerated Culture* (New York: St. Martin's Press, 1992).

[4]Quoted in Douglas Coupland, *Polaroids from the Dead* (London: Flamingo, 1997).

[5]Ibid.

[6]See, for instance, George Barna, *The Second Coming of the Church* (Nashville: Word, 1998).

[7]Douglas Rushkoff, "On Cyberculture," Ziff TV, <www.zdnet.com/zdtv/thesite/0797w1/iview/iview635jump2_070197.html>.

[8]Kevin Ford, *Jesus for a New Generation: Reaching Out to Today's Young Adults* (London: Hodder & Stoughton, 1996), p. 122.

[9]Ibid.

[10]Karen Ritchie, *Marketing to Generation X* (New York: Lexington, 1995), p. 25, quoted in Jimmy Long, *Generating Hope: A Strategy for Reaching the Postmodern Generation* (Downers Grove, Ill.: InterVarsity Press, 1997), p. 39.

[11]Rushkoff, "On Cyberculture," <www.zdnet.com/zdtv/thesite/0797w1/iview/iview635jump2_070197.html>.

[12]Thanks to Lowell Sheppard for this information and translation. Such is the speed of change that a new term, *shinshinjinrui*, has now appeared, describing the generation *beyond* Generation X as "a *new* new type of human being."

[13]Long, *Generating Hope*, p. 12.

[14]David Bosch, *Transforming Mission: Paradigm Shifts in Theology of Mission* (Maryknoll, N.Y.: Orbis, 1991). Bosch's name comes up time and again as an inspiration to those seeking to understand mission to the new generations.

[15]Graham Cray et al., *The Post-Evangelical Debate* (London: SPCK, 1997), p. 2.

[16]Walter Truett Anderson, *Reality Is Stranger than It Used to Be* (San Francisco: Harper & Row, 1990), p. 3, quoted in Michael Riddell, *Threshold of the Future: Reforming the Church in the Post-Christian West* (London: SPCK, 1998), p. 101.

[17]Cray et al., *Post-Evangelical Debate*, p. 2.

[18]Space does not allow a fuller exploration of this idea, but it is essential that we understand the difference between Generation X as a premillennial generation and Generation Y as a postmillennial generation.

Chapter 3: Seven Seas of Why

[1]Alvin Toffler, introduction to *Future Shock* (New York: Pan, 1970).

[2]Leonard Sweet, Aquachurch, <www.aquachurch.com/whatis.htm>.

[3]The concept of surfing is probably the defining image of the junction generations, bringing together this notion of "riding a wave" with the more physical draw of extreme sports, hence the meteoric rise of surf-related clothing brands such as Oakley, Quiksilver and Kangaroo Poo.

[4]Douglas Rushkoff, *Children of Chaos: Surviving the End of the World As We Know It* (London: HarperCollins, 1997), p. 39.

Chapter 4: New Tools, New Rules

[1]Sigvard Strandh, *A History of the Machine* (London: Arrow, 1984), p. 150.

[2]Bill Gates, *The Road Ahead*, <www.roadahead.com>.

[3]Arthur Schlesinger Jr., "Has Democracy a Future?" *Foreign Affairs* (September-October 1997), quoted in Terence Ryan, "The Changing Economy, Information Communication Technology and New Forms of Business Management: What They Could Mean for Education Systems" (paper presented at the Twenty-First Century Learning Initiative conference, Poznan, Poland, April 1998), <www.21learn.org>.

[4]See the Peter F. Drucker Foundation for Non-Profit Management, <www.pfdf.org>.

[5]Peter Drucker, *Post-Capitalist Society* (London: Butterworth-Heinemann, 1994), pp. 53–80.

[6]Ibid.

[7]Ibid.

[8]Ibid.

[9]Ryan, "Changing Economy."

[10]P. William Bane, Stephen P. Bradley and David J. Collis, "Winners and Losers: Industry Structure in the Converging World of Telecommunications, Computing and Entertainment" (paper presented at the Multimedia Colloquium, Harvard Business School, Cambridge, Mass., 1995), quoted in John M. McCann, "Digital Dawn Cyber Trends," <www.duke.edu/~mccann/q-ddawn.htm>.

[11]Charles Handy, *The Age of Unreason* (London: Arrow, 1991), quoted in Danny Brierley, introduction to *Young People and Small Groups* (Bletchley, England: Scripture Union, 1998).

[12]Editorial, *Capital* 83 (August 1998): 42. "Nous sommes en train de vivre une des révolutions les plus rapides de l'histoire humaine" ["We are living through one of the fastest revolutions in human history"].

[13]Alvin Toffler, interview, *New Scientist,* March 19, 1994, pp. 22–25.

[14]Ibid.

[15]Ibid.

[16]Robert Kanigel, *The One Best Way* (New York: Viking Penguin, 1997), quoted in Ryan, "Changing Economy."

[17]Ibid.

[18]Toffler, *New Scientist.*

[19]Gates, *Road Ahead.*

[20]Quoted in Stephen L. Talbott, *The Future Does Not Compute: Transcending the Machines in Our Midst* (Cambridge, Mass.: O'Reilly, 1995), <www.ora.com/people/staff/fdnc/ch06.html>.

[21]Editorial, "The World in 1999," *The Economist,* November 1998.

[22]Gates, *Road Ahead.*

[23]"Gibson introduced the term in his 1984 novel *Neuromancer* after watching young people in a games arcade hunch over their games as if caught up in an imaginary space beyond the screen. Ironically, *Neuromancer* was written on a manual typewriter." Joel Serdlow, "Information Revolution," *National Geographic,* October 1995.

[24]Michael S. Malone, "Chips Triumphant," *Forbes* ASAP, February 26, 1996, p. 74, quoted in McCann, "Digital Dawn," <www.duke.edu/~mccann/q-ddawn.htm>.

[25]Editorial, *The Daily Telegraph* (London), November 8, 1999.

[26]Jim Mallory, "Former Novell Execs Launch Web Venture," *Newsbyte News Network,* December 18, 1995, quoted in McCann, "Digital Dawn."

[27]Quoted in editorial, "Interface," *The Times* (London), September 22, 1999.

[28]Michael Moon, "Dirt-Cheap Bandwidth and the Coming Revolution," *Electronic Buyer News*, January 31, 1994: 44, quoted in McCann, "Digital Dawn."

[29]Editorial, "That Astonishing Microchip," *The Economist* (London), March 23, 1996, quoted in McCann, "Digital Dawn."

[30]Editorial, "The Next Internet," *The Economist* (London), November 1999.

[31]Nicholas Negroponte, *Being Digital* (New York: Alfred A. Knopf, 1995), p. 181, quoted in McCann, "Digital Dawn."

[32]Dr. Kaku can be contacted at <mkaku@aol.com>. Information and a bibliography on him are available at Exploration in Science with Dr. Michio Kaku, <http:www.dorsai.org/~mkaku>.

[33]Michio Kaku, introduction to *Visions: How Science Will Revolutionise the 21st Century and Beyond* (Oxford: Oxford University Press, 1999).

[34]Ibid.

[35]This was first stated in 1965 by Gordon Moore, cofounder of the Intel Corporation. It is not a scientific law in the sense of Newton's laws but a rule-of-thumb which has uncannily predicted the evolution of computer power for several decades.

[36]Kaku, introduction to *Visions.*

[37]See Massachusetts Institute of Technology, <http://web.mit.edu>.

[38]Kaku, *Visions,* p. 26.

[39]Examples drawn from "The Men Who Really Know Your Future," *Focus*, February 1998;

editorial, "Comment Nous Vivrons dans Vingt Ans" ("How We Will Live in Twenty Years"), *Capital* 83 (August 1998).

[40]Throughout this chapter, I have deliberately avoided making judgments on whether new technology is a good or bad thing for society. Melvin Kranzberg, the American historian of technology, hit the nail on the head in forming what he calls Kranzberg's First Law: "Technology is neither positive, negative, nor neutral." A major debate *is* needed lest the technoevangelists lead us into a fool's paradise or the technophobes keep us out of a real one. Our purpose here is not to hold that debate but to identify as objectively as possible the changes that are happening and their likely impact. The world that will be, will be—whether we approve of it or not.

Chapter 5: High-Cyber Diet

[1]This section does not represent a detailed critique of consumerism, which has both positive and negative elements. For better or worse, hyperchoice will shape the expectations of twenty-first-century consumers, and therefore must be taken seriously as an influence on our culture. For a more in-depth analysis of consumerism, see Mike Starkey, *Born to Shop* (Crowborough, England: Monarch, 1989); Oliver James, *Britain on the Couch: Why We're Unhappier than We Were in the 1950s, Despite Being Richer* (London: Arrow, 1998), <http://cgi.pathfinder.com/time/magazine/1997/int/970922/essay.puting_britai.html>; and Tom Sine, *Mustard Seed vs McWorld* (Crowborough, England: Monarch, 1999).

[2]Douglas Rushkoff, "On Cyberculture." <www.zdnet.com/zdtv/thesite/0797w1/iview/iview635 jump3_070197.html>.

[3]Quoted in Sigvard Strandh, *A History of the Machine* (London: Arrow, 1984), p. 6.

[4]John Abbot and Terence Ryan, "Can This Really Ever Happen?" *The Journal of the Twenty-First Century Learning Initiative*, March 1998, p. 1. Available at <www.21learn.org>. Abbot and Ryan's article presents a consistent and compelling analysis of the impact of mechanization on the wider culture and on education in particular. Looking to a postmechanistic future, they say, "The question of battery hens [factory farming] or free-range chickens is critical to a nation's future excellence."

[5]Ibid.

[6]Quoted in John M. McCann, "Digital Dawn Cyber Trends," <www.duke.edu/~mccann/q-ddawn.htm>.

[7]Leith Anderson, *Dying for Change* (Minneapolis: Bethany House, 1989).

[8]Some challenge the notion that there can be real community on the Internet. See, for instance, Stephen L. Talbott, *The Future Does Not Compute* (Cambridge, Mass.: O'Reilly, 1995), chap. 6, for a sobering reminder of the limitations of online relationships ("Community is . . . something to be salvaged from information technology, not furthered by it"). My own experience of eighteen months as a member of a "cyberpub" discussion group has been very positive. Where cyber relationships are complemented by other forms of contact, I believe that the "virtual" element can reach unexpected depths. But cybertouch will never be a total substitute for "skin."

[9]Bob Buford, Texas businessman and author, founder of Leadership Network, quoted in Charles Trueheart, "Welcome to the Next Church," *Atlantic Monthly* (August 1996), <www.theatlantic.com/issues/96aug/nxtchrch/nxtchrch.htm>.

[10]Trueheart, "Welcome to the Next Church."

[11]Douglas Rushkoff, *Cyberia: Life in the Trenches of Hyperspace* (San Francisco: HarperSanFrancisco, 1994).

[12]Douglas Rushkoff, "Lost in Translation," interview by Chris Mitchell, February 1997, *Spike*

Magazine, <www.spikemagazine.com/0297/rush.htm>.

[13]Quoted in editorial, "Beyond 2000," *Time,* November 8, 1999.

[14]Quoted in editorial, "Connected," *The Telegraph* (London), November 18, 1999.

[15]Tim Berners-Lee, foreword to *The World Wide Web Handbook,* by Peter Flynn (Boston: International Thomson Computer Press, 1995), <http://imbolc.ucc.ie/~pflynn>.

[16]Tim Berners-Lee, introduction to *Weaving the Web* (San Francisco: HarperSanFrancisco, 1999). See Tim Berners-Lee's homepage at <www.w3.org/people/berners-lee>.

[17]To say that people "live in" Cyberia is to assert that they increasingly see it as their primary arena of social contact. The expectation that those people will be cranky and isolated and switched off from seeking physical community is proving unfounded. Rushkoff says of the rave scene—the first genuine spinoff of cyber culture—"The fact remains that the first real cultural outgrowth of the computer revolution did not turn out to be the solitary, non-physical experience that many had feared. If anything, it is a reclamation and assertion of the body in the face of our seemingly mechanised computer lifestyles. There is most definitely a thriving cyberculture gaining influence around the world. You just have to get off the computer and out of the house to experience it." Rushkoff, "On Cyberculture," <www.zdnet.com/zdtv/thesite/0797w1/iview/iview635jump3_070197.html>. The challenge to the church is to understand that these people live and breathe the culture of Cyberia.

Chapter 6: Gutenberger & Fries

[1]Joel L. Serdlow, "Information Revolution," *National Geographic,* October 1995.

[2]Quoted in David Lochhead, "Technology and Interpretation: A Footnote to McLuhan," *Journal of Theology* (1994). Also available at <www.religion-research.org/irtc/martin.htm>. Lochhead explains, "Galaxies are always complex, and so is McLuhan's thesis. The 'Gutenberg Galaxy' consisted of the complex social, intellectual, cultural and indeed spiritual changes that accompanied the introduction of printing in western culture."

[3]Ibid.

[4]Serdlow, "Information Revolution," p. 6.

[5]Bill Gates, *The Road Ahead* <www.roadahead.com>.

[6]Lochhead, "Technology and Interpretation."

[7]Ibid.

[8]Quoted in Lochhead, "Technology and Interpretation."

[9]Gates, *Road Ahead.*

[10]Jim Carroll, "The Treachery of the Word, the Tyranny of Choice and Other Areas of Interest" (paper presented at the Whitebread Conference on Youth, London, 1994).

[11]Quoted in ibid.

[12]Auriea Harvey, Entropy8, <www.entropy8.com>.

[13]Auriea Harvey, "Network," interview by Jason Cranford Teague, *The Independent* (London), June 22, 1998.

[14]Ibid.

[15]George Barna, *The Second Coming of the Church* (Nashville: Word, 1998), p. 185.

[16]Ibid.

[17]Alan MacDonald, *Films in Close-Up* (Downers Grove, Ill.: InterVarsity Press, 1991), p. 13. "While we are in this state of dream-like consciousness, film reaches us through a unique combination of story, sound and visual energy to provide a total experience that is brighter, louder and larger than life itself."

[18]"Starwave Teams with Real World Multimedia for new Peter Gabriel Interactive CDRom,"

press release, March 9, 1995, <www.starwave.com/text/starwave/pressrel/gabriel.html>.

[19]Ibid.

[20]Douglas Rushkoff, "Getting Loud: The Pitfalls of Interactive Style," *Levity*, <www.levity.com/rushkoff/getloud.htm>.

[21]Ibid.

[22]Douglas Rushkoff, "The Sorcerer's Apprentice," *Levity*, <www.levity.com/rushkoff/sorcerer.htm>.

[23]Douglas Rushkoff, "On Cyberculture," Ziff TV, <www.zdnet.com/zdtv/thesite/0797ᴡ1/iview/iview635jump3_070197.html>.

[24]Lochhead, "Technology and Interpretation."

[25]Jay David Bolter, *Writing Space: The Computer, Hypertext and the History of Writing* (Hillsdale, N.J.: Erlbaum, 1991), quoted in Janice R. Walker, "Reinventing Rhetoric," 1997, University of South Florida, <www.cas.usf.edu/english/walker/papers/rhetoric.html>.

[26]Quoted in Serdlow, "Information Revolution," p. 9.

[27]Bolter, *Writing Space*.

[28]Charles Henderson, "Sacred Text and Hypertext," About.Com-Christianity, <www.christianity.about.com>.

[29]Thomas Hohstadt, *Dying to Live: The 21st Century Church* (Odessa, Tex.: Damah, 1999).

[30]Charles Handy, "Meeting the Future with a Friendly Face," MCB University Press, <www.imc.org.uk/ais/sub/bulletin/guru-feb/handy.htm>.

[31]Douglas Rushkoff, "A Computer Ate My Book: Part One," *Levity*, <www.levity.com/rushkoff/book1.htm>.

[32]Ibid.

[33]Bill Gates, "Beyond Gutenberg," *The Economist* (London), November 1999.

[34]Ibid.

[35]Ibid.

[36]Quoted in Bolter, *Writing Space*, p. 110.

[37]Stephen Toulmin, *Cosmopolis: The Hidden Agenda of Modernity* (New York: Free Press, 1990), pp. 186–92, quoted in Michael Riddell, *Threshold of the Future* (London: SPCK, 1998), p. 106.

[38]Colin Morris, *God in a Box: Christian Strategy in a Television Age* (London: Hodder & Stoughton, 1984), p. 170.

[39]Joseph Blindloss, "A Censor in Cyberspace," *The Independent* (London), June 22, 1998.

[40]Ibid.

[41]Terence Ryan, "The Changing Economy, Information Communication Technology and New Forms of Business Management: What They Could Mean for Education Systems" (paper presented at the Twenty-First Century Learning Initiative conference, Poznan, Poland, April 1998), <www.21learn.org>.

[42]John Abbot, "Learning Has to Be About More than Just Schooling," *The Journal of the 21st Century Learning Initiative*, (June 1998), p. 1. Also available at the 21st Century Learning Initiative, <www.21learn.org>.

[43]Peter Drucker, *The Knowledge Society* (New York: HarperBusiness, 1993), pp. 53–80.

[44]Gunther Kress, *The Independent* (London), June 11, 1998. Kress is professor of education in relation to English at the Institute of Education, London.

[45]Ibid.

[46]Patrick Dixon, "Internet Statistics: Life in Cyberspace," November 1997, Global Change, <www.globalchange.com/main.htm>.

[47]Bill Buxton, *Social Planning and Communities Along the "Information Highway"* (Toronto: University of Toronto/Alias Research/Xerox Parc, July 1994).

Chapter 7: Screenagers in Love

[1]Jim Carroll, "The Treachery of the Word, the Tyranny of Choice and Other Areas of Interest" (paper presented at the Whitebread Conference on Youth, 1994).

[2]The term *screenager* has its origin, I believe, with Douglas Rushkoff. It describes those raised in the visual environment of MTV, the Internet and video games.

[3]Carroll, "Treachery of the Word."

[4]John Drane, "Was God in Dunblane?" *Baptist Times*, March 21, 1996, p. 8.

[5]David Lochhead, "Technology and Interpretation: A Footnote to McLuhan," *Journal of Theology* (1994).

[6]Amos Wilder, *Early Christian Rhetoric* (London: SCM Press, 1964), p. 59, quoted in Colin Morris, *God in a Box* (London: Hodder & Stoughton, 1984), p. 222.

[7]A version of this story is quoted by Charles Handy in *The Future of Work* (New York: Blackwell's, 1985); another version is in Michael Riddell, *Godzone: A Guide to the Travels of the Soul* (Oxford: Lion, 1992), p. 57.

[8]Michael Riddell, *Threshold of the Future: Reforming the Church in the Post-Christian West* (London: SPCK, 1998), p. 55.

[9]David Hillborn, *Picking Up the Pieces: Can Evangelicals Adapt to Contemporary Culture?* (London: Hodder & Stoughton, 1997), p. 167.

[10]J. Richard Middleton and Brian J. Walsh, *Truth Is Stranger Than It Used to Be* (Downers Grove, Ill.: InterVarsity Press, 1995), p. 69.

[11]Riddell, *Threshold of the Future*, p. 137.

[12]Lesslie Newbigin, *The Open Secret* (London: SPCK, 1995), p. 83.

[13]Brian McLaren, "Story," The Re-Evaluation Forum, Younger Leaders Network, <www.youngleader.org/resources/specialedition/pg3_8.html>.

[14]Walter Brueggemann, *The Bible Makes Sense* (Louisville, Ky.: Westminster John Knox, 1991).

[15]David Bosch, *Transforming Mission* (Maryknoll, N.Y.: Orbis, 1991), p. 353.

[16]Robert E. Webber, *Ancient-Future Faith: Rethinking Evangelicalism for a Postmodern World* (Grand Rapids, Mich.: Baker, 1999), p. 107.

[17]Bobby Maddex, "A God-Shaped Hole: Can U2 and a New Generation of Seekers Ever Fill It?" *Gadfly*, August 1997, p. 26. Maddex adds, "You have this whole generation of seekers who, in some cases, have seen church evolve from the symbolism and mystery of the liturgy to the straightforward logic of revivalism (repent or go to hell) to the entertainment of the rock and roll seeker service. . . . U2 voice perfectly what it feels like to be a believer in a society where our spiritual and cultural options seem used, limited, worn-out" (p. 4).

[18]T Bone Burnett, quoted in ibid., p. 27.

[19]Mark Driscoll, "Multisensory," Younger Leaders Network, <www.youngleader.org/resources/specialedition/pg3_8.html>.

[20]Webber, *Ancient-Future Faith*, p. 108.

[21]Ibid., p. 96.

[22]Jeff Anderson and Mike Maddox, *The Lion Graphic Bible* (Oxford: Lion, 1998).

[23]Press release from Lion Publishing, July 1998, <www.lion-publishing.co.uk>.

[24]Henri J. M. Nouwen, *The Return of the Prodigal Son: A Story of Homecoming* (London: Dartman, Longman & Todd, 1992). A resource for small groups, with audiotape selections

from the book, notes and questions, and ten color prints of Rembrandt's paintings is available from St. Paul's Media Centre, 199 Kensington High St., London W8 6BA.

[25]The painting can be viewed at <www.hermitagemuseum.org/html_en/index.html>.

[26]Leonard Sweet, *SoulTsunami: Sink or Swim in the New Millennium Culture* (Grand Rapids, Mich.: Zondervan, 1999), p. 177.

[27]Newbigin, *Open Secret*, p. 110.

[28]Riddell, *alt.spirit@metro.m3* (Oxford: Lion, 1997).

[29]Ibid., p. 113.

[30]Hillborn, *Picking Up the Pieces*, p. 148.

[31]Webber, *Ancient-Future Faith*, p. 101.

[32]Maggie Dawn in Graham Cray et al., *The Post-Evangelical Debate* (London: SPCK, 1997), p. 37.

[33]Ronald Rolheiser, *The Shattered Lantern* (London: Hodder & Stoughton, 1994), p. 170. Rolheiser is a member of the Oblates of Mary Immaculate and has taught theology and spirituality around the world.

[34]Jean-Pierre de Caussade, *The Sacrament of the Present Moment*, trans. Kitty Muggeridge (London: Fount, 1981), p. 87.

[35]Colin Morris, *God in a Box: Christian Strategy in a Television Age* (London, Hodder & Stoughton, 1984).

[36]David Lochhead, "Technology, Communication and the Future," 1995, InterChange, <www.interchg.ubc.ca/dml/future.html>.

[37]Webber, *Ancient-Future Faith*, p. 45.

Chapter 8: "This Is My Truth, Tell Me Yours"

[1]The chapter title comes from the title of an album by the Manic Street Preachers, 1998. See <www.manics.easynet.co.uk/index2.htm>.

[2]Steven Best and Douglas Kellner, introduction to *Post-modern Theory: Critical Interrogations* (New York: Guilford Press, 1991).

[3]Stephen Connor, *Postmodernist Culture: An Introduction to Theories of the Contemporary* (Cambridge, Mass.: Basil Blackwell, 1989), p. 6.

[4]Best and Kellner, *Post-Modern Theory*.

[5]Jean-Paul Sartre, *Existentialism and Humanism*, trans. Philip Mairet (London: Methuen, 1948), p. 25.

[6]Best and Kellner, *Post-modern Theory*.

[7]Gene Edward Veith, *Postmodern Times: A Christian Guide to Contemporary Thought and Culture* (Wheaton, Ill.: Crossway, 1995), p. 42.

[8]Leonard Sweet, *SoulTsunami: Sink or Swim in the New Millennium Culture* (Grand Rapids, Mich.: Zondervan, 1999), p. 19.

[9]Thomas C. Oden, *Two Worlds: Notes on the Death of Modernity in America and Russia* (Downers Grove, Ill.: InterVarsity Press, 1992), p. 32.

[10]Gene E. Veith, "Post-modern Times: Facing a World of New Challenges and Opportunities," *Modern Reformation*, September-October 1995.

[11]Ibid.

[12]J. Richard Middleton and Brian J. Walsh, *Truth Is Stranger Than It Used to Be* (Downers Grove, Ill.: InterVarsity Press, 1995), pp. 16–17.

[13]Ibid., p. 19.

[14]Tom Sine, "Past Imperfect: Future Tense" (address to Spring Harvest, Minehead, England,

1997). Sine develops the idea that all human cultures are driven by their vision of "the preferred future" and that ours is expressed in exclusively economic terms. See his *Wild Hope* (Crowborough, England: Monarch, 1992).

[15]D. Martin Fields, "Postmodernism," *Premise* 2, no. 8 (1995): 5.

[16]Middleton and Walsh, *Truth Is Stranger*, p. 23.

[17]Veith, *Postmodern Times*.

[18]Christopher Jones, "The Good, the Bad and The-ology," in *Tomorrow Is Another Country* (London: Board of Education of the General Synod of the Church of England, 1996), p. 22.

[19]Dave Tomlinson, *The Post Evangelical* (London: Triangle, 1995).

[20]Jean-François Lyotard, *The Post-modern Condition: A Report on Knowledge,* trans. G. Bennington and B. Massumi (Manchester, England: Manchester University Press, 1984), quoted in Middleton and Walsh, *Truth Is Stranger*, p. 70.

[21]Patricia Waugh, *Postmodernism: A Reader* (London: Edward Arnold, 1992), p. 1.

[22]Veith, *Postmodern Times*.

[23]Michael Riddell, *Threshold of the Future: Reforming the Church in the Post-Christian West* (London: SPCK, 1998), p. 105.

[24]Colin Gunton, *The One, The Three and The Many: God, Creation and the Culture of Modernity* (Cambridge: Cambridge University Press, 1993), p. 105, quoted in Michael Horton, "Where Now? Suggestions for the Way Forward," *Premise* 2, no. 8 (1995).

[25]Quoted in Jimmy Long, *Generating Hope: A Strategy for Reaching the Postmodern Generation* (Downers Grove, Ill.: InterVarsity Press, 1997), p. 69.

[26]Veith, "Post-modern Times."

[27]Riddell, *Threshold*, p. 105.

[28]Middleton and Walsh, *Truth Is Stranger*, p. 62.

[29]Best and Kellner, *Post-Modern Theory*.

[30]Middleton and Walsh, *Truth Is Stranger*, p. 61.

[31]Kevin Ford, *Jesus for a New Generation: Reaching Out to Today's Young Adults* (London: Hodder & Stoughton, 1996), p. 122.

[32]Riddell, *Threshold*, p. 105.

[33]Tomlinson, *Post Evangelical*, p. 140.

[34]Fields, "Postmodernism."

[35]Walter James and Brian Russel, "How Has Postmodernism Changed Education?" in *Tomorrow Is Another Country*, p. 32.

[36]Tomlinson, *Post Evangelical*, p. 140.

[37]Stanley J. Grenz, *A Primer on Post Modernism* (Grand Rapids, Mich.: Eerdmans, 1995), p. 7.

[38]Riddell, *Threshold*, p. 109.

[39]Alisdair MacIntyre, *After Virtue: A Study in Moral Theory* (Notre Dame, Ind.: University of Notre Dame Press, 1984), p. 216, quoted in Middleton and Walsh, *Truth Is Stranger*, p. 68.

[40]Yvonne Craig, "What in the World Is Happening?" in *Tomorrow Is Another Country*, p. 11.

[41]Kenneth J. Gergen, *The Saturated Self: Dilemmas of Identity in Contemporary Life* (New York: BasicBooks, 1991), p. 7, quoted in Middleton and Walsh, *Truth Is Stranger*, p. 53.

[42]Richard Lints, *The Fabric of Theology* (Grand Rapids, Mich.: Eerdmans, 1993), p. 216, quoted in Long, *Generating Hope*, p. 73. It is worth noting that Madonna's latest transition—into motherhood—has by her own admission challenged a self-centered orientation and is leading to a more reflective, "spiritual" body of work.

[43]Bruce Cockburn, "Gavin's Woodpile" (Golden Mountain Music Corporation, 1976), quoted

in Middleton and Walsh, *Truth Is Stranger,* p. 55.

⁴⁴Thomas Hohstadt, *Dying to Live: The 21st Century Church* (Odessa, Tex.: Damah, 1999), p. 2.

Chapter 9: Reimagineering the Church

¹Nigel Wright in Graham Cray et al., *The Post-Evangelical Debate* (London: SPCK, 1997), p. 99.

²Graham Cray, quoted in David Hillborn, *Picking Up the Pieces: Can Evangelicals Adapt to Contemporary Culture?* (London: Hodder & Stoughton, 1997), p. 5.

³Graham Cray in Cray et al., *Post Evangelical Debate,* pp. 2, 15.

⁴J. Richard Middleton and Brian J. Walsh, *Truth Is Stranger Than It Used to Be* (Downers Grove, Ill.: InterVarsity Press, 1995), p. 107.

⁵Ibid., p. 189.

⁶Nick Mercer in Cray et al., *Post-Evangelical Debate,* p. 44.

⁷Walter James and Brian Russel, "How Has Postmodernism Changed Education?" in *Tomorrow Is Another Country* (London: Board of Education of the General Synod of the Church of England, 1996), p. 27.

⁸Kevin Ford, *Jesus for a New Generation: Reaching Out to Today's Young Adults* (London: Hodder & Stoughton, 1996), p. 130.

⁹Michael Riddell, *Threshold of the Future: Reforming the Church in the Post-Christian West* (London: SPCK, 1998), p. 111.

¹⁰Tom Sine, *Cease Fire: Searching for Sanity in America's Culture Wars* (Grand Rapids, Mich.: Eerdmans, 1995), p. 224.

¹¹David Bosch, *Transforming Mission: Paradigm Shifts in Theology of Mission* (Maryknoll, N.Y.: Orbis, 1991), p. 361.

¹²Jürgen Moltmann, *Religion, Revolution and the Future,* trans. Douglas Meeks (New York: Scribner's, 1969), p. 133, quoted in Leonard Sweet, *SoulTsunami: Sink or Swim in the New Millennium Culture* (Grand Rapids, Mich.: Zondervan, 1999), p. 22.

¹³Robert E. Webber, *Ancient-Future Faith: Rethinking Evangelicalism for a Postmodern World* (Grand Rapids, Mich.: Baker, 1999), p. 53.

¹⁴Riddell, *Threshold,* p. 108.

¹⁵Jonny Baker leads the Grace service in Ealing, London. Private conversation.

¹⁶Sweet, *SoulTsunami,* p. 149.

¹⁷Ford, *Jesus for a New Generation,* p. 179.

¹⁸Christopher Jones, "The Good, The Bad and The-ology," in *Tomorrow Is Another Country,* p. 23.

¹⁹Jimmy Long, *Generating Hope: A Strategy for Reaching the Postmodern Generation* (Downers Grove, Ill.: InterVarsity Press, 1997), p. 100.

²⁰Gareth Icenogle, *Biblical Foundations for Small Group Ministry* (Downers Grove, Ill.: InterVarsity Press, 1994), p. 118, quoted in Long, *Generating Hope,* p. 90.

²¹Long, *Generating Hope,* p. 84.

²²Ibid., p. 50.

²³Riddell, *Threshold,* p. 110.

²⁴Nick Mercer in Cray et al., *Post-Evangelical Debate,* p. 60.

²⁵Jones, "Good, the Bad and The-ology," p. 19.

²⁶Fields, "Postmodernism," *Premise* 2, no. 8 (1995): 5.

²⁷Ian Cundy, "Catching the (Last) Post," in *Tomorrow Is Another Country,* p. 90.

Chapter 10: The Power of Globfrag

[1]For a history of the Berlin Wall in words, pictures and music, see <http://members.aol.com/johball/berlinwl.htm>.

[2]Marcus Tanner, "Will the Kurds Ever Be a Nation?" *The Independent* (London), January 15, 1999.

[3]For Ignatieff articles, see <www.oneworld.org/index_oc/issue397/ignatieff.htm>.

[4]Michael Ignatieff, *The Needs of Strangers* (London: Chatto & Windus, 1984), p. 130.

[5]Benjamin R. Barber, "Jihad vs. McWorld," *The Atlantic Monthly* 269, no. 3 (1992): 58.

[6]Ibid., p. 60.

[7]See McDonald's, <www.mcdonalds.com>.

[8]Quoted in Tom Sine, *Mustard Seed vs McWorld* (Crowborough, England: Monarch, 1999), p. 80.

[9]Eugene Linden, "What Have We Wrought?" *Time*, November 1997.

[10]Ibid.

[11]Sine, *Mustard Seed vs McWorld*, p. 22.

[12]Ibid.

[13]Colin Morris, *God in a Box: Christian Strategy in a Television Age* (London, Hodder & Stoughton, 1984), p. 181.

[14]Quoted in Alvin Toffler, *Future Shock* (New York: Pan, 1970).

[15]Gerard Kelly and Lowell Sheppard, *Their Future Our Passion* (Singapore: Youth for Christ International, 1996), p. 31.

[16]Ibid.

[17]Felix 'Machi Njoku, "Watch Out: Globalisation is Re-drawing Africa's Borders," Panafrican News Agency, January 27, 1998, <www.africanews.org>.

[18]Pastor Paul Sweet of the California-Nevada Annual Conference (United Methodist), quoted in Leonard Sweet, *SoulTsunami: Sink or Swim in the New Millennium Culture* (Grand Rapids, Mich.: Zondervan, 1999), p. 369.

[19]Patrick Johnstone, introduction to *Operation World* (Carlisle, U.K.: OM Publishing, 1993).

[20]Ibid.

Chapter 11: Picking Up the Pieces

[1]Robert Beckford, *Jesus Is Dread: Black Theology and Black Culture in Britain* (London: Darton, Longman & Todd, 1998), p. 5.

[2]Ibid., p. 4.

[3]Try it for yourself at Bob Marley, <www.bobmarley.com>.

[4]H. P. Spees, "Evangelizing Young People in Different Cultures" (study paper, convocation of Youth for Christ International, Chicago, 1993).

[5]Tony Lane, *The Lion Concise Book of Christian Thought* (Oxford: Lion, 1984), p. 225.

[6]Kosuke Koyama, *Three Mile an Hour God* (London: SCM Press, 1979), chap. 1, quoted in Lane, *Lion Concise Book*, p. 225.

[7]Spees, "Evangelizing Young People."

[8]*Faith in the City: A Call for Action by Church and Nation* (London: Church House, 1985), p. 315.

[9]Hans Küng, *Christianity, Its Essence and History*, trans. John Bowden (London: SCM Press, 1995), p. 786.

[10]Ibid., p. 788.

[11]James Garbarino, quoted in editorial, *The Independent* (London), April 30, 1999.

[12]Joy Turner, quoted in John Cloud, "Just a Routine School Shooting," *Time*, May 31, 1999, p. 43.

[13]Quoted in Nancy Gibbs, "How to Spot a Troubled Kid," *Time*, May 31, 1999, p. 33.

[14]Oliver James, *Britain on the Couch: Why We're Unhappier than We Were in the 1950s, Despite Being Richer* (London: Arrow, 1998), p. 21.

[15]Ibid.

[16]For background and links to Dr. Campolo's work, see <www.eastern.edu/centers/eape>.

[17]Tony Campolo, interview, *Preparing to Parent Teenagers Seminar* (Youth for Christ, 1996), videocassette.

[18]Michael Riddell, *Godzone: A Guide to the Travels of the Soul* (Oxford: Lion, 1992), p. 14.

[19]James, *Britain on the Couch*, p. 26.

[20]J. Richard Middleton and Brian J. Walsh, *Truth Is Stranger Than It Used to Be* (Downers Grove, Ill.: InterVarsity Press, 1995), p. 77.

[21]Ushio Amagatsu, leader of Japanese dance group Sankai Juku, quoted in editorial, "The Aliens Have Landed," *The Independent* (London), January 15, 1999.

[22]Rupert Cornwell, "Will This Child Inherit His Earth?" *The Independent* (London), July 9, 1998. Visit the Survival International home page at <www.survival.org.uk/about.htm>.

[23]Ibid.

[24]Quoted in John Abbot, "What Kind of Education for What Kind of World" (paper presented at the North of England Education Conference, Sunderland, U.K., January 1999).

[25]Editorial, "Barometer: Inequality," in "Reflections on the 20th Century," *The Economist* (London), September 11, 1999, p. 54.

[26]Rachel Johnnson, "The Picture Still Looks Grim," *Financial Times* (London), January 1994.

[27]Ibid.

[28]Matthew Connelly and Paul Kennedy, "Must It Be the Rest Against the West?" *The Atlantic Monthly*, December 1994.

[29]Ibid.

[30]John Grigg, "What Makes a Great Leader?" *The Times* (London), February 9, 1999.

[31]Mark DeVries, *Family-Based Youth Ministry* (Downers Grove, Ill.: InterVarsity Press, 1994), p. 96.

[32]Editorial, "Young People in 1992: A Survey by the Schools Health Education Unit of Exeter University," *The Sunday Times* (London), January 1993.

[33]Editorial, "Britain's Children Showing Signs of Stress," *The Sunday Times* (London), January 1993.

[34]Juliet B. Schor, *The Overspent American: Upscaling, Downshifting and the New Consumer* (New York: BasicBooks, 1998), quoted in John R. Muether, "Finding Our Way Out of the Mall," *Re:generation Quarterly* 4, no. 4 (1998): 41.

[35]Ibid.

[36]Ibid.

[37]See Café Central at <www.cafe-net.org.uk>.

[38]See David Bosch, *Transforming Mission: Paradigm Shifts in Theology of Mission* (Maryknoll, New York: Orbis, 1991), p. 233: "The concept of pilgrimage often merged into that of mission."

[39]Quoted in Barrie Taylor, "GenX Mission," *EMA Bulletin*, autumn 1998, p. 8.

Chapter 12: Gods R Us

[1]See *Phosphore*, <www.phosphore.com>.

[2]Editorial, "15—20 ans croyez-vous en Dieu?" ("Fifteen-twenty year olds—do you believe in

God?"), *Phosphore*, December 1994, p. 8.

[3]Ibid.

[4]Christopher Dawson, *The Historic Reality of Christian Culture* (New York: Harper/Torchbooks, 1965).

[5]David Bjork, "A Model for the Analysis of Incarnational Ministry in Post-Christendom Lands" (Ph.D. research, Fuller Theological Seminary, 1998).

[6]Michael Riddell, *Threshold of the Future: Reforming the Church in the Post-Christian West* (London: SPCK, 1998), p. 12.

[7]Jacob Needleman and David Applebaum, *Real Philosophy: An Anthology of the Universal Search for Meaning* (London: Arkana [Penguin], 1990), p. 12.

[8]John Drane, *What Is the New Age Saying to the Church?* (London: Marshall Pickering, 1991), p. 239.

[9]Alankentkataxkwe (Star Dancer), "Lenapé Spirituality," Star Dancer at <www.geocities.com/Athens/forum/4438/spirit.html>.

[10]Rupert Sheldrake, interview by Ken Weathersby, *Hootenanny*, <www.hootenanny.com/hoot/3/sheldrake.html>.

[11]For a further exploration of the relationship between science and faith, see Roger Forster and Paul Marston, *Reason, Science and Faith* (Crowborough, England: Monarch, 1999).

[12]Jefferis Kent Peterson, "The New Age Movement: The Self as God," 1997, Scholars Sense, <www.scholarscorner.com/Critical/Newage.html>.

[13]Quoted in Tony Lane, *The Lion Concise Book of Christian Thought* (Oxford: Lion, 1984), p. 215.

[14]Jean-Luc Porquet, "Le New Age, Religion Fast Food," *Phosphore*, December 1994, p. 36. Porquet is the author of *La France des Mutants, voyage au coeur du New Age* (Mutant France—Voyage to the Heart of the New Age) (Paris: Editions Flammarion, 1994).

[15]Porquet, "New Age," p. 36.

[16]Riddell, *Threshold*, p. 115.

[17]John Drane, *Evangelism for a New Age: Creating Churches for the Next Century* (London: Marshall Pickering, 1994), p. 15.

[18]Douglas Coupland, *Life After God* (New York: Pocket Books, 1997), p. 183.

[19]Lesley O'Toole, "Into Battle for a Man of Peace," *The Times* (London), March 31, 1998.

[20]See Shaolin, <www.webcom.com/~shaolin>.

[21]Grace Bradberry, "Monks with a Lethal Habit," *The Times* (London), March 31, 1998.

[22]Isabel Hilton, "The Dalai Lama, Rupert Murdoch and the Forces of Evil," *The Independent* (London), September 22, 1999.

[23]Ibid.

[24]John Drane, "Drane on Culture," interview by Wendy Beech, *YFC Info-View*, April 1996, p. 4.

[25]Myke Johnson, *Wanting to Be Indian: When Spiritual Teaching Turns into Cultural Theft* (Boston: Respect, 1995), p. 1.

[26]John Barry Ryan, "Listening to Native Americans: Making Peace with the Past for the Future," *Journal of Religion and Culture* 31, no. 1 (1996): 24-36.

[27]Dale Stonechild, quoted in *First Nations Gallery Guide* (Saskatchewan, Canada: Royal Saskatchewan Museum).

[28]Johnson, *Wanting to Be Indian*, p. 1.

[29]Paul Vallely, "England's Gentle Revolutionaries," *The Independent* (London), May 27, 1996.

[30]Mitchell Pacwa, S.J., "Catholicism for the New Age: Matthew Fox and Creation-Centred

Spirituality," *Christian Research Journal* (autumn 1992): 14.

[31]Matthew Fox, *The Coming of the Cosmic Christ* (San Francisco: Harper & Row, 1988).

[32]Sheldrake, interview by Ken Weathersby, *Hootenanny.*

[33]Carl G. Jung, *The Undiscovered Self* (London: Little, Brown, 1957), quoted in Steve Schlarb, "Carl G. Jung," <www.geocities.com/Athens/Acropolis/3976/Jung.html>.

[34]Drane, *Evangelism for a New Age*, p. 140.

[35]A New Zealand public holiday celebrating the signing of the Waitangi Treaty between the Maori peoples and the British government.

[36]The Maori are the native tribes of New Zealand. *Pakeha* is the name given to New Zealanders of European origin.

[37]This is Maori for, "We who are many are one body."

[38]Steve Taylor, "Waitangi Day Liturgy," Auckland, New Zealand, 1999. Used with permission.

Chapter 13: Karmageddon

[1]"Soundbites," *Bread for the Journey* 1, no. 2 (1998): 4.

[2]Loren Mead, *The Once and Future Church* (Bethesda, Md.: Alban Institute, 1991).

[3]George Barna, *The Second Coming of the Church* (Nashville, Tenn.: Word, 1998).

[4]Quoted in Martin Wroe, "Life After Death," *Strait Magazine*, February 1990, p. 14.

[5]The Greenbelt Festival in Britain maintains a valuable list of alternative worship sites and resources, with links to a number of U.K.-based services as well as key projects in Australia, New Zealand and the United States. See Greenbelt at <www.greenbelt.org.uk>.

[6]Steve Taylor, "A New (Zealand) Generation Leading the Church into a New (Zealand) Millennium" (paper presented at Younger Leaders Network conference, Seattle, Wash., November 1999).

[7]See Younger Leaders Network at <www.youngleader.org>.

[8]Andrew Jones, e-mail conversation. Contact: <cyberrev@hotmail.com>.

[9]Thomas Hohstadt, *Dying to Live: The 21st Century Church* (Odessa, Tex.: Damah, 1999).

[10]Esther De Waal, introduction to *The Celtic Way of Prayer* (London: Hodder & Stoughton, 1996).

[11]Ian Bradley, *The Celtic Way* (London: Darton, Longman & Todd, 1993), p. 74.

[12]Michael Mitton, introduction to *Restoring the Woven Cord: Strands of Celtic Christianity for the Church Today* (London: Darton, Longman & Todd, 1995).

[13]Michael Shirres, "Inculturation," <www.homepages.ihug.co.nz/~dominic/intro.html>.

[14]Michael Shirres, "My Life," <www.homepages.ihug.co.nz/~dominic/mylife.html>.

[15]Taylor, "New (Zealand) Generation."

[16]Quoted in Helen Chappell, "It's Hip to Be Holy," *New Statesman and Society*, September 8, 1995.

[17]Barna, *Second Coming.*

[18]Ibid.

[19]Martin Scott, Pioneer People. Private conversation.

[20]"When the Horse Is Dead, Dismount," Leadership Network, <www.leadnet.org/d1dnetfax11.html>.

[21]Lesslie Newbigin, *The Open Secret* (London: SPCK, 1995), p. 189.

[22]Paul Tillich, introduction to *The Shaking of the Foundations* (London: Penguin, 1963).

Chapter 14: Pillar to Post

[1]Paul Tillich, *The Shaking of the Foundations* (London: Penguin, 1963), p. 45.

[2]Loren Mead, foreword to Robert Nashjc, *An 8-Track Church in a CD World* (Macon, Ga.:

Smyth & Helwys, 1998).

[3]Cited in Colin Morris, *God in a Box: Christian Strategy in a Television Age* (London: Hodder & Stoughton, 1984), p. 45.

[4]Michael Riddell, *Threshold of the Future: Reforming the Church in the Post-Christian West* (London: SPCK, 1998), p. 2.

Chapter 15: Tsar Wars

[1]For Lindisfarne information, see <www.lindisfarne.org.uk/index.htm>.

[2]Quoted in Michael Mitton, *Restoring the Woven Cord* (London: Darton, Longman & Todd, 1995), p. 15.

[3]Kevin Ford, *Jesus for a New Generation: Reaching Out to Today's Young Adults* (London: Hodder & Stoughton, 1996).

[4]Viv Thomas, *Future Leader: Spirituality, Mentors, Context and Style for Leaders of the Future* (Carlisle, U.K.: Paternoster, 1999), p. 128.

[5]Meic Pearse, introduction to *Who's Feeding Whom?* (Carlisle, U.K.: Solway, 1996).

[6]Jim Partridge, "Spring Harvest" (unpublished paper, July 1999).

[7]See Industrial Society, <www.indsoc.co.uk>.

[8]Thomas, introduction to *Future Leader*.

[9]Editorial, "When the Horse Is Dead, Dismount," Leadership Network, <www.leadnet.org/d1dnetfax11.html>.

[10]David Fisher, *The Twenty-First Century Pastor* (Grand Rapids, Mich.: Zondervan, 1996), quoted in editorial (*Netfax* 49), July 8, 1996, Leadership Network, <www.leadnet.ord/d1dnetfax49.html>.

[11]Quoted in editorial, "Leadership into the 21st Century," *The Times* (London), February 9, 1999.

[12]Quoted in Terence Ryan, "The Changing Economy, Information Communication Technology and New Forms of Business Management: What They Could Mean for Education Systems" (paper presented at the Twenty-First Century Learning Initiative conference, Poznan, Poland, April 1998), <www.21learn.org>.

[13]Steve Taylor, "A New (Zealand) Generation Leading the Church into a New (Zealand) Millennium" (paper presented at Younger Leaders Network conference, Seattle, Wash., November 1999).

[14]Quoted in Leadership Network, <www.leadnet.org>.

[15]Tom Peters, "The Circle of Innovation," audio cassette (abridged) (New York: Random House [Audio], 1997).

[16]Charles Handy, *The Age of Unreason* (London: Arrow, 1990), p. 132.

[17]James Robertson, *The Sane Alternative* (Oxford: Robertson, 1983).

[18]Quoted in Susan MacDonald, "A Duty to Inspire Love and Harmony," *The Times* (London), February 9, 1999.

[19]Ibid.

[20]Quoted in John Abbott, "What Kind of Education for What Kind of World" (paper presented at the North of England Education Conference, Sunderland, U.K., January 1999), <www.21learn.org>.

[21]Loren Mead, foreword to *An 8-Track Church in a CD World,* by Robert N. Nash Jr. (Macon, Ga.: Smyth & Helwys, 1998).

Café.net—a network of Christians active in the future of Europe—is a small organization started by Gerard and Chrissie Kelly to foster innovation and creativity in mission. Our mission statement is this: "We will use every method at our disposal to promote, initiate, nurture and support Christian mission in twenty-first-century Europe."

This mission is implemented in three areas of activity:

Network—bringing together Christians with a passion for Europe and a focus on the future. We link innovative missions projects to one another and to a wider web of prayer.

Exposure—building short-term teams to carry support, encouragement and resources to front-line missions projects in Europe. Café.net trips combine elements of pilgrimage and mission in the "peregrine" ethos, asking participants to "take something with you—bring something back."

Training—providing research, resources and training opportunities specific to the challenges of Christian mission in twenty-first-century Europe.

For details, contact:
Café.net
Chawn Hill Christian Centre
Stourbridge
Chawn Hill,
West Midlands
DY9 7JD, UK
e-mail: <retro@cafe-net.org.uk>
Web site: <www.cafe-net.org.uk>

For comments and questions on the content of *RetroFuture:*
e-mail Gerard Kelly at
<retro@cafe-net.org.uk>

Or visit the book's Web page at
<www.cafe-net.org.uk>